Women and Democracy

Women and Democracy

Latin America and Central and Eastern Europe

Edited by Jane S. Jaquette
and Sharon L. Wolchik

THE JOHNS HOPKINS UNIVERSITY PRESS

Baltimore and London

© 1998 The Johns Hopkins University Press
All rights reserved. Published 1998
Printed in the United States of America on acid-free paper
9 8 7 6 5 4 3 2 1

The Johns Hopkins University Press
2715 North Charles Street
Baltimore, Maryland 21218-4363
The Johns Hopkins Press Ltd., London
www.press.jhu.edu

Library of Congress Cataloging-in-Publication Data will be found at the end
of this book.
A catalog record for this book is available from the British Library.

ISBN 0-8018-5837-2
ISBN 0-8018-5838-0 (pbk.)

Contents

Preface and Acknowledgments

*T*his volume grew out of a conversation between the editors at the 1990 Fourth World Conference of Slavic Studies meetings in Harrogate, England. Each of us had followed gender issues and particularly women's roles in politics in our own regions for some time. In Jane's case, this work focused on women's roles in the transitions from authoritarian governments in Latin America. Sharon's research had focused on the impact of politics on women and women's roles in Central and Eastern Europe during the Communist period. In the months after the fall of Communism in Central and Eastern Europe, it was clear that the change of regime would have important implications for women. In both cases, women were experiencing political and economic transformations, which offered them new opportunities but also presented new constraints.

Intrigued by the similarities and differences in women's roles in the transitions in Latin America and Central and Eastern Europe which a cursory look provided, we decided to explore these experiences more systematically. It was our hope that a comparison of women's responses to dramatic political, economic, and social changes in the two regions would allow us to gain a better understanding of women's roles in each region. We were also interested in what a comparison of women's experiences in the transitions in the two regions would tell us about the nature of the transition processes themselves and about feminist theory. We began this work at a panel that we organized on the subject at the 1991 Annual Meeting of the American Political Science Association and continued it at a conference entitled Women in Political Transitions in South America and Eastern and Central Europe: The Prospects for Democracy, held at the University of California, Berkeley, in December 1992. As commentators on papers we invited from experts on the regions, we asked individuals from varying perspectives: comparative politics and political economy in the two regions; democratic theory; and feminist theory. A summary of conference proceedings is available as a Working Paper of the International and Public Affairs Center at Occidental College.

It was our intention from the beginning of the project to continue this exploration and common discussion of cases in the two regions over an extended period of time in order to allow developments in both regions to unfold. In the five years since the conference, we and the authors of the chapters in this volume have had numerous exchanges that have deepened our understanding of our own cases and regions and those of others. This volume thus is informed by almost a decade of reflection and common discussion. The contributors analyze women's roles in bringing about the transitions from authoritarian and Communist rule and the impact of the early stages of those transitions on women. But they also have been able to take account of the effect of democratization on women's movements in Latin America and of the political, economic, and social transformations that have taken place in Central and Eastern Europe since the end of Communist rule. This study thus is also concerned with the consolidation of democratic political systems in the two regions and with the impact that movement toward consolidation has had on women.

We would like to thank the many individuals that have played a part in and contributed to the evolution of this book. We are especially grateful to Mary Uebersax for her enthusiasm for this project and to the North-South Center of the University of Miami, which provided most of the funding for Jane's travel to Poland, Hungary, and the Czech Republic. We would also like to thank the Department of Political Science, Women's Studies, Center for German and European Studies, and International Area Studies Programs at the University of California, Berkeley, for hosting the conference. We thank Irene Tinker for help in organizing the conference and for providing substantive reflection at various stages in the process. We would also like to thank the International Public Affairs Center and the Department of Political Science at Occidental College and the Institute for European, Russian, and Eurasian Studies and the Elliott School of International Affairs at George Washington University for the research and clerical assistance they provided.

In addition to the authors of the chapters, we would like to thank the following people whose participation enriched our discussions at the conference: Jan Knippers Black, Susan Bourque, Ellen Comisso, Mari Clark, Ruth Collier, David Collier, Beverly Crawford, Albert Fishlow, Kathleen Jones, Terry Karl, Mary Katzenstein, Gail Kligman, Gwen Kirkpatrick, Gail Lapidus, Francine Masiello, José Álvaro Moisés, Lois Oppenheim, Joanna Regulska, Ruth Rosen, Wendy Sarvasy, Philippe Schmitter, Beatriz Schmukler, Molly Shanley, Janos Simon, Jiřina Šiklová, Emily Stoper, Carrie Timko, Joan Tronto, Millidge Walker, Georgina Waylen, Lois West, and Antje Wiener. Joanna Goven, Elisabeth Friedman, Kate Bruhn, and Eva Busza helped the rapporteur. We would also like to thank Henry Tom, our editor at the Johns Hopkins University Press, for his interest and support, and Grace Buonocore, whose sharp eye and persistence made this a better book.

We would also like to thank the research assistants who worked with us, including Naomi Poling Warbasse, Nancy L. Meyers, Zsuzsa Csergo, Spencer Smith, Mark Teele, and Becky Childers at George Washington University, and Allison Giffen at Occidental College, where Tatiana Colombetti, Heather Cummings-Carter, Wendy Clifford, Galeen Roe, and Janet Blum provided research, editorial, and typing assistance.

We owe a special debt to Naomi Warbasse, who, as a graduate student at George Washington, assisted us in organizing the conference and also served as a conference rapporteur. After completing her studies, Naomi became deputy director of the Central and East European Business Information Center at the U.S. Department of Commerce. Tragically, she was one of those who died while on a mission with Commerce Secretary Ron Brown in a plane crash in Dubrovnik on April 3, 1996. This book is dedicated to her memory.

Finally, we would like to thank our husbands and children. Jane is grateful to Abe Lowenthal for his energetic example and always helpful advice and to Chris and Sarah Jaquette, who are finally old enough to view their mother's projects as worthwhile and not just time consuming. John, Michael, and Annie Varnum patiently supported Sharon in this work as in all others.

Women and Democracy

Chapter One

Women and Democratization in Latin America and Central and Eastern Europe

A Comparative Introduction

JANE S. JAQUETTE
AND SHARON L. WOLCHIK

T he last decade has marked a major political watershed. In a few short years, the ratio of individuals living in democracies has risen from one-third to two-thirds of the world's people, and the debate has shifted from the issues of democratic transitions to the challenges of democratic consolidation and the quality of democratic life.

Within that discussion, the comparison between the processes of democratization in Latin America and those in Central and Eastern Europe has drawn significant attention.[1] Yet, despite the participation of women in both sets of transitions and despite the obvious centrality of women to any sustainable process of democratic consolidation, the roles of women in the political transformations of these two regions are rarely examined. The essays in this volume help to fill that void. In doing so they address a range of questions of interest not only to those who analyze comparative politics but also to those who study both democratic and feminist theory. How significant were women's roles in the transitions in each region? How did their participation affect women's activism and the policies directed toward women in the post-transition democracies? What can a comparison explicitly based on gender tell us about the prospects for democratic consolidation and the kinds of democracies which are evolving in Latin America and in Central and Eastern Europe?

The essays in this book are case studies. Each addresses issues of transition and consolidation in a country-specific way, yet the authors were aware of one another's work and had the opportunity to compare their assumptions and to

1

probe their differences.[2] As case studies, however, they are not explicitly comparative. We undertake that task in this introductory chapter.

COMPARING LATIN AMERICA
AND CENTRAL AND EASTERN EUROPE

Early discussions of transitions to democracy were global in scope. Samuel P. Huntington described a "third wave" of democratization, and Francis Fukuyama's now famous reference referred to the demise of Communism as the "end of history" because it marked the end of a fundamental conflict over how modern societies would be organized.[3] The momentum of this democratic wave can be traced from its origins in southern Europe through Latin America and Central and Eastern Europe to the few but important democratizations under way in East Asia. Some argue that the wave is spent, but others project further democratic change in Southeast Asia and in Africa, where South Africa is leading the way.

In addition to the fall of Communism, these ambitious analyses focus on large-scale phenomena, including the spread of neoliberal market reforms, the exponential expansion of communications and communication technologies, and the evidence that such changes are creating a new, truly global society. Norm-setting institutions like the World Trade Organization and the World Bank reinforce global capitalism and global democratization, while nongovernmental organizations that cross national boundaries diffuse new concepts, change expectations, and fuel political participation.

The initial studies of transitions emphasized how pacts and roundtable discussions set the rules of the game for political openings and guaranteed the basic interests of key political actors.[4] The rational choice model effaced the historical differences between countries and regions, and with them the very real difficulties of doing interregional comparisons. Those who criticized the rational choice approach—on the grounds that it privileged elites and narrowed the content of politics to pursuit of individual or group interests—saw an alternative in the solidarity and communitarianism of the new social movements.[5] But this too was a universal model, one that pitted the "genuine" democracy of social movements and civil society against the hierarchies and instrumentalism of parties and the state.

The comparison between Latin America and Central and Eastern Europe is far from straightforward. There are certainly similarities: in both regions, authoritarian rule was successfully replaced by democratic elections. Social movements played an active role in the transitions in both regions, but the crucial decisions resulted from negotiations among key actors. Most of the countries we compare in this volume (Argentina, Chile, and Brazil in Latin America; Poland, Hungary, and the Czech and Slovak Republics in Central and Eastern Europe)[6] are similar in the sense that they compose part of the "semiperiphery"—dependent on an industrialized center but having achieved an appreciable level of industrial production and fairly strong rates of growth during much of the postwar period. The two additional cases—Peru and Bulgaria—are less developed in their region and share other characteristics that differentiate them in regional terms but also suggest similarities between them. In particular, they share characteristics of development and political culture which may compromise democratic consolidation.

In all the cases under review, elements of "civil society" mobilized publicly against authoritarian rule, although the period of state/"society" opposition was shorter in most of the countries of Central and Eastern Europe and longer in Latin America, where (with the exception of Argentina, where the military withdrew after being defeated by the British in the Falklands/Malvinas War) the transitions took several years.

Both types of transition left a legacy of fragility: the abruptness of the transitions in Central and Eastern Europe highlighted the lack of past democratic experience in much of the region and the destabilizing potential of right-wing nationalism. In those countries, such as Poland and Hungary, where the transitions took place more gradually, opposition forces had more experience in politics. However, Communist officials and managers also had more time to translate their political power into economic advantage as the economies privatized. In Latin America the longer transitions facilitated the political reemergence of political parties and gave the social movements substantial political experience, but the ebb and flow of the transition process underlined the ongoing vulnerability of democratic governments to military control. In both regions, moreover, disenchantment set in rapidly, the result of persistent or worsening economic crisis, the pace and uneven results of economic reform, and high expectations for democracy itself.

Yet there are significant contrasts between the two regions which make comparisons difficult. Ellen Comisso summarizes them succinctly: Central and Eastern Europeans recovered national sovereignty and moved out from under Soviet control, whereas Latin Americans recovered popular sovereignty from their military authoritarian rulers. The political spectrum in Latin America is class-based and goes from left to right, while in Central and Eastern Europe political divisions go from *Gemeinschaft* to *Gesellschaft*. In addition, the military is the most important destabilizing factor in Latin American politics but virtually absent as a political force in Central and Eastern Europe. The predecessor regimes in Latin America were based on the military, but in Central and Eastern Europe they were based on Communist parties.[7] Perhaps the most important difference that most analysts recognize is that the Latin American governments are undergoing political *transitions* but the Central and Eastern European societies are experiencing simultaneous economic, social, and political *transformations*.

But important similarities remain. The struggles for democracy have also been struggles for identity,[8] and in both regions (again, with the partial exception of Peru and Bulgaria), post-transition identities were built in part on rejection of the modes and policies of the prior regimes. Because transition politics are periods of crisis and thus of intense politicization, they bring new ideas and institutions into political life. In our view, they provide a rare window on how social structures underlie political structures and practices, and they lend themselves well to a comparative approach that includes gender.

We hypothesized that women would be drawn into politics during the transition and that this involvement, nurtured by a broader international context of women's organizing sparked by the United Nations Decade for Women, would give rise to specific demands for improving the status of women in the post-transition democracies. Among the issues we anticipated would be common to both regions were the political representation of women, women's changing economic roles under conditions of neoliberal economic reforms and globalization, and concerns about the family, including family law and violence against women, and women's reproductive rights.

What these chapters show is that women's political experiences in the two regions were in fact quite different. In both regions, women participated in the oppositional politics of the transition, joining movements that expressed their discontent with existing authoritarian regimes, marching in opposition demonstrations, taking part in strategy sessions, and speaking out. In Latin America, women organized to protest economic conditions and undermined the claims of authoritarian regimes that they were creating the necessary conditions for economic growth. In Central and Eastern Europe women contributed to undermining support for the Communist regimes by fostering values in the home which were not approved by the Communist leadership. In Latin America these strategies of resistance resulted in the mobilization of women around gender issues, whereas the reverse was true in Central and Eastern Europe, where women's movements have been slow to organize after the transitions. There some women expressed their desire to return to the home; others voiced open skepticism about the value of equality in labor force participation and politics, the core goals of Western feminism.

The analysis that follows contrasts the experiences of women in these two regions. It examines explanations for these differences and explores their implications for feminist politics and for the process of democratic consolidation.

WOMEN IN THE DEMOCRATIC TRANSITIONS IN LATIN AMERICA

Women's politicization in the case studies we review here—Argentina, Brazil, Chile, and Peru—provides dramatic support for the model we hypothesized. Women were visible participants in the political oppositions to military rule in these four countries[9] and acted not only as individuals but as participants in a range of social movements, including women's movements. Some joined human rights groups, following the lead of the Mothers of the Plaza de Mayo in Argentina, who marched weekly in front of the presidential palace in Buenos Aires to demand the return of their children who had been imprisoned and tortured or murdered by the military. Poor women in the cities organized boycotts to protest rising prices and communal kitchens to feed themselves during the harsh economic crisis; many of these groups formed federations to increase their political clout. In Brazil, an active day care movement was the basis for cooperation between poor urban women and urban feminist groups. Groups of women, urban and mostly university-educated, some active in political parties and some opposed to such involvement, openly declared themselves feminist and organized explicitly to demand women's rights. Women returning from political exile brought their experiences of American and European feminism into these groups.

What united these women was their commitment to political action to bring about the withdrawal of the military and the return to democratic government. And, although most of these women rejected the term "feminist," their experiences in meeting together outside the home and their growing recognition of their relative powerlessness brought about an awareness of gender issues and a willingness to cooperate with the feminist groups in raising women's issues.

The politics of the transition itself offered unusual opportunities. In many cases political parties were banned, so that social movements, including those championing environmental concerns and human rights as well as women's issues, were at the center of political life. The notion that democracy would be created anew, with much broader representation than in the past, provided an opening for new issues and new ways of doing politics. This rethinking affected politics from top to bottom, as gender issues were included in the new constitutions of Brazil, Peru, and Argentina and changing norms affected the politics of everyday life.

The effects of this mobilization, documented in the chapters in this book, are complex and are still in progress. During the transitions, women cooperated in innovative ways across party and class lines to develop new agendas. Among the many changes that were instituted as a result of this process were the creation of women's ministries; the Brazilian experiment with councils on the status of women to initiate and review legislative proposals; special police stations staffed to aid women victims of rape or abuse; several constitutional initiatives; and changes in marriage and family law, including the legalization of divorce in Argentina. Argentina and Brazil enacted national legislation imposing gender quotas on political party nominations, and in Chile some of the political parties have adopted voluntary quotas to ensure greater representation for women.[10]

The return to democratic politics created unexpected problems for the women's movements and for social movements in general. The politics of the transition had been intense, with a strong emphasis on rhetoric and mass mobilization. Democracy meant that brave concepts had to be turned into workable legislation, that sustained organizational effort would be needed to ensure that women's issues would be taken up by the political parties, and that legislation would be implemented and monitored.

Social movements, which had prided themselves on their autonomy, now found themselves marginalized. And although they viewed themselves as committed to being a moral voice and to providing solidarity to members, they had to confront the need to act like interest groups in order to maintain a political presence. The heady enthusiasm of the transition, with its sense of mass involvement and solidarity, gave way to smaller and more focused efforts. There were serious divisions within the women's movement on the issue of whether to be autonomous or to work with the state and risk being coopted.[11] It proved more difficult to organize women to defend their own interests than to demonstrate against military rule. Nonetheless, there have been significant constitutional and institutional changes, a sustained drive to increase women's political representation, and a widespread political agreement that women's movements have become "political actors," with definable interests and legitimate claims. The test will be whether women can stay organized and sufficiently united to maintain and transform the political space they gained during the transitions.

TRANSITIONS IN CENTRAL AND EASTERN EUROPE

The cases from Central and Eastern Europe suggest a very different trajectory. Women participated in dissident and opposition groups during the transi-

tions, but rarely as women or as feminists. Far from being symbolic of th
as was the case in Latin America, women's claims to equal rights were associated
with the Communist past and thus suspect. In the euphoria about democracy
and markets, it was difficult for women to anticipate how or whether they would
be affected differentially by economic and political restructuring. With no recent
tradition of independent organizing in the region, there were no established
women's movements to participate in the transition or to carry gender issues into
the new democracies.

Instead, many women appeared to reject the "premature emancipation"
they had experienced under Communism. In reaction to the Communist state's
appropriation of the goal of gender equality and the burden which the uneven
pattern of gender role change created for women, many initially expressed a desire not to be pressured to participate in the labor force and in politics.

There are some important exceptions to this generalization, and most
women continue to work outside the home. When conservative, Catholic legislators threatened to pass severe restrictions on women's access to abortion,
women in Poland, the Czech Republic, and Hungary mobilized in protest. In
Central and Eastern Europe, the single most important types of new organizations women formed were made up of women entrepreneurs, in contrast to the
feminist and livelihood groups that characterized women's organizing in Latin
America. Older women, who identified more closely with the social benefits
they had worked for under Communism, pressured governments to retain their
retirement payments and even to lower the age at which they could receive support. Women parliamentarians in Poland organized to form a women's lobby,
and small groups of women have organized in all countries to deal with women's
immediate needs and to take up the slack caused by decreases in social services
and spending on social welfare. But by and large, women did not organize as
women and did not enter the democratic era with new agendas for women.

There are several reasons why activist women in Central and Eastern Europe experienced the transition and the post-transition period quite differently.
Women's relative lack of involvement in organizing cannot be explained by arguing that there was no objective need for them to do so. Communism had not
resolved the "Woman Question," and the turn to the market and the economic
"shocks" prescribed to bring the Central and Eastern European countries into the
global economy had negative implications for women's employment and educational opportunities.[12] Structural adjustment meant cuts in government
spending and thus in government programs including health and child care.
Women were also in a relatively poor position to compete to guarantee their
property rights under plans to privatize state-held assets.[13]

The chapters in this book suggest at least three important reasons why women in Central and Eastern Europe did not mobilize around gender issues. The most powerful explanation is that issues of gender egalitarianism—demands for policies to bring equal rights and full participation for women—were associated with the discredited Communist regimes and not with women's understanding of their own interests. By contrast, in Latin America, women's rights were a new issue, and bringing women's values to bear on politics was one means of differentiating civil society from the hierarchical forms and socially conservative content of repressive military rule. This contrast reinforces Joyce Gelb's observation that successful feminist politics are highly dependent on the broader political context.[14] In Latin America, women's issues were congruent with and symbolic of a larger political transformation, but in Central and Eastern Europe, those few women who did see the transitions in feminist terms were opposed not only by men but by most women as well.

A second barrier to Central and Eastern European women was their lack of experience in organizing combined with their view that there was no need to do so. As Dobrinka Kostova observes in her chapter, women were accustomed to relying on the state. They were aware of the costs of the transition but did not see that women were being singled out.[15] Reka Pignicski has reflected that, as policies changed incrementally, women did not recognize the threat:

> It is indeed difficult to react politically to small steps taken backward; it is difficult to rally around seemingly insignificant negative changes (first slight restrictions in reproductive rights, a chipping away of the family leave subsidies, changes in educational policy that preserve the traditional status of women in certain professions, etc.).[16]

Finally, women in the two regions had very different responses to international feminist currents. For Latin American women, the United Nations Decade for Women, which held its first meeting in Mexico City in 1975, legitimated women's issues and disarmed opponents, particularly on the left, who argued that feminism was a North American or European import not suited to Latin American realities. The timing was significant, as 1975 was the beginning of the process of political opening in Brazil and Peru. The Decade conferences required governments to study and report on the status of women in their countries, which in turn provided the statistical basis for women's claims to resources and egalitarian legislation and involved government agencies and nongovernmental organizations in the ongoing task of monitoring women's progress. Meetings to discuss women's status were allowed by the military regimes and became important though self-censored arenas for political discussion with broader implications for the advancement of civil society.

In Central and Eastern Europe, however, international influences have not been supportive of gender politics, and some of the most outspoken women in the region have complained of heavy-handed attempts on the part of Western feminists to pressure women in the region to conform to their views.[17] Jirina Vrabkova and others have argued that, for Central and Eastern European women, feminism is "just another 'ism'"—and there is little tolerance for any position that is perceived as ideological.[18] In both regions, some of the most visible and active feminist groups have received outside support from private foundations and foreign assistance agencies, which has made them vulnerable to criticism and raises questions about their long-term viability.

FROM DEMOCRATIC TRANSITION TO DEMOCRATIC CONSOLIDATION

The return to democratic politics altered the terms under which women's groups in Latin America engaged in political activity.[19] The success of the prodemocracy effort and the return to party politics reduced the sense of crisis and removed many of the incentives for cross-party collaboration. The women's movement lost momentum, and strategies that had worked well during the transitions did not fit the new political environment of electoral politics and party competition.[20]

Women's movements have tried three main strategies for gaining power under the democratic rules of the game: electoral, bureaucratic, and interest group politics. In Latin America, the electoral strategy has proved slow and frustrating, which is not surprising given the low levels of female representation in the United States and Great Britain, which are mature democracies with well-established feminist movements. In our Latin American cases, the percentage of women elected to the upper and lower houses in the new democracies failed to reach historic highs, and in Uruguay, the country with the longest democratic tradition and a highly educated population, there were no women in the legislature in the first post-transition election. Women's efforts to run as feminist candidates failed in Brazil and Peru,[21] and in her chapter María Elena Valenzuela cites Chilean data showing that more men than women approve of women in public office. Many women elected since democracy was restored have been from conservative parties and have not supported feminist initiatives in the areas of reproductive rights and the family.

Bureaucratic strategies have focused on capturing a part of the state—establishing offices or ministries to identify needs and develop policies for women. The Brazilian councils referred to earlier were established at the state and eventually the national level and were initially very successful. The national council played a critical role in bringing women's issues into Brazil's new constitution, and Chile's women's ministry (SERNAM) launched an ambitious plan to reach out to women at all levels of society and to take the lead in developing new legislation in areas such as family law and violence against women.

What these chapters show, however, is that such institutions cannot operate in a political vacuum. Without ongoing support from well-organized groups outside the government, they are usually dependent upon the support of the president or the ruling party, and that support has proved unreliable, as the cases of Brazil, Argentina, and Chile clearly demonstrate. This situation suggests the need for permanently organized groups that are capable of mobilizing political resources to maintain existing gains and push new agendas, but it is precisely at this level that the loss of momentum and divisions among those who remain active take their toll.

Philippe Schmitter's chapter in this volume addresses issues of representation, arguing not only that some electoral systems (proportional representation and party lists as opposed to single-member district/winner-take-all rules) favor women's electoral success[22] but also that women have a stake in strong party systems that can carry forward a coherent policy agenda. This argument underlines the fact that women need male allies and party support to make new policies and implement them effectively. The chapters in this book reflect some of the frictions that have marked the relations between Latin American women's movements and political parties. The distance between the feminists and the political parties can be attributed not only to the fact that the parties still operate as male-dominated institutions; distance also must be seen as the result of deep divisions in public opinion which make the adoption of the more progressive planks of the feminist agenda politically costly. Taking their cue from successes in Western Europe, several parties in Latin America have adopted nomination quotas to ensure that women's representation will increase substantially over the next several years, and Argentina and Brazil have adopted quota laws that apply to all parties.[23]

In Central and Eastern Europe, women are often depicted as having lost political ground during the transitions. The level of women's participation in national legislatures fell precipitously when democratic elections were held, ranging from 20–30 percent in 1987 in our case studies to less than 10 percent in Poland, Czechoslovakia, and Hungary in 1990. In Hungary, the percentage of women legislators went from 32 percent to 21 percent.[24] As our case studies show, however, the reality is more complicated. Communist legislators did not represent constituencies, as is the case in functioning democracies, but were used by the leadership to legitimate its policies and to promote support for decisions made (by men) at the top. Women's representation brought international accolades during the Communist period, but it was largely window dressing; women were marginalized from the centers of power. The Communists' efforts to bring women into political roles are now portrayed as one more facet of the political hypocrisy of Communist rule, with negative implications for women's future democratic participation.

However, recent elections have seen some recovery. In 1995, women accounted for 10 percent of the legislators in the Czech Republic, 18 percent in Slovakia, 11 percent in Hungary, and 13 percent in both Poland and Bulgaria, even without quotas. These proportions are significantly higher than in our Latin American cases, which range from 5 percent in Brazil to 9 percent in Peru and 14 percent in Argentina, the last due to the early impact of the quota law. To put these numbers in a global context, the figures from Central and Eastern Europe also compare quite favorably with women's proportion of legislators in Great Britain, which was at 7 percent in 1995 (although the recent victory of the Labor Party, which adopted quotas, doubled women's representation to 16% in the House of Commons), and with the nearly 11 percent representation of women in the U.S. Congress, who were elected under a single-member district system and without quotas. However, women's representation in Central and Eastern Europe's legislatures is substantially lower than the proportions of women legislators in the Nordic countries and the Netherlands, which ranged from 29 percent to 39 percent in 1995. If we compare local levels of representation (in city councils, for example), women appear to be doing better in Central and Eastern Europe (15%–20%) than in Latin America (4%–7%).[25]

The conclusion we draw from these data and from the detailed discussions of women's political roles in our case studies is that women's political roles in the two regions are likely to converge much more in the future than they have in the past. Although Central and Eastern Europeans have less experience with civic association, new groups are forming rapidly. There are now more than thirty thousand independent associations in Poland alone, and the number of women's groups is also on the rise. At the same time, women's groups in Latin America are both less mobilized and less effective than they were during the transitions, which narrows the organizational gap between the two regions.

Electoral data indicate that women in both regions are gaining or consolidating a visible presence in national legislatures. These women have the poten-

tial to work together to raise women's issues when there is a consensus (on social welfare issues and violence against women, for example) but will continue
to be divided along party lines, which will restrain progress on issues that appear
to undermine the family or promote an individualistic approach to women's reproductive rights. As politics increasingly reflects new realities and is less shaped
by the desire to reject the Communist past, women in Central and Eastern Europe are becoming more aware of the stakes they have in the new economic
order and the ways in which the new economic, social, and legal reforms affect
them. They are increasingly voting their interests.

Considering possible strategies in this area, we think that the provocative
proposal for state support of interest groups, which Philippe Schmitter discusses in his chapter, should be looked at more closely. Although it could be difficult to implement without creating incentives for state favoritism or new types
of corruption, it does address the fact that women are among the sectors of society particularly disadvantaged by liberal interest group politics. Although
some women's groups have a long organizational history in the established
democracies, in general women have fewer economic resources to devote to
maintaining their own representative organizations, and the more women work,
the less they can make up this deficit by volunteer labor. Schmitter's "popular
corporatism" might be particularly relevant to Central and Eastern Europe, and
Latin America, not only because organizations are weak in general but also because the political culture of pluralism is not well established either in the state
or in society.

Finally, we think it is significant that, in both regions, the debates on "affirmative" or "positive" action have revolved around the issue of party and electoral
quotas and not equal access to educational or employment opportunities. This
continues to be the case despite the fact that women are losing their privileged
position in higher education in Central and Eastern Europe. And in Latin America, as is the pattern in the established industrialized democracies, although
women have achieved virtually equal access to higher education (in Latin America, class, not gender, is the barrier), educational equity has not led to improved
economic status.[26]

ISSUES FOR FEMINIST THEORY AND PRACTICE

We would argue that feminist scholarship employs a model of contemporary
women's political mobilization which has the following elements: women first become conscious of the effects of their political marginalization, most probably in
the context of a larger political crisis, and they then organize to share their aware-

ness and develop political strategies and agendas. They take their issues into the political arena, acting not merely as "interest groups" but with the broader goals of changing both the substance and style of political activity. The explosion of women's movements and the development of a global feminist agenda in the twenty years since the first UN Conference on Women in 1975 have reinforced the view that this model holds and that women's pursuit of full political citizenship is a significant global phenomenon in the late twentieth century.

The experiences of Latin American women's groups in the transitions to democracy are often cited as examples of this trend: they organized independently, provided an arena for political debate in a period when military repression made other forms of public assembly virtually impossible, and brought feminist analysis to bear on larger issues of political transformation. Their experiences reinforce the feminist belief that women's access to power will make a difference, not only for women but for politics.

Further, as Western feminism became less fully committed to a liberal egalitarian agenda, and as many embraced "difference" feminisms, the Latin American experience was, if anything, even more relevant.[27] Latin American women showed that they could enter politics and gain power while defining themselves differently—as mothers, not as "abstract" (that is "male-defined" or "disembodied") citizens.[28] Most Latin American activists followed the example of the Mothers of the Plaza de Mayo of Argentina, framing their interests as mothers of families and not as individuals. Latin American women's movements seemed to be inventing a new kind of feminism, which was at the same time maternal and community-based. Although many women's organizations continued to avoid the term "feminist," which was associated with hostility to men and to the family, women were able to cooperate on some "strategic" gender issues and to oppose patriarchal power, for example, to confront violence against women and to change laws that gave men legal control over family decision making.[29] In making the case for electoral quotas, in general they have not appealed to the norm of gender equality but have argued that the nation and democracy will be better served if women's different voice is represented.

By contrast, the experience of women in Central and Eastern Europe, by appearing to abandon the goals of power and participation for women, challenges the assumption that women will continue to seek full citizenship, even if defined in "difference" terms. Central and Eastern European women seem to be questioning the core feminist tenet that women's confinement to the private sphere is oppressive and women's public involvement in the economy and the polity is liberating. Images of women wanting to return to the home, with their most articulate spokeswomen arguing that they had experienced "too much" equality in work and in politics, challenged the feminist assumption that reversals in women's quest for full citizenship are caused by repression, not by women's free choice.

Although only time will tell, the sharp rejection of Western feminism and its egalitarian goals by Central and Eastern European women in the immediate postauthoritarian period may prove to be in large part a function of the rejection of Communism. Women are not leaving their jobs, and, as noted, women's political representation remains relatively high. The number of women's organizations is increasing rapidly, and women are becoming more engaged at all levels in defining and defending their interests in these rapidly transforming systems.

However, as was the case with Latin American women, the attitudes of Central and Eastern European women with regard to the family will continue to diverge from the Western feminist perspective, which, even at its most "maternal," remains deeply convinced that the family is an institution of patriarchal power. One reason the family is not seen as patriarchal is portrayed in Julia Szalai's chapter in this volume. Szalai describes the family in Hungary as a site of political resistance to Communism and as a much more authentic space for politics than the public sphere. "Home-based female strategies of adaptation" and "family-bound forms of women's self-protection" are still relevant, "despite the collapse of the political regime that inspired their evolution."[30] Szalai's position has been challenged by other scholars such as Joanna Goven, who observes that it was women's invisible work that "maintained the private realm as a functioning and habitable site" for opposition politics and who notes that men emerged from the family into the world of democratic politics carrying "a discourse of anti-feminism that blames women for social disorder."[31] Nonetheless, it appears that, like their Latin American counterparts, women in Central and Eastern Europe are developing a sense of their interests that is compatible with the family, and motherhood, and even with femininity, which has been viewed in the West as a potent symbol of patriarchal power.

There has been very little progress in either region in raising issues of men's equal responsibility in the family, yet gender relations in the family are unlikely to serve as a flash point for feminist consciousness in either region as they did in the West.[32] However, a substantial number of women in both regions seem committed to active lives as workers and citizens as well as mothers. As market economics brings further globalization and continued restriction of government budgets, it will be interesting to observe how the multiple pressures on women are analyzed and confronted by feminists in both regions.

It is not clear that there are off-the-shelf feminist remedies for these issues or that earlier alliances and assumptions will work. For example, Teresa Caldeira's chapter in this volume emphasizes that the initial congruence between women's movements and the human rights movements in Brazil is being tested. When human rights claims were made for political prisoners and for the rule of law against military repression, they were widely hailed as legitimate. However, the efforts of human rights groups to defend ordinary prisoners and improve prison conditions have run up against a negative tide of public opinion that fears rising crime rates and wants to punish criminals, who are mostly poor. Caldeira asks how this lack of respect for individual human rights will affect women's rights and how women's difference discourse about bodies and rights may contribute to the deligitimation of human rights in general.

Maruja Barrig's chapter also raises interesting questions about rights discourse and feminism. Noting that Peruvians (like Brazilians) tend to reject notions of individual legal rights in favor of collective economic and social rights, she argues that democracy, even for women, requires individual decision making and thus requires acceptance of an individual concept of rights. She uses this perspective to explore the circumstances surrounding death of María Elena Moyano, the charismatic leader of the Glass of Milk movement in Peru, who was killed and then blown up in front of her children by members of Sendero Luminoso, Peru's Maoist guerrilla movement. In doing so she reveals and accepts the connections between feminism and individualism which are often glossed over by those who see women's politics as a communitarian alternative to male-defined politics.

INTEGRATING GENDER INTO COMPARATIVE RESEARCH

The comparative literature on democratization has turned its attention from transitions to issues raised by the democratic consolidation.[33] This trend has produced a variety of typologies of consolidation, ranging from the minimal (two sets of elections have been held, and power has changed hands; there is no longer an imminent threat of democratic breakdown) through a spectrum that increasingly attempts to measure the quality of democratic life.

In Central and Eastern Europe, the relative lack of a gender gap between men's and women's votes has obscured the important fact that women constitute a large proportion of the votes in any country. Given that democratic breakdowns have historically been preceded by elections that threaten key interests or divide polities in ways that create coalition governments led by marginal but extreme leaders, it is surprising that so little attention has been paid to women's voting patterns or to gender differences in attitudes toward democracy in this region.[34] Sharon Wolchik's chapter in this volume documents important differences in the issues men and women see as the most critical in the Czech and Slo-vak Republics. However, there are to date few significant gender differences in cit-izens' evaluations of or support for democracy. Renata Siemieńska finds that women in Poland are less likely than men to vote for left-of-center parties, which also seems to be the case in Chile, as Valenzuela notes.

The gender gap has attracted more attention in Latin America. Surveys show gender differences on several issues. The 1988 plebiscite in Chile which re-jected the military dictatorship of General Pinochet depended on the decisions of lower-middle-class women, who were the largest group of "undecideds" as the election date drew near. Survey data, also from Chile, shows that women are less likely than men to support women candidates. But the systematic collection and use of gender-specific data are still lacking, despite their potential importance. Of course, the more fundamental point is that governments cannot claim to be truly democratic if they continue to allow half of their populations to be grossly underrepresented.

One striking characteristic of the consolidation literature is the shift of focus from negotiations and pacts between a small number of elites to concern for the development of a democratic political culture, without which elections and de-mocratic institutions cannot function effectively.[35] Political culture depends on day-to-day habits and social norms that individuals acquire first in families and communities. In fact, a focus on the cultural bases of political and economic reform dominates much of the current literature, including analyses as diverse as Robert Putnam's study of democracy in Italy and Francis Fukuyama's analysis of family structures and economic growth in East Asia.[36] Yet despite the well-documented relationship between the political views of mothers and the social-ization of children, there has been little interest in the family as a site of political and economic socialization, or in the way in which women's attitudes are trans-mitted to children and continue to shape their behavior as adults.[37]

Of the recent wave of books on consolidation, the most thorough effort to identify and relate the different variables and processes that must work together smoothly for consolidation is Juan Linz and Alfred Stepan's *Problems of Demo-cratic Transition and Consolidation*, which compares cases in southern Europe, South America, and post-Communist Central and Eastern Europe.[38] There is not sufficient space here to discuss the gender implications of their work in detail, but we would like to make two points that show the ways in which mainstream analyses would be enriched by incorporating gender perspectives.

Linz and Stepan's initial proposition is that no democracy can be con-structed without the prior existence of a state. They define democracy as "the re-sult of a government that comes to power by the direct result of a free and popular vote," but they emphasize that this government must have "the de facto power to generate new policies" and that the executive, legislative, and judicial bodies cannot share power with other bodies de jure.[39] The latter requirement precludes colonial status or the constitutional right of the military to intervene, and the former assumes that democracy cannot function unless issues of citizenship (the relationship between the "polis" and the "demos") are clearly understood and accepted. Thus Yugoslavia was not a state in their sense, and "stateness" has been enhanced for the Slovaks by the creation of an independent Slovakia. Their use of Benjamin Anderson's notion of the modern state as an "imagined community" further underlines the relationship between identity and stateness and, following Anderson, raises the question of how national identities are constructed and how they condition the prospects for democracy.[40]

Issues of identity and citizenship are politically gendered, with important consequences for women. Valentine Moghadam's work documents the degree to which identities are "found" in what are taken to be "traditional" gender roles and then constructed through the display of those roles to the "outside" world.[41] The radical version of gender identity politics today occurs most obviously in the Middle East, where veiling has become a potent symbol of rejection of the West and the reassertion of Islam. In gender identity politics, as Moghadam observes, "private" choices (of clothing, household management, or demeanor) become powerful public symbols of national character and must be politically as well as socially reinforced. Thus identity politics can severely restrict women's choices and deny them full citizenship, as is now painfully visible in Afghanistan under Taliban rule.

A version of these dynamics has also been at work in Central and Eastern Europe, in conflicts between ethnic groups but also in the politics of competing value systems that are secular, urban, and internationally oriented on the one hand and inward-looking, religious, and rural on the other. Gendered identity politics contributed both to the use of rape as a weapon of war in the former Yugoslavia and to its emergence as a major human rights issue.[42]

Less dramatically, but perhaps as significantly in the long run, nationalist self-definitions that include "appropriate" gender roles limit women's choices in powerful but often subtle ways. These issues are relevant in Latin America as well in those cases in which indigenous groups contest the legitimacy of the state. From a feminist standpoint, indigenous groups are more likely to limit women's autonomous choices. Ironically perhaps, this allows Latin American governments to portray their concern for women's status as "modern," thus legitimating their claims to "stateness" against the "traditional" values of indigenous challengers.

A second point that is worth exploring in Linz and Stepan's analysis is their view that consolidation depends on the mutual interaction and learning be-

tween five different arenas within the nation-state, three of which they charac-
terize as "societies." "Civil society" is differentiated from "political society"
(politicians, parties, and the norms that regulate them), and the two, though separate, cannot be totally opposed to each other. These in turn interact within, develop, and maintain a rule of law "embedded in a spirit of constitutionalism" and
supported by a state that is capable and "usable" by the democratically organized
nation-state.[43] Finally, all of these arenas interact with "economic society," which
mediates relations between the market and the state. This conceptualization offers a creative way to think about markets and states, a central issue for contemporary democracies undergoing economic as well as political transformation,
and to assess possible futures for democratic consolidation.

We agree that conceiving the economic, political, and civil arenas of power
as "societies" is suggestive of the rich background of beliefs, norms and social
sanctions, and supports that distinguish these groups from one another and yet
imply internal and external dynamism—a welcome move away from institutional boundaries toward a concept of political viability that is social at its core.
In that spirit we suggest that it is not only gender blind but empirically inade-
quate to exclude the family as a relevant arena for understanding democratic politics. Conceiving the family as a political arena of power linked closely to the state
is justified by the fact that the state regulates marriage and family law, provides
tax incentives and disincentives, may criminalize abortion, and sets welfare policies. The state intervenes politically in the family with significant consequences
for "private" beliefs and behavior.

But families also influence what happens in the other arenas that Linz and
Stepan identify. Families are the basic units of economic society as consumers
and reproducers of the labor force. Gender roles are carriers of national identity
and thus critical to stateness. Families socialize children, setting and reinforcing
political values. And family values, like economic values, are socially constituted
and reinforced. They are not "natural" but political. An advantage of the Linz and
Stepan approach is that it moves beyond the division between public and private
which has dominated feminist theorizing about politics; it could be developed
to create a much more complex understanding of gender in political life. At the
same time, attention to women's political roles in this broader sense could significantly aid our understanding of democratic consolidation and the many
forms this process may take.

An approach to transition and consolidation politics which picks up on the
earlier promise of social movements is suggested by Douglas Chalmers, Scott
Martin, and Kerianne Piester, who argue that the transitions in Latin America
opened up new possibilities for representation of popular sectors.[44] They differ-

entiate these "associative networks" from the corporatist and clientelist structures common in the past and from "interest groups" in the liberal pluralist sense. Associative networks are independent and decentralized; unlike markets they are based on social ties, not "faceless" interactions; unlike interest groups they "go beyond the strategic bargaining based on fixed interests" to "cognitive politics," a category that includes "perception, social learning and communication."

The approach of Chalmers, Martin, and Piester contrasts with Linz and Stepan's more mainstream institutional analysis in ways that are encouraging to women's participation. What is missing in their analysis, in our view, is the recognition that it was women's large-scale involvement in social movements and women's preferences for nonhierarchical, open, and symbolic forms of politics which were a major factor in their success. Women's ongoing commitment to the kind of social and constructivist politics that make associative networks distinctive will be critical to their evolution and survival.

THE CHAPTERS IN THIS BOOK

The chapters that follow are organized by region, beginning with the Latin American cases, as they are chronologically earlier and also provide the point of comparison from which we look at the Central and Eastern European cases. Similarities among the cases emerge clearly in each region, but so do the subtle differences between case studies. We end with Philippe Schmitter's discussion of women's representation, which grew out of his involvement in our effort to construct a framework for comparing the two regions.

María del Carmen Feijoó's chapter on Argentina sets the stage by putting women's participation in the transition into the historical context of changes in the 1960s. She examines the roles of the Mothers of the Plaza de Mayo and of urban popular groups and takes a close look at the issue of whether women's mobilization as mothers can be a successful strategy for raising gender issues. She traces women's experiences with electoral politics through the development of the quota law that requires parties to nominate women to fill one-third of their candidate slots, and assesses its effects to date. She also discusses the weakness of the women's ministry and the vulnerability of bureaucratic strategies to presidential control.

María Elena Valenzuela traces the history of the Servicio Nacional de la Mujer (SERNAM), a woman's ministry that began with ambitious legislative and social goals but which has struggled with party conflicts and backlash against feminist agenda setting. Although Chilean feminists developed an effective critique of militarism as a result of the hierarchical traditions of Chilean families and society (hence the slogan "Democracy in the Country and the Home"), and although women mounted a detailed "agenda for democracy," SERNAM has been beset by conservative criticism from inside the ruling coalition (where the Christian Democratic Party is in an alliance with leftist parties) and from the opposition as well as by those in the women's movement who feel they have been coopted and ignored. Both Valenzuela and Feijóo discuss how recent developments affected their country's position at the fourth UN conference for women held in Beijing in 1995.

Teresa Caldeira assesses the successes and weaknesses of the women's movements in Brazil, with particular emphasis on the women's councils that Brazil pioneered. Noting the important influence the national council had on the Brazilian constitution but also the lack of implementing legislation, Caldeira documents how and why the councils succeeded or failed, noting particularly the importance of independent organizations in developing new initiatives and keeping up the pressure on those who are working from inside the government, observing with concern the increasing trend toward privatization of government services. Caldeira then develops an extended analysis of the relationship between human rights groups and women's groups, arguing strongly that, in the debate that is occurring in feminist theory about women's bodies and gendered citizenship, the Brazilian experience shows why feminists should support a "bounded" conception of the body and the right to bodily integrity. Women have a direct stake in how these concepts evolve within a democratic context that lacks a deep commitment to individual rights and the rule of law.

Maruja Barrig's chapter looks at Peru in the 1980s, when urban popular movements were locked in a deadly conflict with Sendero Luminoso, Peru's Maoist guerrilla movement. Barrig's analysis touches on several aspects of this conflict, including Sendero Luminoso's appeal to women and the reasons for Sendero's successes. The chapter focuses particularly on the death of María Elena Moyano, which was a shocking blow to the feminist movement in Peru, and discusses the nature of Moyano's relation to her followers and the implications of this case for evolving concepts of human rights and politics in Peru.

Renata Siemieńska's chapter analyzes women's participation and political life prior to and after the end of Communist rule in Poland. Because the Catholic Church played such an important role in the Polish transition, the church's views on gender issues have strongly influenced gender politics since 1989. Economic restructuring has meant somewhat higher unemployment and substantially reduced access to jobs for women. Women lack some of the skills, particularly managerial experience, which would give them opportunities in the privatized economy. Pressure from the church and the Christian parties to "allow" women to return to their traditional roles is further reducing their independence.

Although there are fewer women in parliament than there were under Communism, those who are there are more authentically representative and possess better qualifications for having influence. Siemieńska analyzes many of the barriers that limit women's participation in politics, including the reluctance of party leaders to place women in electable positions on party lists. She also highlights the efforts women in and outside parliament and elsewhere are making to develop a women's lobby to put issues of particular interest to women on the political agenda.

The chapter by Sharon Wolchik looks at the comparative impact that political structure and political values have had in shaping women's political behavior in the Communist and post-Communist periods in the Czech and Slovak Republics. As she notes, women had very few opportunities to be active in autonomous political organizations prior to 1989. Women participated in large numbers in bringing about the end of Communism but soon were marginalized once again from politics. Most women show little interest in politics and do not view the negative impact that the shift to the market has had on certain groups of women in gender terms. The legacy of the old official women's organizations and the association of the goal of gender equality with the Communist system have discouraged most women from participating in feminist or other women's groups. However, though few in number, such groups exist in both the Czech Republic and in Slovakia and have contributed to an increasingly public discussion of gender issues.

Julia Szalai's chapter on Hungary addresses the issue of why women in Central and Eastern Europe prefer to concentrate on their economic and family roles rather than participating in politics or joining women's movements. She argues that, under Communism, the family was a refuge from an intrusive regime that regulated all forms of public behavior. Because they had more flexible schedules, women were able to take advantage of the opportunities in the parallel economy of private plots and small-scale enterprises that served as an escape valve in the 1980s; activities in these areas produced economic growth as well as new opportunities for wealth and prestige. She traces the way in which these experiences had an impact on the broader society as women (and men) used a combination of volunteer labor and local pressure to improve the quality of education and health services at the community level, thereby restructuring a bureaucratic state from below. Together, these experiences changed perceptions of the division between public and private and the value assigned to activities in each sphere. Szalai argues that the lack of women's movements and gender politics in Hungary should be interpreted in light of these experiences, which men and women shared. Still, she notes, women can be organized to protect their interests when the need arises, as the active role women played in the passage of the liberal abortion law in June 1993 illustrates.

Dobrinka Kostova reviews the situation of women in Bulgaria today in comparison with the Communist past. Although individualism and the market are the new ideals, uncertainty about the future has fueled nationalist and ethnic sentiments and created a political climate that makes it very difficult to raise gender issues on their own terms. Kostova documents the way in which women's educational levels and labor force participation increased under socialism, without a corresponding increase in the representation of women in managerial positions. Surveys show that Bulgarians fear unemployment and that ideological support for gender equality has declined. The number of women entrepreneurs is increasing, but from a very small base. Noting that more than 90 percent of women were active in organizations under Communism and thus have had experience with leadership (though often at the local level) and that political activity is expected of women, Kostova explores why women have been much less active than men in democratic politics and discusses the new opportunities for women created by the victory of the democratic opposition in Bulgaria in 1997.

Drawing on his extensive experience with this interregional comparison, Philippe Schmitter addresses the political options available to women to increase women's participation and influence in the democratizing regimes in both regions. He argues that women are more likely to be elected in systems that use proportional representation; that women should prefer parliamentary systems because they are more able to deliver on electoral promises; and that quotas, which are now being tried in several Latin American countries, are an effective method for increasing women's representation. Schmitter speculates about the usefulness of certain kinds of state-supported pluralism by which, for example, citizens could receive vouchers to be used to support the groups of their choice, which would better distribute the economic resources that are the basis of interest group politics and allow women, who are underrepresented in this sector as well as in legislatures, more access.

We believe that this volume provides a rich empirical picture of women's participation in democratic transitions in Latin America and Central and Eastern Europe and a timely assessment of their evolving roles in the processes of democratic consolidation. We are also confident that the comparisons between the two regions which these chapters suggest offer significant challenges to feminist theory and practice, while proving the usefulness of bringing a gender perspective to the study of democratic consolidations.

NOTES

1. There is an extensive literature on democratic transitions. The authoritative work is Guillermo O'Donnell, Philippe C. Schmitter, and Laurence Whitehead, eds., *Transitions from Authoritarian Rule: Prospects for Democracy* (Baltimore: Johns Hopkins University Press, 1986). On this interregional comparison, see Adam Przeworski, *Democracy and the Market: Political and Economic Reforms in Eastern Europe and Latin America* (New York: Cambridge University Press, 1991).

On the relationship between economic liberalization and political reform, see Stephan Haggard and Robert R. Kaufman, *The Political Economy of Democratic Transitions* (Princeton: Princeton University Press, 1995); "Economic Reform and Democracy," a special issue of the *Journal of Democracy* 5, no. 4 (1994); and Joan Nelson, ed., *Intricate Links: Democratization and Market Reforms in Latin America and Eastern Europe* (New Brunswick, N.J.: Transaction Books for the Overseas Development Council, 1994).

Georgina Waylen compares women's roles in the two regions in "Women and Democratization: Conceptualizing Gender Relations in Transition Politics," *World Politics* 46 (April 1994): 327–53. On the implications of globalization for women's organizing, see Sheila Rowbotham and Swasti Mitter, eds., *Dignity and Daily Bread* (London: Routledge, 1994). See also Valentine M. Moghadam, ed., *Democratic Reform and the Position of Women in Transitional Economies* (Oxford: Oxford University Press, 1991).

2. The authors originally exchanged views in a conference held at the University of Calfornia, Berkeley, December 3–4, 1992. In addition to the chapter writers, the conference included commentators from several fields, including the comparative politics of these two regions, comparative studies of women's political participation, and feminist theory (see Preface). Citations of comments from the conference which appear in this introduction are from the conference report, "Women and Political Transitions in Latin America and Eastern and Central Europe" (Naomi Warbasse, rapporteur; hereafter cited as "Conference Report").

3. Samuel P. Huntington, *The Third Wave: Democratization in the Late Twentieth Century* (Norman: University of Oklahoma Press, 1991), and Francis Fukuyama, *The End of History and the Last Man* (New York: Free Press, 1992).

4. See, for example, Adam Przeworski, "The Games of Transition," in *Issues in Democratic Consolidation: The New South American Democracies in Comparative Perspective*, ed. Scott Mainwaring, Guillermo O'Donnell, and J. Samuel Valenzuela (Notre Dame: University of Notre Dame Press, 1992). For a feminist critique, see Waylen, "Women and Democratization."

5. On the new social movements and the expectation that they are creating a new kind of politics which addresses what Jurgen Habermas has described as the "crisis of legitimacy" of the contemporary state, see the special issue of *Social Research* 52, no. 4 (1985), especially the essays by Jean Cohen and Alain Touraine. See also Arturo Escobar and Sonia Alvarez, *The Making of Social Movements in Latin America* (Boulder, Colo.: Westview Press, 1992).

On women's social movements, see Georgina Waylen, "Women's Movements and Democratization in Latin America," *Third World Quarterly* 4, no. 3 (1991). There is no single women's movement or definition of feminism for the region. For a discussion that remains relevant to the contemporary divisions within women's movements in Latin

America, see Nancy Saporta Sternbach, Marysa Navarro-Aranguen, Patricia Chuchryk, and Sonia E. Alvarez, "Feminisms in Latin America: From Bogotá to San Bernardo," in *The Making of Social Movements in Latin America*, ed. Arturo Escobar and Sonia D. Alvarez (Boulder, Colo.: Westview Press, 1992).

The argument in this chapter is that women's movements in both regions operated within a cultural as well as a political set of opportunities and constraints. See Jane Jenson, "Changing Discourse, Changing Agendas: Political Rights and Reproductive Policies in France," in *The Women's Movement of the United States and Western Europe*, ed. Mary Katzenstein and Carol M. Mueller (Philadelphia: Temple University Press, 1987), 64–88.

6. The Latin American case studies were chosen on the basis of their similar transition experiences in the Southern Cone. Argentina, Brazil, and Chile had military regimes of the kind Guillermo O'Donnell labeled "bureaucratic authoritarian"—that is, both repressive and committed to economic policies and political stability in order to encourage foreign investment and economic growth. In general, but particularly in the case of Chile, the military also favored "traditional" values (as opposed to what they characterized as the alien and atheistic values of Communism), which included an emphasis on motherhood and traditional gender roles. Peru's case is different in that the military was leftist rather than rightist in orientation, but the Peruvian transition did involve popular mobilization in favor of democracy, and the rise of women's movements was a very visible aspect of Peruvian politics during and after the transition.

The Central and Eastern European cases of Poland, Hungary, and (initially) Czechoslovakia seemed the obvious countries to compare with the Southern Cone cases in terms of economic and political development, educated and potentially active citizens, national systems of communication which allow political discussion and debate, and the role of civil society in the transition process. With the independence of Slovakia, all have legitimate and uncontested states. The partial exception here is Bulgaria, which like Peru is less developed and more internally divided and which until very recently had weaker prospects for democratic consolidation. In contrast to the situation in Peru, however, women's organizations have not played a significant role to date.

7. Ellen Comisso, quoted in Conference Report. For an argument that emphasized the difficulties in this comparison, see Valerie Bunce, "Should Transitologists be Grounded?" *Slavic Review* 54, no. 1 (1995): 111–27, and Bunce, "Comparing East and South," *Journal of Democracy* 6, no. 3 (1995): 87–100. In reply, see Philippe Schmitter and Terry Karl, "The Conceptual Travels of Transitologists and Consolidologists: How Far to the East Should They Attempt to Go?" *Slavic Review* 54, no. 1 (1994): 173–85.

8. Antje Wiener, quoted in Conference Report, and see the discussion on identity politics and stateness in the section on gender and democratic consolidation below. See also Elizabeth Jelin, ed., *Women and Social Change in Latin America* (London: Zed Books, 1990).

9. Jane S. Jaquette, ed., *The Women's Movement in Latin America: Feminism and the Transition to Democracy* (Boulder, Colo.: Westview Press, 1990); Sonia Alvarez, *Engendering Democracy in Brazil: Women's Movements in Transition Politics* (Princeton: Princeton University Press, 1990).

10. See the discussions in the chapters by Feijoó and Caldeira in this volume.

11. At the 1997 Latin American Feminist Encuentro, "autonomous" feminists criticized women working within the system as "gender technocrats." For an account in English, see *Off Our Backs* (March 1997).

12. This accords with data from the case studies; see also the series of essays written for the UN Seminar on the Impact of Economic and Political Reform on the Status of Women in Eastern Europe and the USSR, Vienna, April 8–12, 1991.

13. These points were emphasized by Joanne Regulska, Joan Tronto, and others in the Conference Report.

14. Joyce Gelb, *Feminism and Politics: A Comparative Perspective* (Berkeley: University of California Press, 1989), 220–21.

15. In Conference Report.

16. Reka Pignicski, "The Making of a Women's Movement in Hungary after 1989," in *Ana's Land: Sisterhood in Eastern Europe*, ed. Tanya Renne (Boulder, Colo.: Westview Press, 1997), 121–32.

17. See comments by Jiřina Šiklová in Conference Report, and Tanya Renne, "Disparaging Digressions: Sisterhood in East-Central Europe"; Laura Busheikin, "Is Sisterhood Really Global?"; and Jiřina Šiklová, "McDonald's, Coca-Cola, Terminator—and Feminism?—Imports from the West," in Renne, *Ana's Land*.

18. Jiřina Vrabková, "Women's Priorities and Visions," in Renne, *Ana's Land*, 73.

19. On women and democratic consolidations, see Georgina Waylen, "Gender and Democratic Consolidation," paper delivered at the 1996 Annual Meeting of the American Political Science Association, San Francisco, August 29–September 1.

20. See Elisabeth Friedman, "Paradoxes of Party Politics: The Impact of Gendered Institutions on Women's Incorporation in Latin American Democratization," paper delivered at the 1996 Annual Meeting of the American Political Science Association.

21. See Maruja Barrig's analysis of the failed effort to elect feminists in Peru in "The Difficult Equilibrium between Bread and Roses: Women's Organizations and the Transition from Dictatorship to Democracy in Peru," in Jaquette, *Women's Movement*, 132–34. Barrig notes that the feminists' insistence on autonomy meant that they did not identify themselves with the United Left in their campaign. However, women who do seek party nominations under proportional representation often find themselves too low on the list to get elected unless their party does unexpectedly well. See also Eugenia Hola and Gabriella Pischedda, *Mujeres, poder y politica: Nuevas tensiones para viejas structuras* (Santiago, Chile: Ediciones CEM, 1994).

22. Wilma Rule pioneered the study of the effects of electoral systems on the election of women; see "Electoral Systems, Contextual Factors, and Women's Opportunity for Election to Parliament in Twenty-three Democracies," *Western Political Quarterly* 40 (1987): 477–86. See also Pippa Norris, "Conclusions: Comparing Legislative Recruitment," in *Gender and Party Politics*, ed. Joni Lovenduski and Pippa Norris (Thousand Oaks, Calif.: Sage Press, 1993), and Robert Darcy, Susan Welch, and Janet Clark, *Women, Elections, and Representation* (Lincoln: University of Nebraska Press, 1994).

23. On the impact of the loss of quotas in Central and Eastern Europe, see Tara L. Jebens and Karen J. Vogel, "Paying the Price: Women and Reform Politics in Eastern Europe," paper prepared for the Western Political Science Association Meeting, Pasadena, Calif., March 17–20, 1995. Rule's recent analysis of elections in Russia argues that women can organize successfully to run women candidates but that electoral thresholds (the requirement that a party must win a minimum percentage of the vote to run candidates in the next election) work against such efforts. See Wilma Rule, "Russian Women's Legislative Comeback: Implications for Developed and Developing Democracies," paper pre-

sented at the Sixth International Interdisciplinary Congress on Women, Adelaide, Australia, April 22–26, 1996; see also Jane S. Jaquette, "Women in Power: From Tokenism to Critical Mass," *Foreign Policy* 108 (1997): 23–37. Quotas for women may prove a less risky strategy for the political parties than taking politically risky stands on controversial gender issues like divorce and abortion.

24. Table A2.4, "Women and Political Participation," in *Human Development Report 1995* (New York: United Nations Development Programme, 1995), 60–61.

25. Ibid.

26. This point is also forcefully made by Rule, who argues that women legislators are needed to initiate antidiscrimination (and sexual harassment) legislation ("Russian Women's Legislative Comeback").

27. Difference feminism embraces the position that women have something unique to bring to the content and practices of political life. Catalyzed by Carole Gilligan's book *In a Different Voice* (Cambridge: Harvard University Press, 1982), which argues for an "ethic of care" as opposed to "an ethic of rights," feminist political theorists have developed the implications of this contrast for feminist political practice. See especially Joan C. Tronto, *Moral Boundaries* (New York: Routledge, 1993). Wendy Sarvasy and Berta Siim have edited a special issue of *Social Politics* 1, no. 3 (1994), "International Studies in Gender, State, and Society," which applies the difference approach internationally. See also Veronica Schild, "'Becoming Subjects of Rights': Citizenship, Political Learning, and Identity Formation among Latin American Women," paper prepared for the 16th World Congress of the International Political Science Association, Berlin, August 21–25, 1994, and Ursula Vogel, "Is Citizenship Gender-Specific?" in *The Frontiers of Citizenship*, ed. Ursula Vogel and M. Moran (London: Macmillan, 1991). For a defense of egalitarian citizenship, see Anne Phillips, *Democracy and Difference* (University Park: Pennsylvania State University Press, 1993), and Mary Dietz, "Citizenship with a Feminist Face: The Problem with Maternal Thinking," *Political Theory* 13, no. 1 (1985): 19–37.

28. The literature on how women's bodies contradict male notions of "universal" citizenship is extensive. For classic statements, see Carole Pateman, *Sexual Politics* (Stanford: Stanford University Press, 1988), and Zillah Eisenstein, *The Female Body and the Law* (Berkeley: University of California Press, 1988). Maternal feminism is one answer to disembodied citizenship; it redefines citizens not as atomistic egos in the "Hobbesian" sense but as caring mothers. See, e.g., Sara Ruddick, *Maternal Thinking: Towards a Politics of Peace* (Boston: Beacon Press, 1989), and Jean B. Elshtain, *Public Man and Private Woman: Women in Social and Political Thought* (Princeton: Princeton University Press, 1981). The issue of the boundedness (or not) of women's bodies and its implications for the rule of law are taken up by Teresa Caldeira in her chapter on Brazil in this volume.

The Latin American practice of maternal citizenship is the focus of several studies on women's political participation in the region, including Patricia M. Chuchryk, "Subversive Mothers: The Women's Opposition of the Military Regime in Chile," in *Women, the State, and Development*, ed. Sue Ellen Charlton, Jana Everett, and Kathleen Staudt (Albany: State University of New York Press, 1989), and Jennifer Schirmer, "The Seeking of Truth and the Gendering of Consciousness: The Comadres of El Salvador and the Conavigua Widows of Guatemala," in *Viva: Women and Popular Participation in Latin America*, ed. Sarah L. Radcliffe and Sallie Westwood (London: Routledge, 1993).

29. Maxine Molyneux distinguishes "strategic" (antipatriarchal) from "practical" (welfare/immediate needs) gender interests in "Mobilization without Emancipation?: Women's Interests, the State, and Revolution in Nicaragua," *Feminist Studies* 11, no. 2 (1985), and argues that in Nicaragua gender was approached in terms of women's practical interests rather than confronting male power. Her position is strongly criticized in Schirmer, "Seeking of Truth." For an account of the debate over maternal politics, see discussion in the concluding chapter of the revised edition of Jaquette, ed., *The Women's Movement in Latin America: Participation and Democracy* (Boulder, Colo.: Westview Press, 1994). On "feminine" politics and democratization, see Anna Jonasdottir, "Does Sex Matter to Democracy?" *Scandinavian Political Studies* 11, no. 4 (1988): 299–321.

30. Julia Szalai's chapter in this volume. For an economic analysis of women's changing status in Hungary, see Maria Lado, "Women in the Transition to a Market Economy: The Case of Hungary," United Nations Regional Seminar on the Impact of Political and Economic Reforms on the Status of Women in Eastern Europe and the USSR: The Role of National Machinery, Vienna, April 8–12, 1991.

31. Joanna Goven, "Gender Politics in Hungary: Autonomy and Anti-feminism," in *Gender Politics and Post-Communism: Reflections on Eastern Europe and the Former Soviet Union*, ed. Nanette Funk and Magda Mueller (New York: Routledge, 1993). For a critical analysis of women's return to the home in the former Soviet Union, see see Tatayana Tolstaya, "Notes from Underground," *New York Review of Books* 37, no. 9 (1990): 3–7. See also Sue Bridger, Rebecca Kay, and Kathryn Pinnick, *No More Heroines? Russia, Women, and the Market* (New York: Routledge, 1996); Vitalina Koval, ed., *Women in Contemporary Russia* (Providence: Berghahn Books, 1995); Anastasia Posadskaya, ed., *Women in Russia: A New Era in Russian Feminism*, trans. Kate Clark (New York: Verso, 1994); and Peggy Watson, "The Rise of Masculinism in Eastern Europe," in *Mapping the Women's Movement*, ed. Monica Threlfall (London: Verson, 1996), 216–31.

32. This view is reinforced by the conclusions of a recent faculty seminar organized by Joanna Regulska, "Locations of Gender: Central and Eastern Europe," held at the Center for Russian and East European Studies, Rutgers University, September 1996.

33. See, e.g., Juan J. Linz and Alfred Stepan, *Problems of Democratic Transition and Consolidation: Southern Europe, South America, and Post-Communist Europe* (Baltimore: Johns Hopkins University Press, 1996); Larry Diamond, "Democracy in Latin America: Degrees, Illusions, and Directions for Consolidation," in *Beyond Sovereignty: Collectively Defending Democracy in the Americas*, ed. Tom Farer (Baltimore: Johns Hopkins University Press, 1996); and Jorge I. Dominguez and Abraham F. Lowenthal, eds., *Constructing Democratic Governance: Latin America and the Caribbean in the 1990s* (Baltimore: Johns Hopkins University Press, 1996). For a discussion of the various meanings of the term "consolidation," see Andreas Schedler, "Concepts of Democratic Consolidation," paper delivered at the 1997 Congress of the Latin American Studies Association, Guadalajara, Mexico, April 17–19, 1997.

34. Two exceptions are J. Á. Moisés of Brazil and Janos Simon of Hungary, who underlined this point and brought their work on gender differences in national and cross-national opinion surveys to the 1992 conference in Berkeley.

35. See Laurence Whitehead, "Political Democratization and Economic Liberalization: Prospects for Their Entrenchment in Eastern Europe and Latin America," paper pre-

sented at the Center for International Studies, University of Southern California, January 1995. Whitehead emphasizes the importance of the "liberal ethos" and makes the case that the regions can be compared on the grounds of a "common European tradition" and a "Christian heritage," noting that "all secured nationhood by emancipation from a past of subordination within European political control" and that "all have a century or more of 'peripheral capitalist' economic history and experience" (37). See also Larry Diamond, ed., *Political Culture and Democracy in Developing Countries* (Boulder: Colo.: Lynne Rienner, 1993). In *Problems of Democratic Transition and Consolidation*, Linz and Stepan speak of actors becoming "*habituated* to . . . the resolution of conflict within the *specific* laws, procedures and institutions sanctioned by the new democratic processes" (6), quoted with emphasis in Schedler, "Concepts of Democratic Consolidation," 20.

36. Robert D. Putnam, *Making Democracy Work: Civil Traditions in Modern Italy* (Princeton: Princeton University Press, 1993), and Francis Fukuyama, *Trust: The Social Virtues and the Creation of Prosperity* (New York: Free Press, 1995). On "subnational" systems, emphasized by Schedler, Putnam, and others, we emphasize the greater representation of women in local politics. See Joanna Regulska, "Transition to Local Democracy: Do Polish Women Have a Chance?" in *Women in the Politics of Postcommunist Eastern Europe*, ed. Marilyn Rueschemeyer (Armonk, N.Y.: M. E. Sharpe, 1994), and "Establishing Democratic Rule: The Re-emergence of Local Governments in Post-Authoritarian Systems," a special issue of *In Depth: A Journal for Values and Public Policy* 3, no. 1 (1993), ed. Richard L. Rubenstein.

37. On the importance of mothers in establishing children's political identity, see, e.g., Kent Jennings and Roger Niemi, "The Division of Political Labor between Mothers and Fathers," *American Political Science Review* 65 (1991): 69–82.

38. See Whitehead, "Political Democratization and Economic Liberalization."

39. Linz and Stepan, *Problems of Democratic Transition and Consolidation*, 3.

40. "A nation requires some internal identification. . . . Without imagined communities there are no nations" (ibid., 22). On stateness: "The criteria of the democratic process presuppose the rightfulness of the unit [nation-state] itself" (26), and "Democracy is characterized not by subjects but by citizens, so a democratic transition often puts the polis/demos questions at the center of politics" (29).

41. Valentine M. Moghadam, ed., *Identity Politics and Women: Cultural Reassertions and Feminisms in International Perspective* (London: Routledge, 1993); Nira Duval-Davis, "The Citizenship Debate: Women, Ethnic Processes, and the State," *Feminist Review* 39, special issue, "Shifting Territories: Feminism and Europe" (1991); and the introduction by Craig Calhoun to his *Social Theory and the Politics of Identity* (Oxford: Blackwell, 1994), 9–36.

42. See essays by Stasa Zajovic, Biljana Regodic, and Tanya Renne in Renne, *Ana's Land*.

43. Linz and Stepan, *Problems of Democratic Transition and Consolidation*, chap. 1, esp. 9–11.

44. Douglas A. Chalmers, Scott B. Martin, and Kerianne Piester, "Associative Networks: New Structure of Representation for the Popular Sectors?" in *The New Politics of Inequality in Latin America: Rethinking Participation and Representation*, ed. Douglas A. Chalmers, Carlos Vilas, Katherine Hite, Scott B. Martin, Kerianne Piester, and Monique Segarra (Oxford: Oxford University Press, 1996), 565.

Chapter Two

Democratic Participation and Women in Argentina

MARÍA DEL CARMEN FEIJOÓ

emocratic transitions, which took place all over the world during the 1970s and 1980s, gave birth to a large literature of in-depth national case studies as well as comparative work on the types of transitions, their actors, dynamics, and outcomes. Implicitly, two opposing paradigms dominated the discussion: one, the paradigm of new social actors, new ways of doing politics, and changed relationships between state and society. Later, this literature focused on how these new movements operated under the rules of the emerging democratic "game." This approach optimistically highlighted the role of social movements and, among them, the role of women's movements in democratic transitions.

The second paradigm was often unable to take into account the fact of a new political arena no longer dominated by political parties nor fully described by negotiations among elites; it was insensitive to the role of new social actors and movements. Both paradigms, however, were continually challenged by the rapid political, economic, and social changes that took place during the transitions and after. Each paradigm produced different expectations and thus different forms of disenchantment with the reality of the forms of politics which replaced the participatory euphoria of the transition period.

Some of these misunderstandings, at least in the Latin American cases, are linked to the biases of the models themselves; others arise from the short time frame of the case studies, which focused primarily on the transitions and not on the "consolidations" that followed. Now, 10 or 15 years later, a reappraisal of these studies is possible in the light of post-transition developments. An analysis of women's social and political participation helps bridge the gap between the two paradigms to assess what has really changed and what we have learned that can empower women in what it is hoped will be stable democratic environments.

The military coup that took place in 1976 followed its tradition, initiated in

1930, of undermining civilian governments. This time, however, it quickly turned into a regime of state terrorism. The military defeat in the Falklands/Malvinas War led in 1983 to the junta's agreeing to give up power and to call elections. Raúl Alfonsín, the candidate of a relatively small centrist party, the Radical Civic Union, won the presidency. President Alfonsín was succeeded by a Peronist candidate, Carlos Menem, in 1989; he was reelected in 1995.

In Argentina, the relevance and diversity of women's experiences and the high-profile role of women from different social classes (especially those in the human rights movements, those who organized against increases in the cost of living, in the resistance against the Falklands/Malvinas War, and in local neighborhood movements) were a notable element of the transition. These experiences have been reflected in several well-known accounts, and the literature on this topic continues to grow.[1] Besides their relevance to scholars, the experience of women's groups such as the Mothers (Madres) and Grandmothers of the Plaza de Mayo inspired similar movements in different places in the world, movements in favor of the defense of life and human rights, struggles against dictatorships, and movements for economic and social rights. Just to cite one example, the Madres of East Los Angeles have also mobilized women on the basis of their roles as mothers, using the Madres' strategies to organize themselves and gain political leverage on issues at the barrio level.

The meaning and potential of political action rooted in women's traditional roles must be analyzed not only from feminist and "feminine" political standpoints but also in the broader context of the social, economic, and political settings that frame their collective action. The relevance of women's activism in the Argentine transition has been stressed, but the context has often been obscured. This chapter analyzes the role of women's organizations in contemporary Argentine history in terms of the particular features of the Argentine transition—a transition that, it is hoped, represents the end to the long cycle of alternation between military and civilian rule which has characterized Argentine political history since 1930. It argues that women's political participation needs to be stepped up to be effectively institutionalized. The political and economic contexts have changed, weakening the forms of "doing politics" appropriate to the transition as they were practiced by both feminist and feminine women's movements. Of those, some remained more allied to autonomous *movimientista* politics, while others were ready to move to more cooperative relations with the state. Despite those differences, the stage was set for the greater political empowerment of women. This discussion among different tendencies is now occurring in other countries in the region and had its most recent expansion in the debate between these groups in the feminist Encuentro that took place in Cartagena, Chile, in 1996.

WOMEN'S POLITICAL PARTICIPATION

Argentine women have a long history of participation in politics, dating from the beginning of the century, in trade unions, political parties, and even feminist movements. This history is often forgotten, but its threads reappear in the fabric of the political history of the country.[2] Excluded from formal politics until 1947, women were active in other ways, especially in trade unions, in socialist and anarchist movements, and in early grassroots feminism. Women were given the vote during the first presidency of Juan Perón (1946–55). In 1951, when they voted and were elected to office for the first time, 29 women were elected to parliament, 18 percent of the total. This high percentage resulted from a quota procedure that was applied to the electoral rosters of the dominant Peronist party and which was intended to elect women from its feminine branch.

To understand modern Argentine history, it is necessary to understand the role played by the armed forces, which undermined the stability of democratic governments.[3] During the fifties, sixties, and seventies, three different military coups, supported by some civilian groups, shut down democratic politics, taking public space from both men and women, most of all those in the popular sectors and working classes. But women, who were such late arrivals to the political arena, were not passive in the face of the political conditions imposed by dictatorship, and many responded with acts of protest and resistance. Popular mobilization and insurgence grew continuously in the 1970s, in a supportive regional context. The military coup initiated the repressive "Dirty War," which was overtly directed against armed groups but which tried in fact to destroy all types of popular organizations, including trade unions, student federations, and even religious and neighborhood organizations.

Although women had played important, if secondary, roles in guerrilla and resistance organizations, their participation did not ensure political recognition. When a democratic government was elected in 1963, after the so-called Peronist Resistance, women held only 0.5 percent of the parliamentary seats. In 1973, when their obvious involvement in the armed struggle made them visible political actors, the percentage of women elected increased substantially but was still only 7.8 percent.

Of course, a full understanding of women's political participation cannot be gained from looking solely at their public involvement. It is necessary to examine their roles in everyday life. The 1960s were an especially important period of changes in the private realm, changes that created a new profile of middle-class and popular-sector urban women. Massive expansion in middle and higher education helped raise women's education levels and favored their incorporation into the expanding labor market. At the same time, traditional family ties began to loosen, helping to democratize gender relations. Free love, the pill, the miniskirt and "flower power" were some of the symbols and ideologies that molded the experiences of middle-class women in this period. Within the family, the bargaining position of working women and working-class housewives improved as a result of their greater economic autonomy. The messages in the mass media favored social as well as economic modernization of "traditional" society. During the late 1960s, these changes laid the foundations for the appearance of new feminist groups. In this context, the military coup of 1966 can be seen as an effort to slow down social change, to mount a cultural backlash, and to stop history.[4]

Women's experiences in the late sixties and early seventies reenacted the complex political history of the decade. In the armed struggle and in different types of partisan political activities (both in political parties and at the grassroots level), those women who became aware of their subordinate position were constrained from expressing feminist views by the influence of both traditional and Marxist thinking. Feminism was rejected as an imperialistic, Eurocentric movement, and women's issues were seen as a "secondary contradiction" to be subordinated to the class struggle.[5]

Nevertheless, women played important roles, and some became national heroines, including the women imprisoned and then killed in 1972 on the navy base in Trelew, where they had been held for their involvement in revolutionary warfare.[6] Women's heroism and their presence in the public arena highlighted their growing political visibility, facilitating their election to parliament the following year. The failure of the male-dominated Left to take gender issues into account at this stage, however, affected the future development of feminist consciousness, which had to overcome the gender-blind militance of popular and leftist parties. Ideologically, feminism focused its attention on the relationships between the public and private, opening up new issues that had been avoided by a left-right debate that was centered on the public sphere.

During the 1970s, as part of the new wave of international feminism and the establishment of the UN Decade for Women (1975–85), new groups appeared which were explicitly feminist, including the Argentine Feminist Union, the Feminist Liberation Movement, and the Argentine Feminist Organization. Some women tried to develop feminist groups linked to or within leftist political parties, such as the Popular Feminist Movement or the Group of Socialist Women. Others formed women's fronts within the parties that, like the Evita Group within Peronist Youth, did not take a stance on feminism but did begin to raise gender concerns. Along with virtually the whole population of the country, these groups were repressed when a military junta established a regime based on state terrorism in March 1976.

In the view of its protagonists, the military takeover was not going to be "just another coup d'état." Using Alain Rouquie's term, the 1976 coup was intended to be "foundational," aiming at nothing less than the reshaping of society and state/society relations. The coup tried to destroy a society that found itself in an obvious political crisis, but one in which the dominant classes feared the possibility that leftist and guerrilla groups might bring about a popular uprising. More than setting out to destroy a "correlation of forces" expressed in terms of a conflict between Left and Right, or to annihilate the guerrillas, the objective of the coup was to destroy a broader process of popular mobilization, following similar military takeovers in Allende's Chile and in Uruguay. This social overhaul could only commence once the military had extirpated the "cancer" of leftist subversion. The supporters of the military regime felt they had the right to decide who should live and who should die, kidnapping individuals without any pretense of legality and imposing a regime of silence and terror on civil society. Argentina became an example of military terror for the whole world.

In power, the armed forces created a hitherto unknown model, kidnapping and torturing those they suspected of leftist sympathies and making "disappearance" a form of political punishment. The term *desaparecidos* will forever be linked to the Argentine experience. Those the government disappeared were usually young men and women—students, militants, and workers, some with their children—who were taken from their homes by parapolice forces, the police, or the armed forces themselves. During the military's Process of National Reorganization, state terrorism resulted in the disappearance of an estimated thirty thousand people.[7]

Women, generally mothers in their forties and fifties, were the first to react. The movement of the Madres and later on the Abuelas (Grandmothers) of the Plaza de Mayo was a brave answer to military terror. Following the path opened by the Madres and the Abuelas, other groups organized to address different political and social issues. Among these, women were especially visible as housewives struggling against increases in the cost of living and women and mothers against the Falklands/Malvinas War and the draft. Feminist groups, whose roots went back to the late 1960s, were reborn. At the same time, as awareness of the problem of discrimination against women grew, it became clear that any future transition to democracy would have to address gender issues.

Along with other social movements, women's movements became visible actors in the transition. Women's experiences made key contributions to the reconstruction of civil society, which appeared with renewed strength after having

survived eight years of the military's efforts to destroy it. In the transition literature, the Argentine case is usually classified as one of "democratization by collapse," resulting from the military's defeat in the Falklands/Malvinas War. But
stressing the external conditions of the military's defeat should in no way detract
from the extraordinary political contribution of the Madres. History will remember them as the first group defiant enough to confront the dictatorship in
the public realm. The feminine presence in crisis is hardly unprecedented; since
the time of Antigone, women have been recognized as capable of extraordinary
deeds in great times of stress. And, since Antigone, it has been recognized that
women bring alternative values and emotions to the public sphere. They may
bring men into the public realm, or even into war, as was the case with Graco's
mother in ancient Rome or with the appeal women made to husbands and sons
during the Spanish Civil War.[8]

What was new in this case was women's capacity to build a movement
from the feelings and emotions that are usually associated with the private sphere
(and which the military had violated when it disappeared the Madres' sons and
daughters) and to sustain and adapt it under particularly repressive political
conditions. Symbolically, their feminine "weakness" became their strength. In this
way, the Madres recast their private identity—motherhood—and converted it to
an effective base from which to enter the public sphere. The legitimacy of their
action was anchored in their historical obligation, legal and moral, to defend their
children. But this mandate took on extraordinary new characteristics once it was
taken out of the private sphere and relocated in the public.

The strategies and the symbolism of confrontation which the Madres developed were unprecedented in the public arena. Appealing solely on the basis of
their identity as mothers, they used symbols such as diapers, which they put on
as handkerchiefs over their heads to symbolize the upbringing of their children.
At the same time every Thursday, they marched silently around the Plaza de
Mayo (in front of the Government House, the symbolic locus of political power)
carrying family photos by which their kidnapped children could be identified.
Thursday at 3:30 P.M. became and continues to be the Argentine symbol of resistance against all types of injustice.[9]

THE TRANSITION

The transition itself was very rapid after General Leopoldo Fortunato
Galtieri's forced resignation from the presidency in June 1982, when the army had
been defeated in the Falklands/Malvinas War. President Reynaldo Bignone was
the last military president; he called for elections, which were held on October 30,

1983, and Raúl Alfonsín was elected with almost 51 percent of the votes. The significance of this return to civilian rule was the profound awareness that had been developing within many sectors of society that this transition should be the last one.

At the same time, there was a new outlook on what a democratic regime should be. As Laurence Whitehead wrote, "Today, in most Latin American countries, especially those that have recently undergone or are still undergoing authoritarian rule, a new factor has emerged. Largely as a consequence of the painful learning induced by the failures of those regimes and the unprecedented repression and violence, most political and cultural forces of any weight now attribute high intrinsic value to the achievement and consolidation of political democracy."[10]

To understand the nature of this transition, it is critical to grasp the meaning and consequences of the positions held by social movements. For the first time in contemporary history, the value of formal democracy was put in first place, without any qualifications: this time it was not democracy as a way to socialism, or democracy as a means to social justice, or democracy as an intermediary step toward a popular regime. This time democracy itself would have the highest value. Although candidate Alfonsín promised that democracy would make it possible "to eat, to heal and to educate," it was clear that it was the democratic process itself, and not its goals as defined by his campaign, which was at stake.

The period between the defeat in the Falklands/Malvinas War and the call to elections was the moment of "opening" or "decompression" (to use Guillermo O'Donnell's terms) which "usually produces a sharp and rapid increase in general politicization and popular activation, the resurrection of civil society."[11] In this moment, the expansion of the membership of the political parties was as important a trend as the appearance of new social movements. When the legal political "game" reopened in 1983, the space that had been dominated by the Madres and other human rights groups, the Permanent Assembly for Human Rights, the Legal and Social Studies Center, the Association of the Relatives of the Imprisoned and Disappeared, and the Service of Peace and Justice (the last created by the Nobel Prize winner Adolfo Perez Esquivel), was reoccupied by the old political parties and interest groups and even some new ones. Trade unions and cultural and social movements linked to different issues emerged as salient actors in the transition process. For the first time in Argentine history, the rebuilding of democracy appeared to be the responsibility of the whole society, not a partisan effort.

Privileged actors in the transition, the new social movements began to feel the competition from the political parties; the challenge was to find ways of matching the interests of the social movements and their new ways of doing politics with the more traditional approaches of the parties. The parties took advantage of the mobilization produced by the social movements, but as they grew stronger, they tended to leave the movements aside. For their part, the new social movements were unable to represent themselves in the parliament, forcing them to deal with the parties in order to have any impact. To a degree, the parties were influenced by the goals of the social movements (which were interest-dominated in terms of getting their goals and patterning new identities) and by their more direct and nonhierarchical political styles.[12]

In this process, women's issues appeared in a variety of party platforms, and almost all the candidates saw that women would be a significant voting force. Women's issues became politicized on various grounds, for example, the appeal to "life" over "politics" as part of a new feminine ethic, in the demand for divorce and in the call for modifications in the family code. Women also appeared as candidates in different party lists and occupied symbolic yet high positions on their candidate rosters, such as vice presidents for some of the small leftist parties. Women showed a new capacity to politicize women's issues in a nonpartisan way and a new ability to permeate traditional structures, including the state.

In the case of women's human rights movements, the novelty was militant motherhood. Motherhood is the most traditional of all women's roles and has often been linked to conservative values: adaptation, conformism, and opposition to collectivist social programs that might threaten the primacy of the family. In these movements, however, motherhood appeared as a striking new identity, capable of sustaining activism and promoting new behavior. Instead of private mourning and passive resignation, the Madres projected themselves assertively into the public realm. If, as I have argued before, this way of entering the public realm could be criticized as a return to a form of *marianismo*, it was hardly a return to the role of Mater Dolorosa.[13]

The second novelty was the way in which, while politicizing their demands, the Madres managed to remain "autonomous," working outside the structures of formal political participation which were being built and rebuilt during the transition. However, like all the other social movements, they were soon confronted with a very different set of political challenges. Social movements, which had developed from the early eighties, were directed toward a range of different objectives and rooted in different identities. They ran the gamut from neighborhood groups addressing local problems and legalizing urban land titles to youth who tried to create a new culture through music. During the transition, each evolved differently, depending on the kinds of demands, and identities were not always articulated according to a predetermined pattern; they often produced different kinds of social and political actions, depending on which element was foremost.

Scott Mainwaring and Eduardo Viola identify four types of relations be-

tween social movements and the democratization process: authoritarian invo-
lution, isolation, cooptation, and new alliances.[14] As cooptation was the most
feared, most groups opted for isolation; a few tried the approach of forging new
alliances. Some groups tried to act as pressure groups, pushing for access to the
political parties and platforms. Others avoided all such contacts, but few actually
joined the parties. In their concern to avoid cooptation, most were also reluctant
to develop linkages with the state.

As the transition and consolidation processes went forward, the debate about
the role of the movements and their relationship to the state became more intense.
As the state slowly developed institutional structures to answer some of their demands, splits and contradictions appeared. Some social movements began to accept the idea that a legitimate democratic state should not be considered the
enemy but rather a powerful tool to reach their goals. Those who stayed apart
were able to preserve their identity, but such a strategy could not begin to close
the deep gap that had opened up between the society and the state.

The answer of the human rights groups, and particularly the Madres, was
to distance themselves firmly from all political organizations. Arguing that the
struggle for human rights was an ethical, not a political, struggle and that it could
not be subsumed under any political current, their decision not to get involved
followed from the decision not to negotiate their demands, including the demand
that their children be returned alive. Other human rights leaders did join some
of the smaller political parties explicitly to politicize human rights issues and link
them to party goals.[15] Still, others entered the National Commission for the Disappeared (CONDADEP), which was created by the state to investigate the dis-
appearances and killings.

However, the decision to stay on the outside was not an easy one. As time
passed, differences sprang up regarding particular steps that should be taken in
the democratic context, for example, whether the Madres would allow the remains of their children to be identified by forensic experts, or whether they
would accept the state's offer to provide monetary indemnification to the families of the disappeared. In 1986, the movement split into two different groups,
the Linea Fundadora (literally Founding Line) and the Asociación Madres de
Plaza de Mayo (Association of the Mothers of the Plaza de Mayo).

In a recent book, Marguerite Bouvard argues that the division was actually
a result of a part of the group trying to endorse the Radical Party then in power.[16]
Using testimonies from different members, she argues that the decision was also
a result of class differences within the group. She finds that the Linea Fundadora
is mostly middle-class women, while the Asociación Madres de Plaza de Mayo
is predominantly made up of women from the popular sectors.

Since 1983, whenever democracy was threatened, women's movements re-mobilized in protest. During the most dramatic moments the country has experienced in recent years, such as the military crisis that occurred during Holy Week in 1987, or when the president decided to release and pardon the officers who had been in jail for their activities during the dictatorship, women went into the streets. As they worked to keep the transition on track, women's groups were also successful in increasing the social awareness of gender issues, as when they mobilized to protest the handling of the case of María Soledad Morales, a young girl who was raped and killed in the province of Catamarca in 1991. Although the case has yet to be solved,[17] it is a good example of the political consequences of organizing to bring private crime to light. In fact, the social protest that arose to press for a resolution of the case brought about the fall of the provincial governor, whom the public accused of being involved in a cover-up.

Economically, the Alfonsín government faced a very difficult situation. As happened elsewhere in the region, Argentina's return to democracy occurred during a period of economic crisis, the worst of the century. The democratic government had to maneuver amid increasing economic demands that had been repressed by decades of military dictatorship.[18]

Under these conditions, it was impossible to fulfill the economic expectations of those who had fought for democracy and who had blamed the military for the economic debacle. The junta that governed from 1976 to 1983 had installed neoliberal economic policies and had eliminated subsidies to domestic industries. The plan was financed by foreign borrowing that sustained the importation of consumer goods. But the neoliberal policies produced declines in productive activity, lowered real incomes, and increased unemployment. To reduce deficits, the military government began to reduce state expenditures in health, education, and welfare, which reduced living standards, particularly in the popular sectors.

As a result of its foreign debt, by 1982 Argentina was in a full-scale crisis, with rapidly increasing levels of inflation. The newly elected democratic authorities had little room to maneuver. After trying to reduce demand, they launched a heterodox anti-inflation plan. An inflation rate of about 5,000 percent per year produced the first food riots in Argentine history (in 1989) and produced widespread disillusionment with the government[19] which prepared the way for President Alfonsín's successor, Carlos Menem, to implement more thoroughgoing structural adjustment in the next presidential term.

The "lost decade" affected different population groups differently. Women and children were particularly hard hit in what was called the "invisible adjustment." Economic crisis, structural adjustment, low wages, and high unemployment gave women much greater responsibility for meeting the basic needs of their families. As households were developing more effective responses to the crisis, women's roles in family survival were enhanced. Traditional strategies were supplemented by new approaches such as communal kitchens and microenterprises, and many kinds of grassroots women's organizations sprang up.

Women in these groups consider their economic activities as a "natural" extension of their maternal role, without overtly challenging the traditional sexual division of labor. But even when this traditional division is accepted, the fact of women coming together becomes a kind of social laboratory where not only survival and poverty issues but also gender issues (such as domestic violence and women's rights) are discussed. Moreover, women's actions in response to the economic crisis copied some of the tactics learned from the women's human rights movements. New components were combined with the old and applied to new situations, such as women who demonstrated against their husbands' unemployment or against layoffs brought about by the neoliberal privatization of state industries.[20]

AFTER THE TRANSITION

The succession of Peronist Carlos Menem to the presidency broke a long tradition of military intervention in politics. In May, Menem received 49 percent of the votes. In July, six months before the end of his term, Alfonsín turned the presidency over to Menem so that Menem and his team could confront the hyperinflation crisis.

The succession reassured many that the process of consolidation was well in place. Sustained high levels of inflation, growing poverty, and recessionary trends, however, made the economic crisis the highest priority issue. But President Menem chose to tackle another problem, the "pacification" of the country, which was still suffering from the wounds of state terrorism. In December 1990, he decreed a pardon for all those in the military who had been tried, found guilty, and sentenced for their part in a criminal conspiracy that had led to the torture and death of thirty thousand *desaparecidos*. The pardon was opposed by millions of Argentines, who had earlier fought the milder amnesty measures that were implemented by the Alfonsín government. In all these instances, women reappeared in the public arena, as social actors in the human rights movements, as feminists, or as representatives of grassroots organizations.

To meet the economic crisis, "lower class women increased their labor force participation, often taking temporary jobs with lower benefits and working longer hours." For middle-class women, the effects were even more dramatic. As male participation in the labor force declined sharply, female participation increased. Between 1974 and 1987, the number of middle-class women in the labor force increased by 33 percent, while the percentage of poor women increased 11 percent. The increase was highest for married women: 53 percent for middle-class women and 33 percent for those in the working class. "Women who were too poor or too burdened with family responsibilities to enter the labor force engaged in survival activities. Food centers or neighborhood food programs, microenterprises and different kinds of neighborhood jobs concentrated women's social energies in response to the challenge of survival."[21]

However, the most striking changes were in the realm of politics. Political parties in Argentina are dominated by men. What impact women have had on them must be traced back to persistent, low-profile feminist militancy and the ability of women's movements to survive after the transition. Although the fragmented feminist groups could not maintain their visibility, they did keep pressing for change, not in response to a well-articulated strategy but tactically, step by step, in response to immediate opportunities.

Just as the threads of the early women's movement keep reappearing in the fabric of Argentine politics, so the renaissance of feminist mobilization during the 1980s can be traced in the politics of Argentina today. Of course, things did not turn out the way many women activists hoped or expected. Instead of a triumphant presence in the public arena, with huge women's mobilizations in support of women's demands, stubborn and modest resistance in a minor key has been the kind of participation which has assured their continued voice in the public realm.

Against all political and economic odds, democracy has survived in Argentina, facilitating women's empowerment and creating opportunities for women to find new ways to participate. There was neither a dramatic advancement of women's causes nor a backlash against them. Instead, there was a slow and progressive struggle to increase the amount of political space in which some women could act.

Collectively, women experienced important changes during the last 10 years. During the first year of the dictatorship, feminists had begun to organize to pursue academic and political goals. The Women's Studies Center was established in 1979 to study women's status in Argentina and to develop political proposals to promote women's rights. The Feminist Liberation Movement was organized in 1981 and called itself the Argentine Feminist Organization. The ATEM November 25 (the Association for the Work and Study of Women) emerged in 1982 as an autonomous group to organize campaigns and seminars and to lobby for Argentine compliance with the UN Convention on the Elimination of All Forms of Discrimination Against Women (CEDAW). Feminists established Women's Place, which offers space for activities and advice to other women's centers on how to organize around feminist themes.[22]

Other groups were formed after the return to democracy, including the Permanent Women's Workshop and the TIDO Foundation, among others. Many women who had been in exile during the dictatorship returned after 1983 and played a prominent role in disseminating feminist ideas. Argentine women were active in regional feminist forums, and the Fifth Latin American and Caribbean Feminist Meeting (Encuentro) was held in 1990 in the Argentine city of San Bernardo. National Encuentros were held beginning in 1985; the last one, held in Corrientes Province, brought together more than six thousand women from feminist groups, grassroots organizations, and political parties.

Although the human rights groups did not engage in the formal politics of political parties and elections, they have continued to play an active role, and their strategies of struggle have been disseminated to other groups, such as housewives opposed to the layoffs of their husbands. Groups that had originally begun their struggle "in defense of life" and against dictatorship extended the scope of their interests to include new issues, including defending young people who were harassed by the police or promoting the cause of women's reproductive rights, or ameliorating the worsening living conditions of the urban poor.

New institutional spaces for women were opened within the state. During Alfonsín's presidency, the government passed a law of compliance with the CEDAW, a divorce law was passed after a contentious public debate, and the existing family law (*patria potestad*) was modified to share custody and family decision making between husband and wife. At the same time, issues of reproductive rights and violence against women began to be addressed. Offices dealing with women's issues were established, first at the federal and then at the provincial level, following the Brazilian model of the *conselhos de mulher*. These offices developed a variety of programs, most with a gender-sensitive perspective, providing assistance to microenterprises, among others. In combination, they represented a highly diversified set of programs responding to women's multiple roles as social actors. International exchanges strengthened the national capacity to address these problems, as in the case of the police stations for women, modeled on the Brazilian *delegacias*.

However, perhaps the single most important change in terms of women's involvement in the public realm was the quota law (Ley de Cupos #24,012) passed in November 1991. This law required that 30 percent of the upper-level positions on party tickets be occupied by women. Female quotas had been tried by the Peronist party in the 1951 elections, when women first had the vote. Law

#24,012 was passed at a time when such affirmative action/antidiscriminatory policies had been tried in many countries. When it was first implemented, the quota law increased women's representation in the Chamber of Deputies from 5.5 percent in 1991 to 12.8 percent in 1993. The struggle against the glass ceiling will continue as more women are nominated and elected under this law.[23]

In 1994, the reform of the old constitution, which dated from 1853 and 1860, would become a major arena for women's lobbying. Constitutional reform was first proposed by President Alfonsín and then by President Menem in order to make reelection of the president, explicitly forbidden by the earlier constitution, possible. A political agreement between the two leaders, the Olivos Pact, led to the passing of law #24,309 to create the procedures for the National Constitutional Reform. The enforcement of the quota law made possible the election of 80 women representatives from a variety of political parties; they constituted 26.4 percent of the constitutional assembly.

Thus, as a result of the democratic game as it has played out in Argentina, women were present at a foundational political event, the writing of Argentina's new "Magna Carta." The women who were elected, and the groups that were working with them, had already shared the same struggles, as party activists, feminists, and members of the human rights movements, and they made an important political difference. They succeeded in creating a crosscutting bloc of individuals, including men, who were deeply committed to further democratization of law and society.

In addition to their role in promoting Argentina's adherence to the CEDAW, women's presence was crucial to the way in which issues (such as the question of whether the "defense of life" should be applied to the unborn and thus block abortion reform) were debated and decided. Although there were few feminists in the assembly, their presence helped pose and deepen a discussion of issues that would have developed very differently had women not been there. The resulting legislation was far from clear, but the debate itself was extremely important.[24] The constitution makes it a responsibility of Congress to address the issue of adequate social support for mothers and children.

As a result of the presence of women and feminists in the assembly, the new constitution includes the principle of affirmative action in the electoral system, which will surely lead to the progressive empowerment of women and increasing attention to women's issues. The provision makes it all the more necessary to deepen the linkages that exist between feminist groups and grassroots women's organizations.

The continued application of the quota law for the election of deputies and senators at the national level has made possible a progressive increase in the number of women in both houses, so that, in the future, there will be a minimum of 30 percent. The results of the implementation of this law are controversial, and there has not yet been a serious analysis of its effect. According to Waylen, even those feminists who are not alienated from participation in the government remain skeptical about the results.[25] Suggestions have been made that the positions are being filled by "private" recruitment (of friends and relatives of male participants) instead of universal criteria of merit. Nevertheless, in the face of this skepticism, it is important to point out that the quota law has opened doors in the party electoral machines for those women who want to make their political careers on the basis of open competition. To meet their obligations under the law, the parties must continue to recruit more women.

The executive is an area, on the other hand, in which women are undoubtedly chosen on the grounds of particular criteria. The power of the presidency in Argentina gives the chief of state very broad leeway in such matters. In fact, the behavior of President Menem, beyond his support for the quota law, has been characterized by his willingness to articulate the interests of the most conservative sector of the female electorate and to give in to groups like the church, historically conservative on matters of women's rights. This can be seen in the mandate the Argentine delegation took to the Population Conference in Cairo in 1994 and the Fourth UN Conference on Women in Beijing in 1995. The delegation not only opposed policies favoring women's reproductive rights but even questioned the use of the term "gender."

Sadly, this put Argentina on the side of countries with the most reactionary views in relation to women's issues. This debate produced a change in leadership in the Women's Council, which serves at the pleasure of the president. A feminist was replaced by a more conservative woman who would represent the president's views. This occurred, however, because the women's organizations and women in political parties who were opposed to these policies were unable to mobilize sufficient pressure to support their position.

WOMEN'S ROLES IN THE TRANSITION: TOWARD SUSTAINABLE DEMOCRATIZATION?

A general assessment of women's roles in the transition and consolidation processes would be cautiously optimistic. Although a broad-based feminist movement has not yet fully emerged in Argentina, a feminist presence and the legitimacy of women's involvement in almost all kinds of activities in the public realm have now been established; all discussions of how Argentine society should be reshaped must now take into account gender issues. In the private sphere, there is a growing awareness of the inequality of gender relationships in the family and the household, which is shown in the growing demands made on those institutions that have been established to respond to domestic violence. Legislation has been changed on crucial aspects of women's position in the family, new issues have opened for women as a result of the economic crisis, and the increasing presence of women in the parliament will ensure that women's agendas will receive greater political attention.

If women's involvement in democratic transitions has been characterized in the past as a crisis response, the evolution of democratic institutions and political culture in Argentina is producing more sustainable forms of empowerment. These changes are not the mechanical results of democratization but the products of persistent collective action. The empowerment that has resulted is not the kind that was anticipated by activists and analysts of the new social movements, nor is it a cautionary tale of state or party cooptation. In fact, a much more complex interaction between the state and civil society has resulted.

It appears that the continuity of the democratic setting is creating an environment in which feminist and women's groups have experienced advances and defeats, but those are part of an ongoing, long-term learning process. When democracy was reestablished in 1983, the women's movements had to learn to play by the rules of the new democratic game. Despite a lack of confidence in some aspects of the political transition, the crisis of representation which affected legitimacy of the political parties, and the fear of state cooptation, the continuity of the democratic process has made it possible to learn a new map of social action. In this process, women must work from several identities at the same time, as feminists, party activists, grassroots or trade union leaders.

This increasingly complex set of identities, alternatives, and experiences demands a continuous rethinking of the challenges and the strategies to meet them. To confront these challenges, women's movements must reshape themselves and ally with other forces in society to effect changes in gender relations. The democracies of Latin America, which some have called "democracies by default" because they survive for lack of any alternative, are not free from potentially fatal threats. The most serious of these is the possibility that they will become democracies in name only, what Guillermo O'Donnell has called "delegative democracies with low intensity citizenship."[26] Gender bias is beginning to be perceived as a significant cause of the low intensity of citizen participation. Permanent feedback is needed—between women's collective actions to exert their rights to citizenship and a democracy that can respond to gender issues—in order to move from a male model of citizenship to one that is truly universal.

NOTES

1. The first contribution on the role of women in human rights movements is the well-known work by Jean Pierre Bosquet, *Las locas de la Plaza de Mayo* (Buenos Aires: El Cid, 1983). More recently, Marguerite Guzmán Bouvard and Marjorie Agosín, *Circles of Madness: Mothers of the Plaza de Mayo* (Fredonia, N.Y.: White Pine Press, 1992).

2. For an overview on women's political participation in Argentina, see, among others, María del Carmen Feijoó, "From Family Ties to Political Action: Women's Experiences in Argentina," in *Women and Politics Worldwide*, ed. Barbara Nelson and Najma Chowdhury (New Haven: Yale University Press, 1994); Carlos Abeijón and Jorge Santos Lafauce, *La mujer argentina antes y despues de Eva Perón* (Buenos Aires: Cuarto Mundo, 1975); Vera Pichel, *Mi país y sus mujeres* (Buenos Aires: La Campaña, 1983); and Marifran Carlson, *Feminism: The Women's Movement in Argentina from Its Beginnings to Eva Perón* (Chicago: Academy Chicago Publishers, 1988).

3. For military intervention, see the classic work by Alain Rouquie, *Poder militar y sociedad política en la Argentina* (Buenos Aires: Emece, 1981).

4. Changes during the sixties are described in María del Carmen Feijoó and Marcela Nari, "Women in Argentina during the 1960s," *Latin American Perspectives*, issue 88, vol. 23, no. 1 (1966). For a gender-blind history of the period, see Oscar Teran, *Nuestros años sesenta* (Buenos Aires: Puntosur, 1991).

5. Ana María Araujo, *Des femmes de l'Uruguay* (Paris: Editions du Seuil, 1980). *Des femmes* has been the first in exploring the complex relationships between guerrilla organizations and women's positions. Later on, Nancy Saporta Sternbach, Marysa Navarro Aranguren, Patricia Chuchryk, and Sonia E. Alvarez, "Feminisms in Latin America: From Bogotá to San Bernardo," in *The Making of Social Movements in Latin America: Identity, Strategy, and Democracy*, ed. Arturo Escobar and Sonia E. Alvarez (Boulder, Colo.: Westview Press, 1992), addressed the same issues in relation to different problems.

6. See Tomás Eloy Martínez, *La pasión según Trelew* (Buenos Aires: Granica Editor, 1973).

7. *Nunca más. Informe de la CONADEP* (Buenos Aires: EUDEBA, 1984).

8. This analysis of women in crisis is historically related to the figure of Antigone. Jean Elshtain's well-known article "Antigone's Daughters" developed this metaphor to describe a female approach to women's involvement in the public arena.

9. For further information on the Madres' resistance and their tactics of entering into public space, see Mónica Gogna, "La ronda de las Madres," mimeo, Buenos Aires, 1986.

10. Laurence Whitehead, "International Aspects of Democratization," in *Transitions from Authoritarian Rule: Prospects for Democracy*, 4 vols., ed. Guillermo O'Donnell, Philippe C. Schmitter, and Laurence Whitehead (Baltimore: Johns Hopkins University Press, 1986).

11. Guillermo O'Donnell, "Resurrecting Civil Society (and Restructuring Public Space)," in O'Donnell et al., *Transitions*, 49–56.

12. See Elizabeth Jelin, ed., *Los nuevos movimientos sociales* (Buenos Aires: CEAL, 1985), and her *Movimientos sociales y democracia emergente* (Buenos Aires: CEAL, 1987) for excellent overviews on social movements and transitions in Argentina.

13. María del Carmen Feijoó, "The Challenge of Constructing Civilian Peace: Women and Democracy in Argentina," in *The Women's Movement in Latin America: Participation and Democracy*, ed. Jane S. Jaquette (Boulder, Colo.: Westview Press, 1994).

14. Scott Mainwaring and Eduardo Viola, "New Social Movements, Political Culture, and Democracy: Brazil and Argentina in the 1980s," *Telos* 61 (1984): 17–42.

15. María del Carmen Feijoó and Marcela Nari, "Women and Democracy in Argentina," in Jaquette, *Women's Movement in Latin America.*

16. Marguerite Guzmán Bouvard, *Revolutionizing Motherhood: The Mothers of the Plaza de Mayo* (Wilmington, Del.: Scholarly Resources, 1994). From our viewpoint, this split will have to be analyzed on a basis other than partisan lines.

17. Juan Carlos Vega, *Catamarca: Un laboratorio social* (Catamarca: Servicio Argentino de Derechos Humanos, 1991).

18. Norberto Lechner, "The Search for the Lost Community: Challenges to Democracy," *International Social Science Journal* 129 (1991), and Elizabeth Jelin and María del Carmen Feijoó, *El ajuste invisible: Los efectos de la crisis económica en las mujeres pobres* (Santiago, Chile: UNESCO, 1989), make the point that "the situation in Latin America, combining the worst economic and social crisis in its history with the greatest strides toward democracy, may seem paradoxical" (Lechner).

19. Juan Carlos Torre and Liliana de Riz, "Argentina since 1946," in *Argentina since Independence,* ed. Leslie Bethel (Cambridge: Cambridge University Press, 1993), thoroughly covers the period, especially focusing on its economic dimensions. On recent changes in the Argentine economy, see William Smith, "State, Market, and Neoliberalism in Post-Transition Argentina: The Menem Experiment," *Journal of Interamerican and World Affairs* (1993).

20. María del Carmen Feijoó, "Women Confronting the Crisis: Two Case Studies from Greater Buenos Aires," in *Emergences: Women's Struggles for Livelihood in Latin America,* ed. John Friedmann, Rebecca Abers, and Lilian Autler, UCLA Latin American Center Publications, vol. 82 (Los Angeles: University of California, 1996), 31–46.

21. Feijoó and Nari, "Women and Democracy."

22. Inés Cano, "El movimiento feminista argentino en la década del 70," *Todo es Historia,* no. 183 (August 1982): 84–93.

23. Consejo Nacional de la Mujer, *Un paso adelante: Sanción y aplicación de la Ley de Cupos* (Buenos Aires: Presidencia de la Nación, n.d.). See Nené Reynoso, "Ley del Cupo: Una prioridad del movimiento feminista," *Feminaria,* year 5, no. 8 (April 1992): 10–12; Jutta Marx and Ana Sampolesi, "Elecciones internas bajos el cupo: La primera aplicación de la Ley de Cuotas en la capital federal," *Feminaria,* year 6, no. 11 (November 1993): 15–17.

24. For a review of the constitutional reform, see María del Carmen Feijoó, "La Reforma Constitucional," *Revista de Ciencias Sociales,* no. 1 (1994): 71–98. A report on recent changes in Argentina may be found in International Women's Rights Action Watch (IWRAW) Country Reports, by Sharon Ladin from the Hubert H. Humphrey Institute of Public Affairs, December 1994. For antecedents of the reform, see Dieter Nohlen and Liliana de Riz, eds., *Reforma institucional y cambio político* (Buenos Aires: CEDES-Legasa, 1991).

25. Georgina Waylen, "Gender and Democratic Consolidation," paper presented at the 1966 Annual Meeting of the American Political Science Association, San Francisco, August 29–September 1.

26. Guillermo O'Donnell, "On the State, Democratization, and Some Conceptual Problems: A Latin American View with Glances at Some Postcommunist Countries," *World Development* 21, no. 8 (1993): 1335–69.

Chapter Three

Women and the Democratization Process in Chile

MARÍA ELENA VALENZUELA

*W*omen's contribution to democratization in Chile began in the late nineteenth century when a group of suffragists tried to register as voters. The reaction was drastic: new legislation prohibiting women's vote was enforced. Only in 1949 was women's right to vote recognized, but their struggle to attain full citizenship continues. Since the return to democracy, there is greater awareness of gender issues and of the need to improve women's rights, but gender equality is not perceived as a prerequisite to the strengthening of democracy. All the key national debates on representational politics are focused on the electoral and presidential systems; they do not include how gender representation is being blocked in a political system that is not integrating women as full citizens.

As a response to military dictatorship (1973–90), a women's movement emerged which confronted political repression, regressive economic policies, and gender discrimination. Women created organizations for human rights, economic survival, and political participation. In this process, women raised their own gender issues, and feminist groups had an important role in the definition of the movement's agenda. Women's mobilization helped to democratize the Chilean political system, making the hidden antidemocratic structures of Chilean life visible and thus debatable and open to change. The very notion of what was a political issue was enlarged. Politics came to mean participation not only in the public realm but also in less traditional activities, such as involvement in social movements, networking, and informal coalition building. However, the peculiar traits of the Chilean transition to democracy inhibited the implementation of a full-fledged women's agenda. The disproportionate veto power of conservative circles and the male domination of political turf are still important obstacles to overcome.

The political dynamics of the democratic transition in Chile encouraged the resurgence of an elitist, male-oriented establishment. The women's movement, which had developed outside the party system, lacked sufficient internal cohesion to confront the system, to bring a substantial number of women into leadership positions, or to press its demands on government agencies, including the newly established women's ministry, Servicio Nacional de la Mujer (SERNAM; National Women's Service). As its ability to mobilize women in the streets, which had been effective during the transition, became less useful as a bargaining chip once democracy was restored, the visibility and impact of the women's movement declined. The successful struggle against authoritarianism which had energized and united the movement dissipated once that goal was accomplished. Without a common enemy, factions reappeared. The common gender identity forged during the transition weakened, to be displaced by other identities, including competing loyalties to political parties.

The cross-party women's political organization that had developed during the opposition period was disbanded, its leaders reintegrated into political parties, governmental posts, and nongovernmental organizations (NGOs). Women's leverage over women's issues weakened. The main trend was the integration of women into mainstream politics, and no accountability mechanism emerged to replace the role that was previously played by the cross-party organization.

The dilemma of autonomy versus subordination, which emerged during the transition, still persists. This tension has fragmented the women's movement and undermines its capacity to become a coherent political force confronting traditional groups. Members of the women's movement as well as those integrated in government agencies have no clear strategy at this time to confront and overcome this situation.

Even though the women's agenda has not been fully implemented since the return to democracy, gender issues have become increasingly visible, expanding women's rights through legal changes, engendering public policies, and showing a new concern for women's political participation. An Equal Opportunity Plan (1994–99) put forth by SERNAM is the most comprehensive agenda for women's rights ever developed in Chile. Its policies include a campaign against domestic violence, the development of a national policy for female heads of households, the revision of educational policies, a program to support pregnant adolescents, training programs on gender issues for public officials, the creation of a national network on women's rights information, and several initiatives to end legal discrimination.

In this chapter, I analyze the development of the women's movement during the military dictatorship, the diversity of its expressions, and the role of feminist groups. The nature and effects of the political transition over the women's

agenda are also studied and the source of resistance to its implementation identified. I conclude with an analysis of the dilemma the women's movement is now
confronting.

THE EMERGENCE OF THE
CHILEAN WOMEN'S MOVEMENT

During the 1960s and 1970s, Chile, one of the few stable democracies in
Latin America, experienced an increasing political polarization. In 1970 a center-left coalition led by the socialist president Salvador Allende was democratically elected. The resulting confrontation between the government and local and
international opposition groups led to a military coup in September 1973, led by
General Augusto Pinochet.

The military dictatorship (1973-89) was a period of hardship, repression,
and misery for important sectors of Chilean society, such as the democratic opposition and the most vulnerable social groups. In addition to repressive policies—the closing of Congress, the banning of political parties, the incarceration
of opposition leaders, massive violations of human rights—the military government enacted a series of neoconservative economic policies. From 1973 to
1981, trade liberalization, a radical imposition of structural adjustment policies,
and the rapid privatization of state-owned industries produced a dramatic increase in unemployment rates. As a result, wage levels fell sharply. As income and
wealth were concentrated in the hands of the few, when the macroeconomic indicators began to improve, living standards of the working and middle classes de-
teriorated.[1] In this context,[2] a women's movement emerged as a response to the
political and economic crisis generated by military rule. These new organizations
revealed the increasing contradiction between the traditional policy of the military government toward women and the new roles they had already assumed.

The military regime developed policies toward women based on a traditional conception of women's roles in society. The government promoted
women's return to family life and discouraged their participation in the workforce and in government, focusing instead on their roles as mothers. This attempt
to return to the past occurred amid conditions that opened opportunities and
even pushed women to assume new roles.

The military's policies toward women contradicted structural trends. The
fertility rate decreased from 5.3 children per woman in 1960–65 to 3.6 in
1970–75 and 2.8 in 1980–85. A rapid incorporation of women in the labor force,
from a 25 percent participation in the seventies to 30 percent in the eighties, was
preceded by an increase in their educational level.[3] The percentage of women in

higher education jumped from 21.4 percent in the mid-1950s to almost 45 percent in the 1980s (Valdés and Gomáriz 1992). These changes modified women's attitudes toward political, economic, and social opportunities and led them to demand more access into the political, economic, and social spheres.

By the mid-1980s, efforts to promote equal rights for women had begun in most Latin American countries,[4] but the Chilean military regime refused even to ratify the UN Convention on the Elimination of All Forms of Discrimination Against Women.[5] Women's mobilization was directed against the political repression of the military government and its regressive economic policies. Through this process, women began to raise their own gender issues. Sharing experiences as women helped them to define their common identity.

During the profound political and economic crisis of the 1980s, new social movements developed in most countries of the region (Escobar and Alvarez 1992), challenging political and economic models in new ways. Amid this crisis, gender identity brought women together across class, age, generation, and ideological differences.

In Chile, as elsewhere in the region, the women's movement had particular strengths: it developed relationships among diverse and divided groups in the opposition and, at the same time, incorporated a gender perspective in the struggle against dictatorship. Feminist ideas helped to shape the social agenda of the women's movement, while the movement of urban poor women provided feminists with popular support and reinforced the movement's political commitment to class issues. The fact that the women's movement grew in the context of the struggle against the Pinochet dictatorship shaped its political nature, provoked and sustained high levels of political mobilization, linked the participation of women from both the working and middle classes, and ensured its close relationship with left and center-left political parties (Chuchryk 1994; Frohman and Valdés 1993).

A number of elements fostered the development of the women's movement. The church provided a sheltering space for the organization of women in poor neighborhoods as well as for the first feminist groups. The UN Decade for Women and the return of exiles with feminist ideas changed the content of the debate and contributed new perspectives and demands to the women's agenda. In Chile as elsewhere in the region, the dictatorship allowed women's organizations to survive and grow while repressing other sectors of civil society.

The dictatorship developed policies toward women which were based on traditional concepts of women's social roles. It aimed to discipline and depoliticize women and to organize a network of female support for the military. In the political arena, the government assigned women the role of educating their children for the *patria* (fatherland), attempting to assure the ideological continuity of the regime. The military gave women a leading role in maintaining traditions but excluded them from the exercise of power (Lechner and Levy 1984; Valenzuela 1987; Munizaga and Letelier 1988; Arteaga 1988). During 17 years of military government, only two women occupied cabinet positions. Moreover, women could not be members of the legislative commissions, which were reserved for the four commanders in chief of the armed services.[6]

Prior to the 1973 coup that brought the military to power, women had mobilized politically only twice; during the suffrage movement and during the Popular Unity (Allende) period from 1970 to 1973. Although there had been a period of intensive activity supporting women's right to vote (passed in 1949), a period of "feminist silence" followed. Despite the fact that important democratic changes had occurred between 1950 and 1973—broader access to education and health, higher standards of living, moderate but sustained economic development, and increased political participation of new social groups such as peasants and poor urban migrants—the problem of gender inequality was not addressed.

During the Popular Unity period, some women organized an antisocialist movement, Poder Femenino, and demanded protection for women's traditional roles against what they perceived as the economic and social threats of Allende's socialist policies. But, paradoxically, 20 years of "feminist silence" came to an end during the military dictatorship, and the women's movement expressed itself in different forms. Some women organized themselves for the return to democracy; others defended human rights; still others developed ingenious survival strategies to endure the economic crisis and the effects of the regime's social and economic policies on the poor. They mobilized against dictatorship and through this process began to redefine their relationship to politics. Some of these groups took feminist positions, questioning authoritarian relations in all areas of society and arguing that the concept of democracy must embrace not only traditional issues of politics but social and cultural structures as well. As the different groups came together in opposition to dictatorship, their actions played an important role in the reappraisal of women's contribution to politics.

As authoritarian political and economic policies decomposed and atomized the social fabric, a virtual explosion of women's organizations occurred, making possible greater autonomy for women. Both opposition and government groups started to develop new organizations directed by and composed of women, beyond the traditional tutelage of the male-dominated ones. Serious tensions emerged between women's organizations and opposition political parties, especially from 1973 to 1983, when the parties had no legitimate channels for expression and the social movements provided the forum for political debates. After 1983, when political parties began to reorganize, they tried to assert firmer control over women's organizations.

HUMAN RIGHTS ORGANIZATIONS:
NEW ROLES OF WOMEN IN POLITICS

Shortly after the coup of 1973, women whose families had suffered directly from human rights abuses began to organize in order to engage in solidarity work. Mothers, wives, or daughters of the disappeared, executed, imprisoned, and politically repressed joined in organizations such as the Organization of Family Members of the Detained and Disappeared, the Organization of Family Members of Political Prisoners, and the Organization of Family Members of the Politically Executed.[7]

These organizations were predominantly composed of women who had little previous political experience but who were able to develop public activities denouncing and opposing the military as did the Madres of the Plaza de Mayo in Argentina. They mobilized, calling upon their maternal roles and denouncing the dictatorship, which, despite its public commitment to preserve traditional family values, used state terror to invade the private sphere of the family in order to maintain political control.

Although these organizations were not seeking to break the barrier between public and private, they actually did so, establishing at the same time a new pattern that challenged the traditional role of women in politics. These groups were not focused on gender issues, but they initiated a strong and visible presence of women in the struggle against dictatorship.

ECONOMIC SURVIVAL ORGANIZATIONS:
SEEDS FOR THE DEVELOPMENT OF GENDER IDENTITY

Structural adjustment policies designed to cope with the debt crisis in the 1980s led to new high levels of unemployment and brought heavier demands on women. The deteriorating economic situation led large numbers of poor urban women to initiate collective strategies for survival. They created thousands of economic organizations including subsistence and craft workshops, soup kitchens, and "collective shopping" programs (Hardy 1988; Razeto 1990). The significant increase of women's work within and outside the home has been called the "invisible adjustment" through which women compensated for the disruptions occurring in the labor market and society at large.

Even though new economic organizations created by women had survival as their main focus, they were able to make a further step forward by developing a gender identity that facilitated the growth of a women's social movement. Survival organizations were created in poor neighborhoods supported by the Catholic Church and by NGOs working on women issues.

Although these women's organizations did not propose to end gender discrimination as the middle-class feminist movement did, their new tasks and responsibilities changed their attitudes toward women's issues and gave their members a greater sense of personal worth. Women's experience of leaving their homes, making contact with other women who were suffering the same problems, and discovering their own unsuspected capacities and abilities to cope with the economic crisis had an important impact on their lives, even challenging power relations in their families.[8] Many of them learned to recognize their own oppression as a point of departure for political action.

FEMINIST GROUPS: COMMITTED TO GENDER AND CLASS

Contemporary feminism emerged in Chile in the late 1970s, during the dictatorship, showing the close ties that linked patriarchy and military rule. Some of these women had been politically active in the Left, where they had played peripheral roles and experienced gender discrimination. Others had been in exile and had been exposed to the influence of feminist thinking in Europe and North America. In 1977, middle-class professional women created the Circle for the Study of Women, the first feminist organization of this period. They argued that authoritarianism characterized Chilean society at all levels, including the family, and sought more active roles for themselves incorporating a gender dimension into political life. Other feminist groups emerged as well. Some were created by poor women who developed "popular feminist" organizations. The slogan "Democracy in the Country and in the Home," which integrated gender issues and the struggle against dictatorship, was assumed by the entire women's movement.

Although Chilean feminism maintained a commitment to social change, there were tensions between feminists and women in political parties, in what was perceived as the opposition between "feministas y políticas" (Kirkwood 1990). Many feminists sought autonomy and feared being controlled by political parties as had happened after women won the right to vote in 1949. They did not trust the parties to promote cultural change to oppose patriarchy. However, those feminists who were affiliated with political parties did consider the parties useful tools in meeting the demands of women. They remained loyal to both their parties and feminism, observing what was called "double militancy." The opposition between autonomy and integration into political parties expressed a tension between insulated women's groups who wanted to remain as such and those who wanted to introduce feminism into the political agenda, participating in traditional male arenas.

From the very beginning feminist groups assumed they were involved in a confrontational movement, challenging not only patriarchy but also the most important paradigm of male domination, the military state. As a consequence of their opposition to military rule, feminists joined forces with other opposition groups in denouncing social, economic, and political oppression, introducing a feminist component the opposition was lacking.

The first women's movement platform was the Manifesto Feminista, released in 1983, anticipating most of the issues that developed later. It linked authoritarianism and patriarchy and brought attention to violence against women while raising more traditional feminist themes such as the discrimination against women in politics, law, and education. In 1984, MEMCH-83, the umbrella organization for various women's groups, developed the Plataforma de la Mujer Chilena (Chilean Women's Platform), closely following the contents of the UN Convention on the Elimination of All Forms of Discrimination Against Women (1979). The Pliego de las Mujeres (Women's Document) was presented in 1986, in association with the Asamblea de la Civilidad, a multipartisan organization that represented different sectors of Chilean society who were demanding the return to democracy.

A major step was taken in 1988, when the women's movement went beyond gender denunciation and developed a proposal, the Demandas de las Mujeres a la Democracia (Women's Demands to Democracy), which focused on three different areas: civil rights, reproductive and family issues, and labor rights. It was an attempt to link the women's agenda to the broader political and social agenda for the transition to democracy. The logical conclusion of this effort, and a significant step toward building a women's agenda, was the set of proposals prepared by the Concertación Nacional de Mujeres por la Democracia (CNMD) in 1989, which identified a number of gender-specific public policies to be implemented by a democratic government.

Feminism had an undeniable impact on the political agenda of the transition. During the presidential and congressional campaigns for the December 1989 elections, "gender" was recognized as a political category for the first time in Chilean history. In this context the women's movement was able to include its demands in the program of the democratizing coalition. The large and active Chilean women's movement saw the return to democracy as an important opportunity to reach the goals of power sharing they had sought during the 17-year dictatorship.

CHILEAN DEMOCRACY AND THE PROBLEM OF IMPLEMENTING THE FEMINIST AGENDA

The capacity of the women's movement to organize and mobilize women had important consequences for the Chilean transition. Women's political influence grew out of their capacity to draw up an agenda, negotiate it with political parties, and establish open channels of communication and participation within the newly reorganized political institutions.

Thanks to women's mobilization for democracy and their limited but significant influence in the democratizing coalition, gender demands were included in the democratic agenda in 1990, and a new cabinet-level governmental agency—SERNAM—was created to implement a program for women.

Social inequality had long been an issue in Chile, but feminist demands put inequality in a broader context, focusing attention on those social institutions that reproduce discrimination: family, the educational system, political parties of all ideologies, the state apparatus, and the legal system. This broad agenda inevitably produced a debate on how to establish a 'successful strategy to bring about change.

In this context, the discussion on how to use the political moment to promote changes in women's status blurred the division between autonomous and institutional groups, making possible the integration of even the most independent groups into the preparation of the democratic agenda (Serrano 1990). Women from various groups discussed issues such as the specificity of women in politics, women's alliances, and the scope of negotiable and nonnegotiable issues. A majority decided they should organize to play a role in politics, filling government posts to advance the women's agenda. However, subsequent negotiations with the political parties about how to increase women's representation were difficult. The visible role women's organizations had played in the transition was not enough to open up the male-controlled party structure.

The experience of the Comando de Mujeres por el No (the Women's Command for the No—an opposition alliance that campaigned successfully against the continuation of military rule under Pinochet in a plebiscite held in 1988) was created by the party leadership and was composed of female representatives of political parties not linked to the women's movement. The Command had little power; the opposition alliance lacked a gender perspective; and the visibility of women during the campaign was lower than it had been when the opposition operated through social movements. After the victory of the "No" campaign, opposition parties created the Concertación de Partidos por la Democracia (CPD; Coalition for Democracy), a center-left coalition that won in the December 1989 elections. At the same time, women created the Concertación Nacional de Mujeres por la Democracia (CNMD; Women's Coalition for Democracy) as an autonomous women's coalition. It included political party members, feminists, and women from nongovernmental organizations who, after their experience in the Women's Command, decided to create an independent political caucus to negotiate with the democratic coalition. Policy recommendations were developed in the areas of education, health, family, communications, labor, art and culture, political participation, peasants, shantytown women, legislation, and the creation of a bureau in charge of gender issues (Montecino and Rossetti 1990).

The CNMD also aimed at supporting women's candidates and at making gender issues visible for the whole society. Among their achievements was that the presidential candidate, a traditional and Catholic Christian Democrat, adopted the women's demand for "Democracy in the Country and in the Home" as his own (Aylwin 1989).

The Women's Coalition's agenda was presented to the CPD, not as a matter to be discussed inside the parties but as an already legitimated set of women's demands. The strategy was a success: the government program of the CPD included a chapter on women incorporating most of the demands, and it recognized the need to enforce gender-specific public policies. For the first time, gender issues were part of the national debate, and even the right-wing presidential candidate, Hernan Buchi (supported by Pinochet), had to include equal rights for women in his platform.[9]

The CPD agenda made it a priority to "fully enforce women's rights taking into consideration the new role of women in society and overcoming any form of discrimination." Despite the CPD's support for antidiscrimination policies, some of its constituent parties were critical on the grounds of "family rights." The compromise was to add: "In addition, the government will enforce the measures required to adequately protect the family" (interview with Soledad Larraín, leader of the CDP, and from the official text of the law creating SERNAM [#19.023], published officially on January 3, 1991). The CPD announced its intention to implement the proposed goals through legal changes, through a program to encourage the social participation of women, and by creating a national office for women (SERNAM) in charge of promoting, coordinating, and monitoring the enforcement of the new policies toward women.

The women's movement assumed that the return to democracy would lead to an expansion of rights and democratic procedures and that women would be eventually incorporated as full citizens. For this purpose, the government was considered a gender-neutral tool available to be used to carry out political commitments.

The first disappointment was that, despite the public commitment of the government to women's issues, only 1 woman was appointed at the cabinet level: the director of SERNAM; of the vice-ministers, only 3 out of 27 were women; and no female was appointed among 13 governors.[10] At the second term of the democratic coalition, electing Eduardo Frei to the presidency in 1994, the situation improved, as 3 women were appointed as ministers—among them the former minister of SERNAM at the Justice Department—and 1 governor. At the present time, women hold 35.2 percent of the intermediate positions in the state bureaucracy, a proportion that increases at lower levels of the decision-making structure.

Though limited, the incorporation of women in government had an important impact. A number of professional women who had been active in the women's movement were appointed to government posts. They began to introduce a gender perspective into policy making and gave the role of women in government more visibility.[11] But when it came to enforcing changes within the state, women confronted barriers from within and without. Institutions such as the Catholic Church, which has significant influence in national politics, reacted vigorously against the more progressive elements of the women's agenda. Despite its early support, the church hierarchy proved antagonistic toward the feminist agenda, using its veto power (together with other conservative elites, some of them inside the ruling coalition) in key areas such as divorce and reproductive rights. As the feminist agenda confronted deeply held social values, it encountered resistance not matched by the experience of other groups who were also seeking change. Implementation proved to be even more difficult as the strength and visibility the women's movement had achieved during the transition ebbed away. Most troubling of all, women lost the pluralist ideological space in which they had been working out their own issues. The Women's Coalition for Democracy (and other women's umbrella organizations) never regained its earlier high-profile role as the political parties and the government promoted their own platforms for women. The difficulty of reaching consensus further sapped the movement's momentum.

Under these conditions, women's organizations needed to revise their previous strategy. They faced a new confrontation between those groups who championed greater autonomy and who criticized the previous process, and the "institutionalists," who had gained greater access to political parties and government. At the core of this debate was a disagreement about the usefulness of institutionalizing the feminist agenda within the government. Some regarded it as an important achievement of Chilean feminism; others considered it a trap because only noncontroversial issues were incorporated and women's capacity to demand radical changes was substantially reduced (Waylen 1994).

From 1990 on, the actual incorporation of women's demands into the democratic agenda was only partial, owing to the negotiated characteristics of the Chilean transition. The military had withdrawn from power on its own terms, forcing the opposition coalition to compromise. Although massive urban mobilizations for the return to democracy in 1984–85, propelled by citizens' rejection of massive violations of human rights, had forced the Pinochet government to initiate a political liberalization process, the military government retained some social and political support, as shown in the 1988 plebiscite,[12] in which it was not clear until the vote itself that Pinochet would be defeated.

One outcome of this process was a semidemocratic political system that overrepresented right-wing parties and gave them a veto power. This veto power was guaranteed by an electoral system in which 30 percent of voters elect 50 percent of parliamentary seats, and 25 percent of the senators in the upper house are appointed, and which requires a high number of votes for constitutional change, making it very difficult to modify the constitution.[13] Under the terms of withdrawal the commanders in chief of the armed forces cannot be removed by the elected president, and half of the members of the Central Bank board of directors were to be appointed by the military government.[14]

The transition to democracy after the 1988 plebiscite gained momentum with the 1989 presidential election and the inauguration of the new government in March 1990. However, the transition did not occur at a single moment but involved several interrelated and not always consistent processes. As the political transition moved forward, other cultural, economic, and social developments failed to keep pace, and the possibilities for organizing consensus around gender issues sharply decreased. Women's demands would require broad support in order to be enacted and then implemented. But gender issues brought out the veto power of minorities and raised issues that disrupted the alignment of the traditional political parties.

One reason why women's proposals were seen as controversial is that they were associated with the secularization of Chilean society; they compelled Chileans to confront values that had gone unquestioned in the past. The modernization process enforced by the military and technocratic elites during the period of authoritarian rule had produced important economic and social changes, but it was carried out by appeals to conservative values and religious tradition. Conservative social values were emphasized in order to give stability during rapid economic change. In contrast, women's demands confronted the traditional value system, challenging male control over the process of democratization and threatening the most conservative sectors.

Those who had supported the authoritarian regime could be expected to oppose the proposals of the women's movement. But there also was resistance inside the ruling coalition. In addition to the Catholic Church, which had played a progressive role in the transitional period but which openly opposed the women's agenda,[15] within a government composed of Christian Democrats and center-left parties, it was logical that there would be divisions between the Catholic and secular sectors.[16]

The result was a permanent tension between the government and Chilean conservative circles over whether and how to implement women's demands. Aylwin's government responded by distancing itself from the more radical feminist content of the women's agenda; its public policies for women became increasingly specific and technical. To incorporate a gender dimension permanently into public policies, President Frei (1994–) was persuaded to include the Equal Opportunity Plan into his programmatic agenda. The plan gained new momentum—in a highly controversial context—during the preparatory activities for the UN's Fourth World Conference on Women in Beijing, held in September 1995. Women's issues, which had become almost marginal to the national agenda, gained a new high profile. Catholic groups, supported by the most influential part of the media, orchestrated a national debate that resulted in a Senate resolution against the more feminist posture SERNAM had developed for Beijing. Paradoxically, in the midst of this ideological confrontation, the government did not abandon its position but sharpened its strategy and pushed for public policies that favored increasing women's participation in decision making.

Since the return to democracy, however, the women's movement itself has been largely absent from politics. Even though there are an important number of grassroots women's organizations, they do not provide active or consistent political support for those working on a women's agenda within the government (Jaquette 1994). In these conditions, SERNAM has come to play a de facto leadership role by default, blurring its functions as a government institution and as a representative of the women's movement.

INSTITUTIONALIZING WOMEN'S PARTICIPATION: THE NATIONAL WOMEN'S SERVICE (SERNAM)

One key demand women did achieve was to create a ministry to guarantee the incorporation of women's issues into government policies and to encourage women's active participation in social, economic, political, and cultural development. SERNAM was established in accordance with the commitment made to the CNMD for a national office of women. It was legally created on January 3,

1991, with a regional and decentralized structure. It has independent executive and financial powers, and it works with different ministries and municipalities. It undertakes a variety of studies to coordinate policies carried out by different ministries and public services.

The first measure taken by the democratically elected government regarding women's issues was President Aylwin's submission of a bill to Congress to create SERNAM. The women's movement specifically requested that SERNAM be created by law and not by presidential decree, on the theory that the office would then be a permanent state organization that could not easily be discarded at the whim of the executive—a crucial weakness of a similar strategy adopted by Brazil's feminists.

Two months before the election a seminar was held to learn from the best practices in Brazil, Argentina, and Spain. Current and former heads of governmental women's offices in those countries participated in this meeting. Mariana Aylwin (the daughter of the elected president) and Soledad Larraín, both leaders of the women's movement, later went to Spain to look at the structure and activities of the Spanish Instituto de la Mujer. SERNAM was first established by executive decree in March 1990. A talented Christian Democratic lawyer— Soledad Alvear—was appointed as its head. Her deputy, Soledad Larraín, was a feminist socialist psychologist with long experience in the women's movement. From the beginning, the bill to create SERNAM was controversial and produced a major debate in Congress. Although SERNAM's formal charge was to enforce the 1980 Convention on the Elimination of All Forms of Discrimination Against Women (which the military government had ratified in December 1989) and to protect the family, the opposition declared SERNAM a threat to the maintenance of the family and social order.

The projected involvement of women who were both feminists and leftists in SERNAM was sufficiently threatening to mobilize the opposition. Right-wing parties opposed the creation of SERNAM on the grounds that it would infiltrate women's groups and subvert the family. They also feared that the center-left government would seek to manipulate women through SERNAM, as the military government itself had done through a state-supported system of mothers' clubs under Pinochet. After a series of negotiations, the functions and personnel of SERNAM were cut back, and it could no longer carry out its own programs. Although the director remains a member of the cabinet with the status of a minister, SERNAM is administratively under the Ministry of Planning.

When SERNAM was legally created, it had a staff of 59 people, a small budget of $2 million, and $1.5 million in international funding. In response to ongoing pressure SERNAM's annual budget has increased more than six times in six years. However, conflicts between the governmental coalition and the opposition and within the coalition itself have made it easier for the coalition to reach agreement on the economic program, political reforms, and the institutionalization of the democratic process than on women's issues.

Serious tensions appeared when nonconsensual issues such as divorce and abortion were raised. Some felt that, because such issues were not included in the governmental program, they were not a priority for the government and SERNAM should not take them up. Others argued that failure to move forward on these issues would alienate SERNAM from the women's constituency that had called for its creation.

These differences persist. Divorce is still not legal in Chile, and it was not incorporated in the agenda of either Aylwin or Frei, since no agreement could be reached in the CPD. However, in 1997 the House voted (by a small margin) to discuss the subject for the first time since 1914. Although more than 50 percent of the population supports a divorce law, the pressure of the Catholic Church and conservative groups across the political spectrum has delayed its discussion and is blocking any meaningful action. Therapeutic abortion was banned in 1989 by the military dictatorship, and penalties for abortion were increased. This is such a divisive issue that no initiatives have been posed in Congress, although it is well known that about 150,000 illegal abortions are performed in Chile every year.

Nonetheless, during Aylwin's term, SERNAM was able to implement important gender-specific policies proposed by the CNMD and outlined in the demands presented by the feminists in 1988. It operated to some extent like an interest group, engaging in lobbying activities to transform the demands of women into legislative gains and public policies.

At the beginning, SERNAM focused its action in three main areas: campaigns to increase gender awareness, issue and targeted group programs, and legal reforms. In 1993, the last year of Aylwin's term, SERNAM was able to organize a master implementation plan. The Equal Opportunity Plan for Women, 1994–1999, had a clear feminist orientation and included legal, cultural, economic, political, and social issues to be addressed through a set of public policies (SERNAM 1994). After the Beijing conference the plan, enriched with the conference's recommendations, identified the priority areas of education, labor, and political participation and cross-issue areas such as poverty and the family.

Although the political goals in the first presidential term (1990–94) were political reforms and human rights issues, SERNAM and the government were able to develop a common strategy to have several bills approved, including the elimination of gender discrimination in the civil and criminal codes and new regulations favoring women in the labor code. In 1992 an equal rights amendment, in a package with other important constitutional reforms, was sent to parliament. The whole package was rejected because no consensus was reached with the opposition. The amendment was sent again in 1995 and is expected to be discussed during the 1997 term. Despite the symbolic and legal importance of an equal rights amendment to the women's movement, women did not actively lobby or mobilize to reintroduce it. SERNAM also sent a bill to modify the property rights of married women, still regulated by the Civil Code of 1855. The bill went up to the Congress in 1991, but it was not approved until 1994 because of the overloaded schedule of the Congress and the relatively low priority given to this issue by the government and the parliament.

Tied to this bill was a proposal to modify the adultery law. According to Chilean law, adultery by a woman can result in five years of imprisonment, but a man convicted of adultery can only receive a maximum of one and a half years in jail, and only if he was carrying on an openly bigamous relationship. The bill proposed depenalizing adultery on the ground that it was a private matter. After much debate the law decriminalized adultery and established equal civil penalties for men and women in extramarital relationships.

Among the legal reforms sought by the CPD, the modification of the labor code had been among the top priorities. The military government had enforced a highly regressive code. Negotiations to have female workers' rights incorporated into the bill started before it was sent to the Congress. SERNAM held discussions with the Ministry of Labor and with the pro-government Union Federation, the Central Unitaria de Trabajadores (CUT). Neither the ministry nor the CUT considered women workers' rights an important issue. SERNAM succeeded in raising issues of the rights of seasonal and domestic workers,[17] both groups mostly composed of women. A paternal leave policy was also approved,[18] but Congress failed to establish new regulations for home workers. The proposals regarding domestic workers and home workers provoked heated controversy. Representatives from different parties—even some belonging to the ruling coalition—opposed establishing the same minimum wage for domestic workers as for other workers, fearing that it would provoke a negative reaction from the middle class. Opponents argued that the government should not establish standards for home work in order to compete successfully in the international economy, which depends on cheap labor.

Other important initiatives were developed by SERNAM and are still under discussion in Congress. These are a bill to penalize sexual assault and sexual harassment, a proposal forbidding pregnancy tests to hire women, and another bill to equalize the status of children born inside and outside wedlock.

To incorporate a gender perspective into public policies, SERNAM started a new series of programs, perhaps most important of which is the network of Information Centers on Women's Rights (CIDEM), which promote grassroots women's organizations and encourage communication and cooperation between the state and the women's movement. They publicize information about women's rights and provide a channel for women's demands to establish a stable feedback between public policies and women's needs and interests. The centers were modeled on institutions with similar characteristics in other countries, specifically Spain, and were completely funded by donations from abroad. Because of their strong gender focus, it was unlikely that they would have been selected as priorities under the national budget. Foreign funding from foundations committed to women's rights made it possible to avoid congressional debate on their goals and activities. In its second year, this program began to receive some government funding, but its goals were scaled back to providing information on government programs and women's rights to individuals, rather than promoting women's grassroots organizations. From the third year onward, most of the financing has come from the fiscal budget.

In the framework of poverty alleviation policies, a program for poor women heads of households was implemented, coordinating and focusing resources from different ministries to empower women and provide tools to overcome poverty through employment opportunities (Valenzuela, Venegas, and Andrade 1994). To make this program possible SERNAM had to confront conservative groups opposed to the recognition of single mothers. This program was finally approved and later incorporated into the National Program on Poverty (Programa Nacional de Superación de la Pobreza), producing for the first time an antipoverty policy with a gender perspective. In this context, a program for seasonal workers, aimed at providing child care and tools, was also implemented.

Domestic violence was also a high priority for SERNAM. A policy was developed within the human rights context based on previous experiences of women's NGOs working in this area. Two representatives[19] introduced a bill on domestic violence in 1991, with the sponsorship of SERNAM. However, as in the case of the reforms to the civil code, the discussion took longer than expected, and it was 1994 before it was finally approved. A comprehensive program, including training for police and other public officials, followed up with legal and technical assistance to the municipalities that established centers for battered women, was launched with substantial success. Research showing the dimensions of this problem in Chile helped to legitimate the issue.

Reproductive rights were partially addressed through SERNAM's teenage pregnancy program. Working with the Ministry of Education, it abolished the rule—enforced by the military dictatorship—prohibiting pregnant teenagers from attending schools. This action was followed by an interministerial program, coordinated by the ministries of education and health, to provide sex education to teenagers, a highly controversial issue for conservative sectors.

To link the government with grassroots women's organizations another type of institution was created, the Programa de Desarrollo de la Mujer (PRODEMU; Program for Women and Development). This was a nationwide private nonprofit corporation, funded by the government and directed by the first lady, to support women's organizations. However, the women's movement did not consider PRODEMU, an organization intended to support poor women economically rather than change gender relations, as part of its strategy. In its turn, SERNAM, without well-established communication mechanisms with grassroots women's organizations, did establish a close collaboration with es-tablished NGOs working on women issues. This functional separation deep-ened the divisions in the women's movement, however, and made it difficult to monitor SERNAM and the implementation of the Equal Opportunity Plan.

The marginal role of the women's movement in the current political agenda shows how difficult is to represent women's interests in a context dominated by political parties. Women are not experts in traditional politics, and women's is-sues are not considered relevant by party structures. Similarly, women's access to decision making is limited, excluding women from the main national political is-sues. Women do not have strong organizations outside the government able to support SERNAM in its negotiations with other ministries and with Congress or to make it accountable. One explanation for their low capacity for negotiation is that the problem can be found at the origin of the movement, during dictator-ship, when women entered politics as mothers, emphasizing family and com-munity needs but not their own interests (Jaquette 1994). However, the feminist groups did not fail to raise gender issues, so other explanations must be sought for their lack of involvement.

POLITICAL PARTIES AND
WOMEN'S PARTICIPATION

Unlike most other Latin American countries, Chile has been characterized by the strength of its party system. After 17 years of military dictatorship, political parties reappeared without meaningful modifications in their political leadership. As indicated, "Chilean parties from the earliest days in the mid-nineteenth century have been highly and even deliberately intrusive institutions seeking to reach deeply into the workings of civil society. . . . Parties have almost always been the major mechanisms to channel and shape emerging interests" (Scully 1995, 100).

Gender-based politics appear in parties when women realize that they can be—and actually want to be—in leadership positions but realize that they are barred by their sex (Sapiro 1991). This happened with the left-wing parties, where women's "positive action" plans were successful at promoting quotas for women candidates to party leadership. Since most political parties have resisted incorporating women on equal terms, the women's movement has been weakened as a political force. The question of whether autonomously organized groups of women can be more successful in the struggle for power than those who join preexisting structures was fiercely debated during the transition and remains a controversial issue today. Although radical feminist groups have insisted on remaining independent of parties, significant numbers of women who define themselves as feminists have joined them, intending to struggle for greater power and for recognition of women's issues within the parties and using them to achieve their political ends.[20]

This process has left autonomous feminist groups as well as popular women's organizations largely isolated, strengthening the conventional view that women in politics are not interested in competing with men. Even though there is a growing consciousness and a sense of common identity based on gender awareness,[21] feminism is still perceived by large segments of the political spectrum and by much of society as an anti-male movement that does not represent the majority of women. The persistence of traditional values and attitudes concerning the role of women in society has made the work of feminist pressure groups more difficult.

The democratic transition was energized by the women's proposals to democratize politics, but democracy has helped restore the role of the traditional political organizations more than it has helped the women's movement. The parties showed a relatively open attitude toward incorporating women's issues, but they did not give priority to these issues and tended to exclude the more controversial demands such as those linked to reproductive rights and empowerment. Women as individuals were not incorporated into the higher levels of decision making, and the CNMD failed to find effective ways to negotiate the full empowerment of women inside the political parties. As a consequence, it did not have enough leverage to increase the number of women on the legislative candidates lists or for government posts. Instead, the interests of traditional pressure groups inside the political parties prevailed. Therefore, the political representation of women, an important measure of women's power, did not improve substantially with the return to democracy.

During and after the transition, the active mobilization of women's organizations and their capacity for protest had caused most parties on the left and in the center to become interested in women's issues and to incorporate women's demands into their platforms in varying ways and degrees (Molina 1989). Yet, although more women seemed to be in formal leadership positions, political power eluded them. Subtle discrimination mechanisms operated strongly in all parties (Hola and Pischedda 1993). The few women leaders who managed to overcome these barriers encountered additional difficulties. They lacked experience in the dominant style of political negotiation and sometimes failed to manage key aspects of their political campaigns, especially campaign finance.

Different strategies have been used by women to reach decision-making levels in their own parties. Following the successful experience in Europe, affirmative action was promoted by feminist groups inside some parties. After the 1988 plebiscite, the two most important leftist parties—Partido por la Democracia (PPD) and the Socialist Party (PS), now in the ruling coalition—agreed to incorporate 20 and 25 percent quotas respectively for women in leadership positions.[22] Further, the PS created a vice presidency for women in 1992 to ensure that gender issues would be mainstreamed in the party. The Christian Democratic Party decided to maintain its Women's Department and continued to debate the use of quotas, while the rightist Renovación Nacional (National Renovation Party) created a department for women and the family.

As a consequence, the PPD and the Socialist Party have women at all decision-making levels, but fewer than in the Humanista-Verde (Humanist-Green) alliance, a small party that is the only one that has gender equality as a primary goal. Right-wing parties have a few women at decision-making levels. In the centrist Christian Democratic Party the participation of women at top levels is also low, although higher than in most right-wing parties. Because of class differences, women's rank-and-file participation in political parties is much higher in right-wing parties—about 50 to 60 percent—than in the Christian Democratic Party, while in the Socialist Party the overall female membership is lower (Muñoz and Wojciechowski 1996).

All things considered, there has not been significant progress in politically empowering women after the return to democracy. Quotas did dramatically change the likelihood that women would be nominated by some of the smaller parties to run for Congress, yet despite these measures, a critical mass of women has not yet emerged to influence party politics. Because very few ran for office, the proportion of women in Congress is low, even lower than before the military

Table 3.1

WOMEN IN PARLIAMENT, 1951–1994

Year	Chamber of Deputies			Senate		
	Total	Women	%	Total	Women	%
1951–53[a]	147	1	0.7	45	0	0.0
1953–57[b]	147	1	0.7	45	1	2.2
1957–61[c]	147	3	2.0	45	0	0.0
1961–65[d]	147	5	3.4	45	0	0.0
1965–69[e]	147	12	8.2	45	2	4.4
1969–73[f]	150	9	6.0	50	1	2.0
1973[g]	150	14	9.3	50	1	2.0
1990–94[h]	120	7	5.8	47	3	6.4
1994–98[i]	120	9	7.5	47	3	6.4

Source: Servicio Electoral.

[a] 1946–52, President Gabriel Gonzalez Videla, Radical, supported by a center-right coalition.
[b] 1952–58, President Carlos Ibanez, Independent, supported by populist center-right coalition.
[c] 1958–64, President Jorge Alessandri, Independent, supported by a right-center coalition.
[d] 1964–70, President Eduardo Frei, Christian Democrat, supported by his center party.
[e] 1970–73, President Salvador Allende, Socialist, supported by a center-left coalition.
[f] 1970–73, President Salvador Allende, Socialist, supported by a broad center-left coalition, removed by a military coup on September 11, 1973, led by General Augusto Pinochet.
[g] 1990–94, President Patricio Aylwin, Christian Democrat, supported by a center-left coalition (CPD).
[h] 1994– , President Eduardo Frei Ruiz Tagle, Christian Democrat, supported by a center-left coalition (CPD).
[i] PS (Socialist Party), PPD (Partido por la Democrácia; Party for Democracy), and PH (Partido Humanista; Green Party) are the left-wing party members of the ruling coalition Concertación del Partido por la Democrácia (Coalition of the Party for Democracy), while the PDC (Partido Democrata Cristiano; Christian Democratic Party) is the center party and the most important of the coalition. RN (Renovación Nacional; National Renovation) is the most important right-wing party.

coup in 1973, when there were 14 representatives. Only 6 women were elected to the 120-member House in 1990 (5.8%) and 9 in 1994 (7.5%), while 3 out of the 47 seats in the Senate are held by women (6.4%). The proportion of women elected to local councils in municipal elections increased from 11.6 percent in 1992 to 13.7 percent in 1996. Women accounted for 17.7 percent of council candidates in 1996 but only 11 percent of parliamentary candidates in 1993.

Two women legislators elected to the House of Representatives in 1989—Adriana Muñoz and Laura Rodríguez—were feminists and had long been members of the women's movement. They introduced important initiatives, such as a divorce bill (Rodriguez) and bills on domestic violence and therapeutic abortion (Muñoz). Unfortunately Laura Rodríguez died in 1992 before she had finished her legislative term. Adriana Muñoz stood for reelection in 1993 and lost, owing in part to lack of support within her own Socialist Party. The most conservative presidential candidate, Jose Piñera, focused part of his campaign on personal attacks on Adriana Muñoz for her abortion initiative. In the new parliament, inaugurated in March 1994, two leaders of the women's movement were elected representatives: María Antoineta Saa, a feminist-socialist, and Mariana Aylwin, a Christian Democrat who had played an active role in the CNMD. Fany Pollarolo, an active member of a women's group for human rights ("Mujeres por la Vida"; Women for Life) and later an advocate of women's issues, was also elected.

Under democracy, the political parties have recovered their traditional role as mediators between the state and civil society. But they still discriminate against women, and politics is still considered a male activity. As a consequence, there is a prevailing prejudice against women's participation in public life. For women who do participate, family connections play an important role. Of the two women elected to the Senate, one is the daughter of former president Frei. The daughter of General Fernando Matthei, a former military junta member, was elected to Congress in 1989 and reelected in 1993. Mariana Aylwin, the daughter of President Aylwin, was also elected to Congress in 1993.

How are female candidates seen by female voters? If the support received in congressional elections after the return to democracy is any indicator, women do not necessarily "vote woman." What is surprising is that right-wing female candidates (who did not raise women's issues) received higher support from women than from men, while left-wing female candidates (the ones who do raise women's issues) received more male than female votes. What is especially significant is that the two women who considered themselves feminists and who openly raised gender issues (Adriana Muñoz and the late Laura Rodríguez) received the lowest support from women compared with the support they received from men, reinforcing the historical view that Chilean women are more politically conservative than men in the voting booth.

Despite that female membership is higher in right-wing parties, there is a lower representation of women at decision-making levels. Out of the nine representatives in the House, only three (30%) belong to the right-wing parties, a much lower proportion than the one they show as a whole in the House (around 45%). At the same time, in the Senate, the only two female elected senators are members of the CPD (Carmen Frei from the Christian Democratic Party and María Elena Carrera from the Socialist Party). Female leaders from right-wing parties are just starting to complain about this situation, attributing their lack of opportunity to the discrimination women face in politics.

Table 3.2

ELECTED WOMEN REPRESENTATIVES, 1989

Candidates[a]	Votes (%)		
	Men	Women	Total
Adriana Muñoz (PS)	32.7	27.7	30.2
Maria Maluenda (PPD)	30.9	28.0	29.4
Laura Rodríguez (PH)	32.4	27.7	29.9
Eliana Caraball (PDC)	26.3	26.7	26.6
Evelyn Matthei (RN)	40.8	43.4	42.3
Angelica Cristi (RN)	30.8	37.3	34.3
Marina Prochelle (RN)	23.4	30.4	27.0

Source: Servicio Electoral, 1989.

[a] The Christian Democratic Party (Partido Democrata Cristiano or, PDC) is the center party and the most important of the coalition. RN (Renovación Nacional; National Renovation) is the most important right-wing party.

The electoral behavior of women is consistent with their political preferences. Female membership is higher in right-wing parties and lower in left-wing parties. The lower representation of women at decision-making levels in right-wing parties is due to the fact that their participation is organized around traditional instead of feminist values and expectations.

CONCLUSIONS

The advancement of women's rights has been strongly supported by democratization processes in Chilean society and politics. An increasing visibility of gender issues and the solidification of women's rights through legal reforms are engendering public policies. However, these improvements have been made in a context of an unsolved tension between the women's movement's autonomy and its dependence on government policies.

The women's movement emerged and consolidated during dictatorship. It filled the vacuum left by the retrenchment of political parties. In this context the women's movement operated with a high degree of autonomy vis-à-vis political parties, and women played their roles through innovative mechanisms and in new political arenas.

Under new democratic conditions social movements have been replaced in their representational roles by political parties. The options that the women's movement faced were to integrate its organization into the male-dominated spaces of politics or keep itself uncompromised but isolated on the periphery.

Could women promote social changes from outside politics? Could they play the power game without loosing autonomy? A large majority took the latter option without perceiving all the dangers and limitations this option implied.

Political elites resisted the integration of women into politics, particularly at the decision-making level, where real power is at stake. Where women are integrated they have played important roles in gradually moving the gender agenda forward. Political rhetoric and practices remain traditional, and there is no social recognition of the need to integrate women politically. Instead, there is some general support for women on the grounds that women dignify politics because of their superior ethical standards. With this bias, for women to play this political role in arenas where ethical standards are not highly honored means by definition that they will be marginalized.

In the late 1980s the integration of women into politics implied a negotiation of the gender agenda between the new democratic government, the democratizing coalition (CPD), and the women's organization (CNMD). After the disappearance of the women's political organization and the integration of their leaders in political parties, governmental posts, and NGOs, women's leverage as a group weakened. For those who did become integrated into power politics, there was no accountability mechanism to replace the role previously played by the CNMD.

Although important changes with clear feminist content have been implemented, other more controversial changes closely linked to women's control of their sexuality, reproduction, and access to power have been put aside. The secular nature of feminist demands confronted conservative groups that resented these demands and responded aggressively. Some demands, such as abortion, have simply been eliminated from the national agenda.

Under these conditions the women's movement leadership role was taken over by SERNAM. Even though the existence of SERNAM is extremely positive for women and gender interests, it has important limitations. It is restricted by the current rules of the political game and expresses the ideological contradictions also observed inside the ruling coalition. It is also restrained by the bureaucratic dynamics that impose an institutional pace and styles of work which are often incompatible with feminist expectations.

The dilemma between autonomy and subordination has not yet been resolved. This tension continues to divide the women's movement and conspires against its capacity to develop itself as a relevant political actor with the strength to confront traditional groups. Members of the women's movement as well as those integrated in government agencies have no clear strategy to confront and overcome this situation, which is true not only for the women's movement but more generally for all the major social movements in Latin America.

NOTES

1. While in the period 1971–73 income concentration (Gini index) was 0.4474, in the period 1977–81 this index reached 0.51. Thus, in the period 1971–73, the poorest 50 percent of the population earned 19.04 percent of national income; the poorest 20 percent, 4.18 percent; and the wealthiest 10 percent bracket, 32.39 percent of national income. Between 1977 and 1981, the poorest 50 percent received 16.16 percent of national income; the poorest 20 percent, 3.66 percent of national income; and the richest 10 percent, 40.02 percent of national income (Mujica and Larrañaga 1992).

2. A military junta took power on September 11, 1973. In 1988 there was a plebiscite to decide on the continuation of the regime up to 1996. The plebiscite was won by the opposition, and in December 1989 presidential and parliamentary elections were held. The democratically elected transitional president—Patricio Aylwin—and the Congress took power in March 1990 for a four-year term. In December 1993 a second government of the Concertación was elected for a regular six-year term—headed by President Eduardo Frei—to run the country until March 2000.

3. Women with higher education increased their participation in the labor force at the highest rate. In the late eighties, their economic participation rate was more than 50 percent.

4. As an expression of this interest in different countries national commissions for the improvement of women's status were created. In 1983 the Committee on Women in Bolivia was created; in 1985, the National Council on Women's Rights in Brazil; in 1986, the National Center for the Development of Women and the Family in Costa Rica and the Dirección Nacional de la Mujer in Ecuador; and in 1987, the Instituto Nicaraguense de la Mujer.

5. The convention was finally ratified in December 1989, a few days before the presidential and congressional election.

6. This was an important step back, considering that in the last democratic parliament there were 15 women among the senators and deputies.

7. For a detailed analysis of human rights organizations, see Fruhling 1989.

8. For a detailed analysis of women's economic organizations, see Serrano 1990.

9. Yet gender issues did not determine the general climate of the presidential campaign, which was mainly focused on human rights and democracy and economic and social issues.

10. The governmental agenda, however, established that "the incorporation of women in all levels of society would be promoted," including their participation in the state administration and in the political posts.

11. This was especially the case for Maria Antonieta Saa, longtime leader of the women's movement, who was designated mayor of Conchali, the largest working-class municipality in Santiago at that time. She introduced several gender-specific policies, among these the first center for battered women in Chile.

12. Although Pinochet's bid to extend his term for eight more years was rejected, the military government was still backed by a significant 42 percent of the population.

13. The constitution was drawn up by a committee appointed by the military government and approved in a plebiscite held without voter registration and without guarantees of a free election.

14. Central Bank's council members remain in their posts for eight years, and the nominations should be approved by the Senate. The commanders in chief of the armed services will remain in power until 1998, if they were in their posts before March 10, 1990, or will have a four-year term—not removable by the president—if they were nominated after this date by elected governments.

15. The current conservative position of the Vatican on these issues and its pressure over the Chilean Catholic Church hierarchy have been shown during the Cairo Conference on Population and the Women's Conference in Beijing.

16. An example of this are current alignments around the divorce law, which are crossing political parties from the Right, Center, and Left.

17. Congress approved the establishment of regulations to protect seasonal workers, recognizing their right to unionize, to have a labor contract, and to safe working conditions. Maximum daily working hours were established, and a minimum salary was set for the first time, although it was only 75 percent of the minimum wage of other workers.

18. The father has the right of 1 day paid leave when the child is born and 90 days of paid maternity leave due to the mother if she dies in childbirth. Paid leave to attend a sick child can also be taken by the father if the working mother is not using it.

19. Sergio Aguilo and Adriana Muñoz, both from the Socialist Party.

20. The institutionalization of NGOs in contrast to independent or radical feminism has been studied by several scholars (Alvarez n.d.). The cleavage between them was clearly stated during the last Latin American Feminist Congress in Cartagena, Chile (November 1996).

21. Among the most consensual issues are those related to women's labor conditions and the elimination of legal discrimination.

22. These affirmative action measures do not extend to candidate selection.

REFERENCES

Alvarez, Sonia. N.d. "Latin American Feminisms 'Go Global': Trends of the 1990s and Challenges for the New Millennium." Manuscript. Also in *Cultures of Politics/Politics of Cultures: Revisioning Latin American Social Movements*, ed. Sonia E. Alvarez, Evelina Dagnino, and Arturo Escobar. Boulder, Colo.: Westview Press, 1997.

Arteaga, Ana María. 1988. "Politícizatión de lo privado y subversión del cotidiano." In *Mundo de Mujer: Continuidad y Cambio,* ed. CEM. Santiago: Ediciones CEM.

Aylwin, Patricio. 1989. Speech at Teatro Caupolican. Santiago, August 29.

Chuchryk, Patricia M. 1994. "From Dictatorship to Democracy: The Women's Movement in Chile." In *The Women's Movement in Latin America: Participation and Democracy,* ed. Jane S. Jaquette, 63–108. Boulder, Colo.: Westview Press.

Escobar, Arturo, and Sonia E. Alvarez, eds. 1992. *The Making of Social Movements in Latin America: Identity, Strategy, and Democracy.* Boulder, Colo.: Westview Press.

Frohman, Alicia, and Teresa Valdés. 1993. "Democracy in the Country and in the Home: The Women's Movement in Chile." Documento de trabajo, Serie Estudios Sociales. Santiago: FLACSO.

Fruhling, Hugo. 1989. "Nonprofit Organizations as Opposition to Authoritarian Rule: The

Case of Human Rights Organizations in Chile." In *The Nonprofit Sector in International Perspectives*, ed. Estelle James. New York: Oxford University Press, 358–76.

Hardy, Clarisa, Mariana Schkolnik, and Berta Teitelboim. 1988. "Pobreza y trabajo." Serie Trabajo y Democracia. Santiago: Academia de Humanismo Cristiano-PET.

Hola, Eugenia, and Gabriela Pischedda. 1993. *Mujeres, poder y política: Nuevos tensiones para viejas estructuras*. Santiago: Ediciones CEM.

Jaquette, Jane. 1994. "Women's Movements and Democracy in Latin America: Some Unresolved Tensions." In "Women and the Transition to Democracy: The Impact of Political and Economic Reform in Latin America." Working paper, series no. 211. The Latin American program, Woodrow Wilson International Center for Scholars, Washington, D.C.

Kirkwood, Julieta. 1990. *Ser política en Chile: Los nudos de la sabiduría feminista*. Santiago: Editorial Cuarto Propio.

Larraín, Soledad. 1994. Interview by the author.

Lechner, Norbert, and Susana Levy. 1984. "Notas sobre la vida cotidiana III: El disciplinamiento de la mujer." Serie Material de Discusión. Santiago: FLACSO.

Molina, Natacha. 1990. "El estado y las mujeres: Una relación difícil." In *Transiciones: Mujeres en los procesos democráticos*, ed. Regina Rodríguez, 85–98. Ediciones de las Mujeres no. 13. Santiago: ISIS Internacional.

Molina, Natacha, and Patricia Provoste. 1995. "Igualdad de oportunidades para las mujeres: Una oportunidad para la democracia." Documento de Trabajo. Instituto de la Mujer, Santiago.

Montecino, Sonia, and Josefina Rosetti. 1990. *Tramas para un nuevo destino: Programas de las Comisiones de la Concertación de Mujeres por la Democracia*. Santiago: Sin Editorial.

Mujica, Patricio, and Osvaldo Larrañaga. 1992. "Políticas sociales y distribución del ingreso." Serie Documentos de Trabajo, no. 106. BID, Washington, D.C. March.

Munizaga, Giselle, and Lilian Letelier. 1988. "Mujer y régimen militar." In *Mundo de Mujer: Continuidad y Cambio*. Santiago: Ediciones CEM.

Muñoz, Adriana, and Scarlett Wojciechowski. 1996. "Importancia de una ley de cuotas en Chile." Working paper. IDEAS, Santiago.

Razeto, Luis, Apolonia Ramírez, and Roberto Urmeneta. 1990. *Las organizaciones económicas populares, 1973–1990*. Santiago: PET.

Sapiro, Virginia. 1991. "Gender Politics, Gendered Politics: The State of the Field." In *Political Science: Looking to the Future*, vol. 1, ed. William Crotty. Evanston: Northwestern University Press.

Scully, Timothy. 1995. "Reconstituting Party Politics in Chile." In *Building Democratic Institutions: Party Systems in Latin America*, ed. Scott Mainwaring and Timothy Scully. Stanford: Stanford University Press.

SERNAM. 1994. *Plan de Igualdad de Oportunidades para las mujeres, 1994–1999*. Santiago: SERNAM.

Serrano, Claudia. 1990. "Entre la autonomía y la integración." In *Transiciones: Mujeres en los procesos democráticos*, ed. Regina Rodríguez, 99–106. Ediciones de las Mujeres. Santiago: Isis Internacional.

Valenzuela, María Elena. 1987. *La mujer en el Chile militar: Todas íbamos a ser reinas.* Santiago: CESOC.

———1990. "Mujeres y política: Logros y tensiones en el proceso de redemocratización." *Proposiciones No. 18: Chile, Sociedad y Transición,* ed. José Bengoa. Santiago: Ediciones Sur.

Valdés, Teresa, and Enrique Gomáriz, comp. 1992. *Mujeres latinoamericanas en cifras, Chile.* Santiago: Instituto de la Mujer de España and FLACSO Chile.

Valenzuela, María Elena, Sylvia Venegas, and Carmen Andrade, eds. 1994. *De mujer sola a jefa de hogar: Género, pobreza y políticas públicas.* Santiago: SERNAM.

Waylen, Georgina. 1994. "Women and Democratization: Conceptualizing Gender Relations in Transition Politics." *World Politics* 46 (April).

Chapter Four

Justice and Individual Rights

Challenges for Women's Movements and Democratization in Brazil

TERESA P. R. CALDEIRA

omen's movements have played an important role in Brazilian democratization.[1] Frequently, this role is described as the capacity of these groups to create new institutions within the state, such as the Councils on the Rights of Women and the women's police stations. On other occasions, it is presented as their great ability to mobilize public support and lobby the Congress or join international networks of women's associations and influence the framing of both national and international documents in UN-sponsored conferences. The diverse Brazilian women's movements offer a strategic perspective from which to look at democratic consolidation for two reasons. On one hand, they force us to conceive of democratization as a process that extends well beyond the institutionalized political system. In fact, if women's movements are contributing to the democratization process, it is not so much because of women's ability to join institutionalized politics but because of their continuous capacity to create new spaces for articulation and mobilization and to provoke transformations that affect cultural patterns of inequality and authoritarianism embedded in everyday life. On the other hand, however, while they do this, women's movements face restrictions that indicate the limits and the main challenges of an effective democratization in Brazil. These limits relate to the delegitimation of the justice system and of individual and civil rights, dimensions that traditionally constitute the cornerstone of a feminist agenda. As they act to transform these dimensions, women's movements contribute to the expansion of civil citizenship in Brazil and simultaneously expose both the discriminations suffered by women and other minorities and the precarious side of the democratization process itself.

To make these claims, I look at the relationship between women's move-

75

ments and the process of democratization in Brazil from four interrelated perspectives. First, focusing on the women's movements, I address their changing organizations and relationship with the state, their capacity to influence public
policies and to continuously re-create spaces for political mobilization. Second,
I analyze the disjunctive character of Brazilian democracy,[2] that is, the fact that
although it has democratized at the level of the political system, Brazilian society continues to be plagued by violence, human rights abuses, and the delegitimation of the justice system, all of which affect the situation of women. Third, I
discuss how the women's movements have been struggling for the legitimation
of rights in this disjunctive democracy and therefore expanding the scope of citizenship. Finally, I let the experience of Brazilian women's movements talk back
to feminist theory and democratization theory, and I raise a series of questions
about the models that usually frame how we think of women's rights.

WOMEN'S MOVEMENTS:
DIVERSITY AND INNOVATION

Instead of attempting to summarize the history of the women's movements in the Brazilian democratic consolidation, by building on conclusions of
previous studies, I seek to reveal the way in which the women's movements construct their own spaces to articulate gender-specific claims and to press for the
expansion of citizenship rights.[3] I talk about women's movements in the plural
to emphasize the very diverse character of the organizations dealing with
women's issues. They include feminist groups, mostly but not only composed of
middle-class professionals; working-class women's groups that do not call themselves feminist but which have worked for a gender-specific agenda, such as
campaigning for day care centers and health clinics with special programs for
women; and, more recently, women-oriented nongovernmental organizations
(NGOs). The last have professional and paid staff, are usually supported by international funds, implement specific projects and offer diverse types of services,
and have been skilled at lobbying governmental institutions. The boundaries between these diverse types of organizations are not always clear-cut.

I start by considering women's movements' relationship with the state during the process of democratization, that is, from the period of transition from
military to civilian rule to the present.[4] The women's movements had the highest visibility and the greatest political space in the postmilitary Brazilian state
during the rule of the first elected state governors (1983–87) and the first civil
president (1985–90). The first Council on the Feminine Condition (Conselho da
Condição Feminina) was created in the state of São Paulo in 1983 by Governor

Franco Montoro, the first elected governor after the military rule, in response to demands by feminist groups.[5] The representatives of the feminist movement who constituted its first members were able to use the council to press their agenda, primarily in the areas of women's health, family planning, and day care. The council was also associated with another institutional invention: the women's police stations (Delegacias de Defesa da Mulher), which have female staff and specialize in cases of violence against women. The political success of both generated a proliferation of similar institutions in various states and cities. Today there are 10 state councils (including São Paulo's), 23 municipal councils, and the federal-level National Council for the Rights of Women (Conselho Nacional dos Direitos da Mulher), which was created by the first civil president, José Sarney, in 1985. Since the opening of the first women's police station in 1985, 8 others have been created in the city of São Paulo, 11 in the other municipalities of the metropolitan region, and another 104 in the interior of the state. Moreover, 20 of Brazil's states have created women's stations.

Comparing the history of the various councils, Danielle Ardaillon demonstrated that they have had different connections to party politics and changed according to political conjunctures. These factors generated substantial differences in their performance. Although the first São Paulo council and the first National Council were largely made up of feminists and were constituted to fulfill their demands, various succeeding councils were created by governors and mayors (including conservative ones) without consulting the feminist organizations. They tended to become party enclaves within the state bureaucracy, and their capacity to articulate a women's agenda and to promote institutional changes has been severely limited. This leads to the conclusion, drawn by both Danielle Ardaillon and Sonia Alvarez, that the maintenance of a feminist agenda and the achievement of policy transformations depend less on the existence of an institutional space per se than on the relationship of this space to autonomous feminist and women's organizations. This conclusion coincides with internal evaluations of the participants of feminist movements. Since the beginning, feminists have had ambiguous relationships with the spaces opened within the state and the political parties. Many opposed this participation and decided not to support it. Most, however, ended up engaging in some sort of participation in institutional politics while emphasizing the "autonomy of the movement," that is, the need to maintain an independent space of organized women if they were to be able to press a genuine feminist agenda.[6] The expression "double militancy" accounts for the participation in both spheres, the state or political parties on the one hand and the feminist movement on the other.

The combination of feminists' use of specific institutional spaces within the state and grassroots and lobbying work of autonomous women's organizations succeeded best during the constitutional assembly meeting in the late 1980s, in which there were only 26 women out of a total of 559 representatives. Formed at that time by a strong group of feminists, the National Council was able to coordinate a campaign to introduce a series of women's demands in the new constitution of 1988 and to lobby successfully for their approval. The Women's Network (Rede Mulher), integrated by seven hundred women's groups around the country, collected approximately forty-three thousand signatures for a popular amendment called "Rights of Women" (Direitos da Mulher) and another thirty-two thousand for the amendment "Health of Women" (Saúde da Mulher). At the end, the "Lipstick Lobby" (Lobby do Batom), as it became known, contributed to the approval of various articles guaranteeing equal rights for men and women and people of all races and specific women's provisions, such as maternity leave of 120 days, paternity leave of a week, the right to divorce, and equal rights for men and women inside the family.[7] The new constitution also defined the state as responsible for creating the means to curb domestic violence and for providing couples with the means to exercise a free decision on family planning. Abortion, which was also included in the "Health of Women" amendment, was not approved but was not prohibited either, which left space for its approval in enabling legislation.[8]

After this success story, however, feminists lost many of their institutional spaces, both at state and national levels. In the state of São Paulo, for example, the successor of Governor Franco Montoro, Orestes Quércia, decided the nominations for the council according to party lines (called *fisiologismo* in Brazil) and did not select feminists named by women's movements. Moreover, he cut the budget and shrank the scope of the council's activities. Since 1987 the council has been hamstrung and has had little political visibility. At the national level, it was not necessary to change presidents to change the character of the council. The same government that gave the first and second presidents of the council the power to act also provoked the resignation of its feminist members in 1989 after a newly appointed Ministry of Justice (to which the council is subordinated) cut its budget and administrative support. A new council was designated, but it was formed exclusively by women (mostly lawyers) who had no connections with the feminist movement. The council disappeared as a political actor.

In sum, the existence of institutional spaces for women per se does not mean much. The success of a women's agenda depends both on the organization of autonomous women's movements capable of demanding and monitoring feminist action inside the state and on political support from the governors or presidents. In the early 1990s, in the absence of these two connections, most women's councils lacked effectiveness in implementing policies for women. In the mid-1990s, some of the councils, including the National Council after the election of Fernando Henrique Cardoso in 1994, were again staffed by feminist teams. Nevertheless, the relationship that the new councils maintain with the organized feminist movement is quite different from and much less organic than that of the first councils.

Considering the case of the National Council, there are at least two reasons that explain the differences between its recent version and the first ones, and these differences indicate the changes that occurred in the women's movements during the last decade. The first is that, after the National Council fell apart in 1989, feminists created an alternative institution to coordinate their attempts at influencing public policies: the Forum Nacional de Presidentas de Conselhos da Condição Feminina e Direitos da Mulher (National Forum of Presidents of Councils on the Feminine Condition and Rights of Women). In the absence of an official space, feminists engaged in local actions in different states created their own autonomous space of articulation. It continues to exist up to the present, in spite of the revitalization of the National Council, whose members were appointed with little consultation with the organized feminist movements. The second reason is that since the late 1980s feminists have reinvented their forms of organization and their strategies to influence public policies.

During the early 1990s, women multiplied the places and spaces in which they act and from which they circulate their discourses.[9] Many of the feminists who left the councils and who had provided important and visible leadership spent some time outside political institutions. Some continued to be committed to institution building, but of different types. They created women's studies centers in universities (there are now more than 20); some started the publication of a new journal, *Estudos Feministas*, which was the first women's journal in Brazil to call itself feminist. Most important, however, women created numerous nongovernmental organizations, indicating their increased professionalization and specialization. NGOs specialize in various areas, although there is a concentration in issues of reproductive rights, health, and environment. Some of these areas, especially reproductive rights, have been given priority by international funding agencies working in Brazil. In various cases, it seems that these NGOs are receiving development and public policy funds that used to be directed to government agencies before but which are now directed to these organizations because they are thought to be more flexible and efficient.[10] This illustrates the tendency toward the privatization (and consequent selectivity) of social programs which has accompanied the adoption of neoliberal policies by various states in Latin America, which involves the dismantling of their welfare structure, and the delegitimation of social rights.

In addition to being a required format for obtaining external funding, NGOs are also the basis from which women have organized effective transnational networks and lobbied at international forums.[11] These new organizations with their complex international networks have proved to be efficient in influencing public policies and governmental decisions without necessarily being inside the state. The feminist participation in the preparation of UN conferences since 1992 exemplifies this trend.[12] On these occasions, and especially at the Beijing conference, Brazilian feminist groups and NGOs actively participated in international and regional networks to prepare for the meetings and showed an impressive presence (three hundred representatives of NGOs from Brazil went to the parallel forum in Huairou, China).[13] Moreover, feminists were able to influence decisively the position of the Brazilian government. For the Conference on Women, as well as for the other UN conferences since 1993, the Brazilian Foreign Affairs ministry invited members of NGOs and feminists to write reports, to help to shape its official position, and to be part of the official delegation. In sum, feminists have continued to be influential in state politics in spite of the fact that they were not occupying positions within the state or even within the elected representative system.

Despite this successful influence, the intense NGO-ization of the women's movements raises important questions that constitute the main concern of some feminist critics in the late 1990s.[14] First, the dependence on external funding comes with the increasing ability of the granting agencies to set the priorities of NGO activities and therefore with the disempowerment of local women to determine their own agenda. Second, the transfer of what used to be public policies or public development projects to private organizations opens space for the reproduction of inequalities and privileges among women instead of contributing to their erosion. Moreover, it obviously changes the framing of some of the struggles undertaken by women, as they are no longer conceived as struggles for citizenship rights but framed as disputes for private resources. Third, at the same time that feminist discourses achieve wide circulation and are absorbed and incorporated into the media and into official and governmental documents, they are also tamed, selected, and resignified, losing radicalism and transformative power, as Sonia Alvarez and Veronica Schild demonstrate.[15] Fourth, the rapid professionalization and formalization provoked by the proliferation of NGOs break down the traditional connections that many middle-class feminists have maintained with working-class women for a long time, alienating the latter from the movement's new activities, most clearly from transnational networking.

Among the women's groups organized in the early 1980s there were several groups of working-class women which did not consider themselves feminist.

Women constituted a large part of the participants in the urban social movements that changed the political scene in the late 1970s and early 1980s.[16] Middle-class feminists, most of them connected to a left-wing politics, have always made a point of articulating their struggles with working-class women. This was especially important in the late 1970s and early 1980s, and one of its symbols is the Movimento de Luta por Creche (Day Care Movement) in São Paulo. In the late 1980s, however, not only did the organization of popular social movements diminish, but the linkages between working-class women and middle-class feminist groups became more fragile. The working-class women who continue to be active are more likely to be found working for NGOs, usually in secondary or voluntary positions, instead of in neighborhood associations. This has happened despite a severe economic crisis that worsened the situation of poor women.

This economic crisis provoked high inflation (up to almost 2,500% in 1993), unemployment, and an increase in the number of people living below the poverty level. Moreover, in recent years, the already iniquitous distribution of wealth in Brazil was aggravated. The Gini coefficient in the metropolitan region of São Paulo grew from 0.516 in 1981 to 0.575 in 1991.[17] In the last decade, according to IBGE (Instituto Brasileiro de Geografia e Estatística; the national census bureau), the proportion of income in the hands of the richest 1 percent of the Brazilian population grew from 13.0 percent in 1981 to 17.3 percent in 1989. At the same time, the proportion of income of the poorest 50 percent of the population dropped from 13.4 percent in 1981 to 10.4 percent in 1989. According to Lopes, the effects of the economic crisis were more perverse on the households headed by women.[18] This type of household increased considerably in the last years: they constituted 10.7 percent of the total number of households in 1960 and 20 percent in 1989.[19] In 1989, 33 percent of the households headed by women were living below the poverty line, compared with 23 percent of the total number of households.[20] Despite the worsening living conditions of the poor urban population and especially of poor women, the last decade has not witnessed the same level of organization of social movements which existed in the previous decade.

The one exception is the groups representing African Brazilians. Probably one of the most important innovations of women's movements in recent years is the development of a series of NGOs and groups addressing the situation of black women. These groups carved out their space in the intersection of the feminist movement and the black movement, struggling to show to both how their specific problems had been systematically neglected. In fact, in the last decade, the combination of the efforts of African Brazilian women and the availability of unprecedented data on discrimination against the black population resulted in an awareness about the dramatic situation of black women and led to the organization of important black women's groups. These data show, for example, that households headed by women are more frequent among black households than among white households (21% compared with 14%). Moreover, they indicate that almost half (49%) of the households headed by a black woman are below the poverty line.[21]

With the decline of working-class social movements, the various Afro-Brazilian women's groups represent today probably the most important challenge to the reproduction of class and power inequalities inside the women's movements. The left-wing gesture of middle-class feminists toward the working-class women seems to have lost power after the NGOs with their specialized (mostly middle-class) staff replaced the looser organizations of social movements as the dominant type of women's organization. In this context, organizations became socially more homogeneous, and the black women's movements may fulfill the role of reminding white middle-class women of social inequalities and keeping them in check.[22]

In summarizing what happened with women's movements of various sorts and their relationship with state institutions and public policies in the last decade, three conclusions are clear. First, women's organizations became more diversified and dispersed. However, this diversification did not mean more social heterogeneity but exactly the opposite, with the exception of the case of black women's groups. Second, although many of the institutions created within the state for the articulation of a women's agenda either lost power or were abandoned by feminists, the latter continue to influence public policies and the state and to expand women's rights. Third, women's influence does not translate into participation in the institutionalized political system (electoral politics and political parties), where the presence of women continues to be low.

Between 1950 and 1980 Brazil had only 11 women in Congress. After the 1980s, this situation improved a little. In 1982, 8 women were elected to Congress, and in 1986, 26 were elected to the constitutional assembly (only 5% of the total). In 1990, 30 women deputies and 2 women senators were elected (5% and 2.5% of the total of their respective houses). In 1994, 5 women were elected to the Senate (6.2%), and the representation in the House increased to 6.8 percent. At state and city level, the representation of women is not more impressive than at the federal level, although it has also been increasing. Moreover, political parties continue to be male spaces in which women's careers face incredible obstacles. A federal law of 1995 established a quota of 20 percent for women in political parties' lists of candidates in municipal elections and the quota is beginning to have some impact.[23]

Looking at women's roles in current transformations of Brazilian society from the narrow perspective of institutionalized politics one can arrive at the wrong conclusion that feminist groups "have not been contributing to the democratization of the political struggle in its strict sense, through the intervention into the country's political agenda, the involvement in political disputes, the expansion of respect for human rights, or the constitution of a new level of equality for the so-called general interest."[24] Arguments such as this miss women's movements' innovations and contributions to democratization and cultural change, basically because they look for them in the wrong places. Instead of exploring the effects of the new political spaces and practices that women have been creating, they want to find women where men have always been, participating in traditional ways in institutionalized politics.

In the last decades, although women's participation in institutionalized politics improved only marginally, the situation of women changed considerably,[25] and feminist ideas spread and were absorbed in various dimensions of Brazilian society. On the one hand, studies with participants in various types of social movements in Latin America show that this participation provoked transformations in women's lives, even when gender was not an issue in the movements in which they were engaged.[26] Women in these movements especially value their new relationships, the opportunity to get out of the house, to ask questions, learn, and grow, to explore the public space, to question structures of authority both public and private. They feel empowered by their participation, and this feeling guides them both in questioning domestic relationships and in changing state agencies and the services they provide. On the other hand, feminist ideas are no longer something to be found only in women's movements: they are everywhere in people's minds, in the mass media (in famous soap opera characters or in advertisements of all types of products), in the actions of individuals who do not think of themselves as feminists. This means that they are dispersed and articulated in many different ways. These are all indications of a fact that should be obvious by now: that feminist politics is also a cultural politics. Feminism and women's movements are at their best when they create new spaces and resignify everyday practices and people's lives, not only when they expand representation within political institutions narrowly defined. The most powerful contribution of Brazilian and Latin American feminisms and of all types of women's organizations to the democratization of their societies has been their creativity and ability constantly to reproduce their gender-specific agendas and their experiences of personal growth, transformation of everyday life, and solidarity in a variety of spaces and organizational forms.

If we agree that one of the most important dimensions of women's movements has been to transform cultural values and everyday lives, then we can also see how the NGO format is problematic. Although NGOs are very effective in their lobbying activity, it seems that their more professional organizations leave less space for the kind of experiences of learning and growing which women who engaged in social movements value so much. This is especially true in the case of working-class women who are increasingly alienated from those institutions. As NGOs become the main form under which women organize, they may be losing important spaces for transforming their everyday lives and practices.

Another problem in current developments in women's movements concerns the content of a gender-specific agenda. I suggested earlier that women's movements' ability to set their own priorities may be decreasing owing to the higher dependency on external funding. Moreover, there are some areas in which a feminist intervention, although crucial, is impeded by structural features of Brazilian society. From my perspective, one of the main challenges of Brazilian women's movements is to affect the perception of individual rights, justice, violence, and conceptions of the body. This is the case not only because civil rights constitute the cornerstone of any feminist agenda and because women are victims of various sorts of violence but also because this is the area in which Brazilian democratic consolidation is weakest. It seems to me that women's movements occupy a crucial position in relation to this issue, as they are one of the few social movements addressing this central dimension of any democratic consolidation.[27]

DISJUNCTIVE DEMOCRACY AND THE DELEGITIMATION OF JUSTICE AND CIVIL RIGHTS

The analysis of the development of Brazilian democracy since the end of military rule in 1985 reveals the coexistence of various processes of opposed meanings: some of them can be considered to expand citizenship and guarantee rights, while others clearly jeopardize rights and the rule of law. The most innovative process of the expansion of citizenship rights was that associated with the urban social movements and the minorities' movements of the late 1970s and early 1980s. Dominated groups succeeded in gaining legitimacy for the idea that they had the "right to have rights," and during the last two decades social movements of all sorts emerged and expanded. At the same time, trade unions gained independence from the state (to which they were connected by the corporatist model), reinvented their forms of organization and leadership, and contributed significantly to the creation of new political institutions such as the PT (Partido dos Trabalhadores; the Workers' Party). Freedom of expression, the end of press censorship, the guarantee of democratic electoral procedures in which cases of corruption are rare, free party organization, and routine functioning of the legislative branch at all levels are other signs of the expansion of citizenship. Nevertheless, at the same time, Brazilian society has been marked by attacks against institutions representing the rights of minority groups and by massacres of prisoners, children, rural workers, indigenous people, and common citizens committed not only by the police but also by private guards and vigilante groups. In sum, in the last two decades many events led to the expansion and consolidation of political and social rights and of democratic institutions, while others led to disrespect for individual, civil, and human rights.

James Holston and I developed the concept of disjunctive democracy in order to account for these contradictory processes and for one of the most intriguing features of Brazilian democratic consolidation: the fact that violence, both civilian and of the state, has increased considerably after the end of military rule and the routinization of democratic procedures at the level of the political system.[28] In other words, in Brazil political democracy did not bring respect for rights, justice, and lives but exactly its opposite. With the concept of disjunctive democracy we want to achieve at least two things: first, to highlight the fact that democratization is not a totally coherent process in which all aspects of social and political life change in one direction; and second, to force the theorization of democracy as a broad social process rather than only as a political process. In order to make this consideration we obviously go back to T. H. Marshall's classic distinction between political, civil, and social rights.[29] Separating these spheres allow us to identify where the main problem seems to be. In the case of Brazil, it seems to lie in the sphere of individual and civil rights and in the institution in charge of guaranteeing them: the justice system. In fact, civil rights have not been effectively woven into the fabric of Brazilian citizenship. Instead, the protections and immunities they are intended to ensure as constitutional norms are generally perceived as privileges of elite social statutes and thus of limited access. They are not, in other words, appreciated as common rights of citizenship.[30]

There is a tendency in the social sciences, and especially in studies influenced by T. H. Marshall, to think of the expansion of rights and democratization as complementary processes, perhaps because they take on the British experience as a model.[31] Countries such as Brazil and many others in the Third World confirm the variety of historical forms of the expansion/retraction of citizenship rights. Social rights—mainly connected to labor rights—expanded in Brazil and other Latin American countries before other rights and even during dictatorships that suspended political rights. Moreover, in populist dictatorships such as those of Vargas in Brazil and Perón in Argentina, social rights were presented as a gift from above given to those below instead of the result of struggles from the working classes, as was the case in Europe. In Latin America countries, political rights have had a convoluted history of going back and forth, of being guaranteed and taken away until they got to the current stage in which they are largely legitimated and exercised. Individual and civil rights, however, have always remained underdeveloped, together with the justice system, which is, in principle, the institution in charge of assuring them. In Brazil, the sphere of individual rights is extremely weak at this moment if compared with other areas of citizenship. It problematizes both the disrespect for individuals—their rights and their bodies—and the weakness of a justice system made to serve the elites and repeatedly adapted to serve different dictatorships.

There are many ways through which we can demonstrate the uneven evaluation of different types of rights. One of them is a survey conducted by the Instituto Brasileiro de Opinião Pública e Estatística (IBOPE; Brazilian Institute of Public Opinion and Statistics) for the Commission of Justice and Peace of the Archdiocese of São Paulo in 1989. This survey asked a sample of the populations of São Paulo, Rio de Janeiro, and Recife to evaluate a series of rights in terms of which were more important and which were more frequently violated. In the final classification of 36 rights, it is clear that those rights that are most legitimate are collective and social services (retirement, education, health assistance, housing, social security, child assistance, and public security). Those rated least important were political and civil rights (to vote, to participate in organizations). This response may result from the fact that, at the time the poll was taken, in the late 1980s, political rights were not being denied to the citizens. At the same time, however, abuses by the police were intense, and perceptions that the judiciary system was biased were widespread. But this was not enough to give any of the rights associated with control of the police and the justice system (fair trial, not to be tortured, not to be killed by the police, not to be imprisoned without a mandate) significant rating, meaning that they continue to be considered not important.[32]

The delegitimation of justice and civil rights in Brazil has numerous dimensions. A discussion of four of them is sufficient to demonstrate the perversities generated in a context in which rights become privileges and in which injustice and impunity rule. The first is the widespread lack of confidence in the fairness of the justice system. Justice is thought of as a privilege for the rich, who can either pay for or avoid it. It therefore further reinforces already devastating levels of social inequality. The second dimension is the routine abuses and human rights violations practiced by the police. They not only beat and torture but kill. In some recent years, they killed more than 1,000 civilians in the metropolitan region of São Paulo alone; in 1992, the number reached 1,470, a figure probab unequaled anywhere worldwide, especially under democratic rule. This includes 111 prisoners killed in one afternoon in São Paulo's largest prison in October 1992. In April 1997, prime-time television broadcast scenes of harassment, torture, and a killing of poor workers by São Paulo military police. They have done this with impunity, on the one hand, because military policemen have not been under the jurisdiction of the civil courts. A special military court usually acquits policemen, arguing that they have killed in self-defense and in the line of duty.[33] More important, however, the police continue to kill because the population believes in the use of violence as a means of controlling high rates of crime and basically because they think that because the justice system does not work, it is better to kill bandits right away.[34]

This brings us to the third dimension: a significant part of the population opposes the defense of human rights. The contestation of human rights symbolizes in a clear way the limits of the democratization process in Brazil.[35] Human rights have not always been opposed in São Paulo. On the contrary, respect for human rights helped galvanize the political movement that led to the end of the military regime. The change in meaning happened after political prisoners were freed (the amnesty bill was approved in 1979) and human rights groups turned their attention to common prisoners, who continue to be tortured and to live in degrading conditions to this day. In fact, the association of human rights with the defense of "criminals" was a very successful right-wing ideological strategy in a context of increasing fear of crime. What made it possible was the exploitation of some of the perverse characteristics of the justice system and the delegitimation of civil rights. Because most people believe that justice is a privilege of the rich, the opponents of human rights argued that if the majority of the population do not have their rights respected, why should criminals have the privilege of having their rights respected? Why should they have good living conditions in the prisons while the majority of the population is suffering? Why should they be treated with humanity when the workers' everyday experience with the police is one of harassment and violence? Sometimes conservative politicians justified their opposition to human rights of prisoners by positioning them against the social rights of the majority of the population. They argued that to assure prisoners good living conditions would spend money better used to provide hospitals, nurseries, and asylums for the majority of the population. In this right-wing rhetoric, the defenders of human rights were transformed into people struggling against the rights of honest citizens and in favor of crime.[36]

The fourth dimension is the privatization of justice, revealed both in people's resorting to private security and in the walling off of cities. The combination of fearing the police and distrusting the justice system leaves people feeling terribly vulnerable. Although some are resigned to this feeling, others seek alternatives that are usually outside the law. In one alternative, people consider reacting privately and taking justice into their own hands. Such vigilantism is usually an alternative more at the level of discourse than of practice, although the number of lynchings has, in fact, increased significantly in the last decade. Another alternative is support for police use of deadly force against alleged criminals, and it is in this context that the police violence is admired by the population. Private measures to deal with crime also include the ubiquitous walls and bars people put around their houses and apartment buildings. These barriers are dramatically changing not only the landscape of Brazilian cities but also the social interactions that occur in their public spaces. In these cities of walls, residents have high levels of suspicion and change their habits to avoid interactions in public, especially with people perceived as different. The walls not only separate residents but also create fortified enclaves such as shopping centers and office complexes where entrances can be controlled and social homogeneity guaranteed. Fear of crime in this sense legitimates practices of segregation and considerably changes the character of public space.[37] The walls come with a large variety of technologies of security and the hiring of doormen and private guards. As in many other countries, they help to multiply the profits of the rapidly growing industry of private security. This industry has various faces in Brazil, as it adapts to serve different social classes. At various levels, however, it mixes with the illegal actions of the police, as a significant proportion of private guards are off-duty policemen, frequently working with police guns. The working classes who cannot afford these services may benefit from the vigilance of *justiceiros* (literally, justice makers) hired by local merchants; but they are just as likely to suffer the adverse consequences.

In sum, these four dimensions indicate unmistakably the extent of the delegitimation of justice and civil rights in Brazilian society. Although in various dimensions Brazilian society has clearly democratized in the last decade, the fields of justice and civil rights represent a space in which democratization has still not occurred and in which rights have been openly contested. In fact, they constitute the most significant obstacle for the consolidation of a democratic society in Brazil. Individual rights traditionally constitute the cornerstone of a feminist agenda. It is important, then, to investigate how the women's movements relate to this dimension of citizenship and to the challenges it presents to democratic consolidation.

WOMEN'S MOVEMENTS AND THE STRUGGLE FOR RIGHTS IN A DISJUNCTIVE DEMOCRACY

The history of Brazilian women's movements since the mid-1970s both reflects and challenges the disjunctive process of democratic consolidation. Contemporary Brazilian women's movements came into existence in the mid-1970s during the process of transition from military rule and inside the opposition movement that overthrew it. In that context, they basically engaged in two types of struggles. On the one hand, they opposed the military regime and demanded political rights (to vote, to elect executive officers, to organize in political parties, and so on). As part of this opposition, women organized the Movimento Feminino pela Anistia (Feminine Movement for Amnesty) in 1975, demanding the liberation of political prisoners and the respect for their human rights. On the other hand, women struggled for the expansion of social rights that directly affect women's lives. They demanded facilities for collective use (such as day care centers, clinics, police stations) and social services and influenced the conception of public policies. Both types of struggles were quite successful: on the one hand, the opposition movement succeeded at making the military leave power, political liberties were reinstalled, and the amnesty law was passed; on the other hand, day care centers, health clinics, and women's police stations were built in large quantities in various cities, and the women's movements influenced the approval of the Programa de Asistência Integral à Saúde da Mulher (PAISM; Program for Integral Assistance to Women's Health) and other state-level programs based on a view of women's health which was inspired by the feminist rhetoric and which even included the notion of reproductive rights.

Social rights are historically the most legitimate aspect of Brazilian citizenship. In fact, the sphere of collective or social rights has traditionally been not only the main area of articulation for the left wing and for labor movements but also the sphere in which the state, in its populist-corporatist incarnation, was accustomed to answering public demands or even creating them.[38] It made sense, then, that women's movements (and social movements in general) were first organized in this more legitimate field and that the way in which the opposition shaped its demands in the late 1970s and the immediate response of the state were innovations within a well-known pattern. The demands of the social movements in general, as well as of women's movements, were largely demands for collective rights. Even during military rule, the state started to grant these rights, undoubtedly anticipating that elections would be reinstated. Various administrations, especially at the local level, not only provided new facilities for collective use demanded by the women's movements but also created various types of citizens' councils to deal with different public policies (health was again an important area, but there were also councils to deal with education, sanitation, environment, children, the rights of women, and the like). In sum, it was through the field of social rights that women first challenged the state and then entered the state, as they framed their gender-specific demands in terms of demands for social rights and collective services. It continues to be in this sphere that women have concentrated their lobbying efforts and have been most successful.

In contrast, the success of women in gaining their political rights has been more ambiguous. Women were the majority of the participants in almost all types of popular movements, but many continue to believe that political parties are not for them but constitute male universes.[39] Although middle-class feminists, especially those on the left, challenged the dominant ideologies of their parties (which considered gender a secondary issue to be addressed only after the main revolutionary issues of "general interest" had been taken care of), and although they disrupted some of the organizational gender hierarchies, the participation of women in institutional politics continues to be low.

Even though women's movements mainly framed their initiatives as demands for social rights and collective services, they have also always addressed issues related to the sphere of individual rights and the protection of women's bodies. This is especially clear in the intervention of feminists and NGOs in the areas of reproductive rights, legal changes, violence against women, and racism against black women. Reproductive rights are the main theme of feminist groups in the 1990s. It is a traditional area of interest for feminists and the state.[40] It is also probably the area in which there is more work by NGOs and therefore more available funding, and it has been at the center of women's disputes internationally, as the controversies at both the Cairo and the Beijing UN conferences attest. In the Brazilian case, the state has taken various initiatives to develop public health policies for women, some influenced by feminist activity and discourse. The 1988 constitution establishes that the state is responsible for providing couples with the means to make free decisions on family planning.

The evidence shows that women from all social classes in Brazil have been changing their reproductive practices. Brazil has become an exemplary case of a sharp decrease in fertility rate in a short period of time, despite the lack of a strong policy of population control. The fertility rate dropped from 5.8 children per woman in 1970, to 4.3 in 1975, and to 3.6 in 1984, which means a decline of 37 percent in 15 years. Preliminary estimates for 1991 indicate a fertility rate of at most 2.9 children per woman. This change was possible in part because of the increase in the availability of medical services that affected especially women and their perception of their bodies. The change can only be fully understood, however, if one assumes significant changes in women's perceptions and attitudes and a complete reassessment of the value of large families.[41] Although there is information on the policy-making aspects of family planning, very little is known about how the changes in this area reflect changes in women's perceptions. Apparently, the assertion of the right to make decisions about reproduction is a crucial dimension of women's individual control over their bodies and lives, but the little information available on how these decisions are being made raises questions about the level of control women have over their reproductive choices and about the extent to which they can protect their bodies. In fact, I argue that although the new reproductive practices could be considered to expand notions of individual rights and control of women's bodies, there are many grounds on which to question the quality of this control.

The most important indicators of this are data on the use of birth control and on births. By 1986, 70 percent of married women (either officially married or cohabiting) between 15 and 54 years old were using some kind of birth control. The main method, used by 44.4 percent of women, was sterilization (tubal ligation), followed by the pill, used by 41 percent of women.[42] In 1991–92, in the northeast of Brazil (the poorest region of the country), the proportion of sterilization reached 63 percent (compared with 36.1% in São Paulo), and the data indicated that 19 percent of women in the northeast were already sterilized before they turned 25 (compared with 10% in São Paulo). The percentage of female sterilization for all countries worldwide is 15.7 percent and for all developed countries 7.6 percent. In China, where the state has a very aggressive policy of population control, the proportion is 49.1 percent.[43] These practices of birth control are accompanied by another striking fact: in Brazil, birth through a cesarean section is becoming more common than natural birth. In the state of São Paulo (the richest state of the country) in 1992, 53.4 percent of all births occurred through cesarean section. Its high proportion is associated with the prevalence of sterilization, as most of the tubal ligations (75% in 1986 in all of Brazil, 83% in São Paulo) occur during a cesarean section.[44]

These data are revealing in various ways. First, they illustrate a serious problem of public health and the existence of a medical class that is using cesarean sections far more than is medically necessary and which does not provide alternative means of birth control. Second, they indicate that this is especially true in the poorest region of the country. Third, and most important for the perspective of women's control of their bodies, the above data indicate that Brazilian women are taking radical steps to control their reproduction, in terms of both the irreversibility of the method and the amount of intervention in the body which is required. In other words, women's reproductive decisions are being e in ways that normalize drastic interference in the body. Reproduction is not the only area in which this interference occurs. Plastic surgery of all types is also very common among the middle classes, who can afford such operations. Very little is being done so far to change this culture of sterilization and radical interventions on the body, a culture that seems to be quite pervasive in Brazil and which goes beyond the question of women's bodies.

In fact, these radical interventions and manipulations of the body may be taken as normal in the context of a wide and complex cultural pattern with quite diverse expressions, some extremely violent and negative and others perceived as attractive features of Brazilian culture.[45] My hypothesis is that the delegitimation of individual rights in general is a counterpart of what I call the unboundedness of the body in Brazilian society. The unbounded body is a concept that has two complementary sides. On the one hand, the unbounded body has no clear barriers of separation and avoidance; it is a body permeable and open to intervention and upon which manipulations by others are not seen as problematic. On the other hand, the unbounded body is unprotected by individual rights and indeed results historically from the lack of their enforcement. In Brazil, where the judicial system is openly discredited, the body (and the person) is in general not protected by a set of rights that would bind it, in the sense of establishing barriers and setting limits to the interference, intervention, or abuse of others. To me, the unboundedness of the body is expressed in the disrespect of human rights and the widespread opposition to them, the killings by the police, the use of physical violence as a ubiquitous form of punishment of children of all social classes, the defense of death penalty, domestic violence against women, and the medical practices just described. Moreover, it is expressed in those features that, as the saying goes, "make Brazil Brazil": in Carnival and its mixture of bodies, in the open sensuality and exhibition of the body and what is frequently described as a flexible sexuality, in the valorization of the proximity of bodies, and so forth.

Violence against women is an obvious area of the manifestation of this complex pattern of relations and one that has always been an issue for women's movements. However, to bind women's bodies with individual rights in the context of this cultural pattern is not a trivial undertaking. Women and men are victims of violence in Brazil, although of different types. Men are the main victims of homicides and police abuses, whereas women suffer more from domestic violence. Statistics are precarious in this regard, as there is only a national survey on victimization, part of a household survey (PNAD) in 1988.[46] It shows that while men are victimized mainly in public spaces (54.73% of the cases on streets), women are mostly victimized inside their homes (48.2%). The main aggressor of both men and women is someone known to them (33.9% of the cases of aggression involving women and 43.6% of the cases of aggression involving men), but while only 10.68 percent of men are victims of a relative, for women the figure is 32 percent. Most of the victims of physical assault never take their case to the police authorities (62.37% of the men and 58.48% of the women), and therefore crime statistics do not reflect most of the cases. The main reason why people do not go to the police is their lack of confidence in the police and the feeling that it is better to avoid them (31.78% of the men and 38.1% of women).

The invention of the women's police stations is probably the most famous creation influenced by the women's movements to deal with violence against women. Although there are no studies assessing their impact as yet, it is known that in 1986, the year after the creation of the first women's police station in São Paulo, reported rape increased 25 percent. Obviously, a trust in the police is crucial for the enforcement of rights. However, it is also necessary to have legislation and the means to enforce it. Women succeeded in having many of their issues incorporated into the 1988 constitution, but most have yet to come into legal force owing to the lack of enabling legislation. One of the main things to be changed is the version of the Penal Code which is still in effect from 1940 and, in addition to having articles that contradict the 1988 constitution, has several significant flaws. These include an article that defines rape as a crime against custom and not against a person. In the same category are crimes such as "unusual sexual acts," seduction, prostitution, and oral sex. Moreover, the code maintains a difference between "honest" and "dishonest" women. These classifications reveal a great deal about Brazilian conceptions of sexual roles, sexuality, and individual rights. According to the Penal Code, in the case of rape the judicial object to be protected is custom, not the woman's body. Moreover, the aggregation of crimes in the category "custom" and the use of concepts such as "dishonest" women illustrate how women's sexuality in Brazil is conceived of as something to be controlled; thus it shows how far women still are from having their integrity and personal rights recognized, from having their bodies legally bounded.

In countries such as the United States, in which the justice system is highly legitimated, where individual and civil rights have a strong tradition (which does not mean that they are always respected and, furthermore, equally respected for all social groups), and where feminists have been extremely active in struggling for the judicial protection of women's bodies, the body is basically conceived and experienced as bounded today. People learn not only to keep a certain distance around their bodies unconsciously and to respect this distance around other people's bodies but also to rely on the justice system to protect their bodies' boundedness and privacy. The criminalization of sexual harassment is an important example of the continuous boundedness of women's bodies. In Brazil, feminist movements, and especially feminist lawyers, have been active in making suggestions and trying to approve changes in the ordinary legislation. The Forum of Presidents of Councils on the Feminine Condition elaborated a feminist proposal for the reformation of the Civil Code and the Penal Code and presented it to the national Congress on March 1991. This proposal suggests the elimination of the category "crimes against custom" and the inclusion of rape in the category "crimes against person." A similar proposal circulating among feminist groups suggests the creation of the category of crimes of sexual harassment and family violence and proposes the legalization of abortion.[47] In May 1997, the reformation of the Penal Code was still under discussion. It seems that there is a consensus among the members of the commission in charge of proposing a new code about the need to eliminate the category "crimes against custom." However, the majority of the members of the commission, which has had only one woman, are in favor of considering abortion as a crime.

Another indication of women's fragility in the justice system and of the fact that their bodies are not legally bounded is that until very recently Brazilian trials allowed the "legitimate defense of honor," a legal argument used to acquit men who kill their wives. In such cases, the character of the victim is under trial, as the persecution tries to prove that her "disloyal," "dishonest," or "deviant" behavior justified the killing. After much pressure by women's groups, the Brazilian Supreme Court outlawed this argument in 1991, declaring that "homicide cannot be seen as a normal and legitimate way of reacting to adultery" and that "what is defended is not honor, but self-esteem, vanity, and pride of a master who considers his wife as property." Despite this historic ruling, however, the man whose acquittal had been appealed to the Supreme Court and whose case generated this ruling—a man who stabbed to death his former wife and her new husband—was again acquitted of the double homicide on a retrial in the original state court and with the use of the same argument of "defense of honor." This is a clear indication that the question is not only to change the legislation but to transform the practice of justice and the cultural context in which it finds legitimation.[48]

To bind or secure women's bodies (or those of people in general) with rights is a huge task. In Brazil, the difficulties faced by both feminists and defenders of human rights in their efforts to protect people's bodies and lives are a clear indication of the dimension of this task and of the precarious conditions of civil citizenship. They are therefore an indication of the disjunction of the democratization process. In Brazil, democracy is basically nonexistent in relation to the protection of bodies, privacy, and individual rights. Women and especially feminists have been among the main agents addressing such issues and, by raising issues few other movements have addressed, they have been contributing to a movement to expand civil citizenship. Women's movements have been innovative and have helped to give more meaning to Brazilian democracy. Nevertheless, the previous discussion also indicates that the enforcement of these rights and the acceptance of new understandings of the body and the law have a long way to go.

PUSHING LIMITS AND TESTING BOUNDARIES

To say that feminist practices (including feminist theory) are shaped by the different contexts in which they develop in spite of the existence of what one might call a common feminist agenda is probably an obvious statement. However, it is interesting to reflect on some of the specificities of Brazilian women's movements and their implication for both democratic and feminist theory. I have argued that women's movements in Brazil play a crucial role in democratic consolidation as they both reveal and challenge some of the limits of this process. I have also argued that the main challenge for both women's movements and the democratic consolidation is to change the civil sphere of citizenship, that is, the sphere of justice, law, and individual rights in which violence and abuses of various sorts constantly threaten citizens, their lives, and their bodies. Finally, I have also suggested that the focus on civil citizenship allows for reconsiderations in the way in which we theorize about democratic consolidation, forcing us to look beyond the political system and into broad cultural patterns. I want now to focus on some themes that present the opportunity for discussion within feminist theory.

An important theme in contemporary American feminist theory is the definition of rights in the context of struggles for equality. The development of theoretical arguments shifting the discussion of rights and equality to the question of difference exemplifies feminists' intervention both in theoretical debates and in the political struggles for equality. Although Brazilian women's movements have been struggling for many rights that are difference-specific, this theoretical debate has been almost nonexistent in Brazil. It is worth exploring this difference. A possible explanation for the absence of this debate is the relative unimportance of notions of individualism, individual rights, and equality when compared with the notion of social rights. I have argued that many gender-specific demands of women's movements have been framed in terms of collective rights and have been legitimated in these terms. One may argue, however, that this legitimacy has a suspicious history. I mentioned that since the populist dictatorship of Getulio Vargas in the 1940s, there have been various laws guaranteeing specific rights to women. They were mainly labor laws and included not only rights of paid pregnancy leave and of breast-feeding during the working hours but also the right for women to retire earlier than men in any type of job and provisions that keep women out of night shifts and out of some occupations. It is not difficult to detect the intentions of these gender-specific laws: women have been protected by a patriarchal state and society because they have been considered weaker and less capable for certain occupations and because their roles as mothers have always been considered crucial for society and therefore in need of special protection.

Women have used this type of imagery for their own ends in the social movements: they have legitimated both their going out of the home to become involved in politics and their demands for services and rights in terms of their role as mothers. The arguments they often use can be summarized in these terms: it is because they are responsible mothers that they organize social movements to demand what is needed to improve the lives in their neighborhoods for their families.[49] This process of participation, however, changes their lives and their perceptions of their traditional roles; women in working-class neighborhoods themselves describe this process as learning and growing and becoming liberated.[50] Nevertheless, this has not led them necessarily to talk in terms of equality. If we observe how women shaped their struggles, it is clear that, especially in the case of the social movements, women have demanded what they saw themselves as being entitled to (as mothers, first of all; or as poor mothers) but did not frame their demands in terms of equality. Women workers ask for equal pay for equal work but have not questioned their different rules of retirement or night shifts, for example. In fact, I think it is possible to argue that the question of equality has never been as central as the question of entitlement in Brazilian women's struggles. As a consequence, the notion of gender-specific rights as rights to difference becomes legitimated but not as a critique of liberal notions of equality as sameness.[51] Rather, they are uncriticized developments of a patriarchal-paternalistic tradition.

If this tradition has not yet been directly confronted by middle-class feminists, one can hope that it will be addressed by the emergent African Brazilian women's groups. For these groups, racism brings the issue of difference and inequality to the forefront. Moreover, as they set out to deconstruct traditional paternalistic notions of racial democracy, chances are that they will unravel other paternalisms as well and deal more directly with the question of inequality. One result may be that African Brazilian women will have the power to bring forward one of the most troublesome "absences" of Brazilian feminism: a discussion of the widespread reliance on the work of maids, who are disproportionately African Brazilian women.

Although most women who work outside the home (including feminists) continue to rely on the work of a housekeeper, there is very little investigated or written about how class and race inequalities are reproduced among women. There is also very little discussion about changing men's roles in domestic life, precisely because the domestic work is done by a housekeeper. In all these dimensions, the issue of equality (or of inequality) is hidden by the presence of some patriarchal or class privilege. In sum, what I am arguing is that in a society such as Brazil's, in which the equality of individuals is not the most central progressive theme and in which inequalities and privileges are reproduced even when it may appear that they are being contested, bringing the issue of equality (and of individual rights) to the forefront of feminist debates could have far-reaching effects.

Let us now turn again to the question of individual rights and the unbounded body. My argument about the unbounded body and its association with violence and the delegitimation of individual rights in Brazil carries a negative evaluation of the unbounded notion of the body and favors boundedness as a guarantee for the protection of persons and bodies. However, as I deal with these issues for the Brazilian case, I am also reminded of some critiques of the model of the bounded body and of the bounded self which underlie the notions of individual rights in American society. For example, feminist theorist Jennifer Nedelski argues that the prevalent notion of rights in American constitutional tradition is that of rights as boundaries and derives from the property model.[52] In this tradition, individual rights are conceived as property rights in one's body, and the protection of individuals and their autonomy as the erection of walls. In her critique of boundary images as the model for conceptions of rights, self, and autonomy, Nedelski argues that they cannot be very useful, especially for women and their bodies, given elementary facts such as pregnancy and intercourse. She argues instead for a more flexible model for the body and for the self, a model focused on connection, contact, relationship, and permeable boundaries. I cannot avoid being skeptical of Nedelski's alternative for the Brazilian case, especially because I have come to believe that its more flexible and unbounded model not only is the counterpart of much violence in various areas of social life but also is inherently violent, especially against women and children. Moreover, as flexibility comes with great inequality in social relations, the permeability works only in one direction, that is, from dominant to dominated, without any institutional restraint (boundary, wall) to the former's power to abuse. Thus, I tend to advocate more rather than less boundedness for the body, especially when it involves relationships between unequals.

As I continue to investigate these questions and let the American and the Brazilian cases talk to each other, I cannot avoid thinking that to advocate more flexible models for the body means completely different things in a context in which civil rights and justice are legitimated and in a context in which they are delegitimated. In fact, my argument is that the dominant experience of these rights is inseparable from certain conceptions of the body. The culture that produces unbounded bodies is unlikely to have strong civil rights and vice versa. If this is true, and if the link between flexible boundaries and violence exists, which I think it does, how can we think of a model of citizenship and individual rights which is at the same time more protective and less discriminatory for women? Can a model both provide boundaries for women's bodies to protect them from sexual harassment and not penalize them when they get pregnant (by forcing them to see their more flexible bodies in terms of disability)? How can we think of rights and autonomy without reinforcing class and gender barriers in very real contexts of social inequality and gender oppression? Can we think of a model that can at the same time leave space for the proximity of bodies and sensuality and yet enforce the respect for privacy, individuality, and human rights? Does the control of violence and abuse require rigid, clearly defined boundaries? Can we develop a model of citizenship and individual rights which is flexible and at the same time efficient for the control of violence? These are some of the questions the struggles of women in the process of democratization of Brazilian society could pose both to theories of democratization and to feminist theory.

NOTES

1. I thank Jane Jaquette for her careful reading of this chapter, her comments, and her editorial suggestions. I thank James Holston for many illuminating discussions about citizenship and rights. This chapter was originally written in 1992 for the conference "Women and Political Transitions in South America and Eastern and Central Europe: The Prospects for Democracy," which generated this volume. It was substantially revised in 1997 to be brought up to date for publication. The results bear the marks of its double incarnation.

2. This notion is developed in James Holston and Teresa P. R. Caldeira, "Democracy, Law, and Justice: Disjunctions of Brazilian Democracy," in *Fault Lines of Democratic Governance in the Americas,* ed. Felipe Agüero and Jeffrey Stark (Miami: North-South Center and Lynne Rienner Publishers, 1997).

3. The most complete analysis of Brazilian women's movements in the democratizing process is Sonia Alvarez, *Engendering Democracy in Brazil: Women's Movements in Transition Politics* (Princeton: Princeton University Press, 1990). For some internal views, see Vera Soares, Ana Alice Alcantara Costa, Cristina Maria Buarque, Denise Dourado Dora, and Wania Sant'Anna, "Brazilian Feminism and Women's Movements: A Two-Way Street," in *The Challenge of Local Feminisms: Women's Movements in Global Perspective,* ed. Amrita Basu (Boulder, Colo.: Westview Press, 1995), 302–23, and Maria Aparecida Schumaher and Elizabeth Vargas, "A Place in Government: Alibi or Conquest?" *Estudos*

Feministas 1, no. 2 (1993): 449–60. See also Annette Goldberg, "Feminismo no Brasil contemporâneo: O percurso intelectual de um ideário político," *BIB* 28 (1989).

4. The military rule in Brazil lasted from 1964 to 1985. The long period of transition to democratic rule is called *abertura* (literally, opening) and started in the mid-1970s.

5. For a detailed history of the Councils on the Feminine Condition, see Sonia Alvarez, "Contradictions of a 'Women's Space' in a Male-Dominant State: The Political Role of the Commissions on the Status of Women in Postauthoritarian Brazil," in *Women, International Development, and Politics: The Bureaucratic Mire*, ed. Kathleen Staudt (Philadelphia: Temple University Press, 1990, and Danielle Ardaillon, "Estado e mulher: Conselhos dos Direitos da Mulher e Delegacias de Defesa da Mulher," research report, Fundação Carlos Chagas, São Paulo, 1989.

6. On the importance of the issue of autonomy, see Alvarez, *Engendering Democracy*; Soares et al., "Brazilian Feminism"; and Schumaher and Vargas, "Place in Government."

7. For a summary of the provisions in the 1988 constitution guaranteeing women's rights, and for a discussion of current needs of change in the ordinary legislation to make it coherent with the constitutional principles, see Florisa Verucci, "Women and the New Brazilian Constitution," *Feminist Studies* 17, no. 3 (1991): 551–68.

8. On the history of the struggle for legal abortion in Brazil, see Leila de Andrade Linhares Barsted, "Legalization and Decriminalization of Abortion in Brazil: Ten Years of Feminist Struggle," *Estudos Feministas* 0, no. 0 (1992): 169–86.

9. Sonia Alvarez has a very insightful interpretation of the recent transformations in her analysis of Latin American feminists' participation in the Beijing conference. See "Latin American Feminisms 'Go Global': Trends of the 1990s and Challenges for the New Millennium," in *Cultures of Politics/Politics of Cultures: Revisioning Latin American Social Movements*, ed. Sonia E. Alvarez, Evelina Dagnino, and Arturo Escobar (Boulder, Colo.: Westview Press, 1997).

10. Cf. Schumaher and Vargas, "Place in Government," 362–64. For an analysis of health NGOs, see Nathalie Lebon, "Professionalization of Women's Health Groups in São Paulo: The Troublesome Road towards Organizational Diversity," *Organization: Rewriting Globalization* 3, no. 4 (1996): 588–609.

11. See Alvarez, "Latin American Feminisms," for an analysis of this global activity.

12. The UN conferences (and related programming activities) in which Brazilian feminist organizations had important participation and were able to influence both the official documents and the parallel NGO forums are the 1992 World Conference on Environment and Development in Rio de Janeiro; the 1993 World Conference on Human Rights in Vienna; the 1994 International Conference on Population and Development in Cairo; the 1995 World Summit for Social Development in Copenhagen; and the 1995 Fourth World Conference on Women in Beijing.

13. The Beijing conference was preceded by various meetings both in Brazil and in Latin America. In Brazil, the preparation was coordinated by the Articulação de Mulheres Brasileiras (Articulation of Brazilian Women), which organized meetings in 25 Brazilian states involving the participation of more than 800 organizations and which received 22 documents diagnosing the situation of women in Brazil (Maria Aparecida Schumaher, "América Latina mais Intograda," *Estudos Feministas* 3, no. 2 [1995]: 427–32). See ibid. and Vera Soares, "O contraditório e ambíguo caminho para Beijing," *Estudos Feministas* 3, no. 1 (1995): 172–79, for accounts of the preparation and of the Brazilian participation.

See Alvarez, "Latin American Feminisms," for an analysis of this participation from a Latin American perspective.

14. The transformation of social movements into NGOs is not a dominant trend of the women's movements alone but is a characteristic of the spectrum of social movements. On this aspect, see Leilah Landim, "A invenção das ONGs: Do serviço invisível à profissão sem nome" (Ph.D. diss., Universidade Federal do Rio de Janeiro, Museu Nacional, 1993), and Rubem César Fernandes, *Privado, porém público: O terceiro setor na América Latina* (Rio de Janeiro: Relume-Dumará, 1994).

15. See Alvarez, "Latin American Feminisms," and, for the case of Chile, Veronica Schild, "New Subjects of Rights? Women's Movements and the Construction of Citizenship in the 'New Democracies,'" in Alvarez, Dagnino, and Escobar, *Cultures of Politics*, and Veronica Schild, "NGOs, Feminist Politics, and Neo-liberal Latin American State Formations: Some Lessons from Chile," *Canadian Journal of Development Studies*, special issue (1995): 123–47.

16. For an analysis of women's participation in social movements in São Paulo, see Teresa Pires do Rio Caldeira, "Women, Daily Life, and Politics," in *Women and Social Change in Latin America*, ed. Elizabeth Jelin (London: Zed Books, 1990).

17. The Gini coefficient varies from 0 to 1. It would be 0 if all people had the same income and 1 if one person concentrated the whole national income. For Brazil, the Gini coefficient was 0.580 in 1985 and 0.636 in 1991. Sonia Rocha, "Pobreza metropolitana e os ciclos de curto prazo: Balanço dos anos 80," *IPEA: Boletim de Conjuntura* 12 (1991): 38.

18. Juarez Rubens Brandão Lopes, "Brasil 1989: Um estudo sócioeconômico da indigência e da probreza urbanas," *NEEP: Cadernos de Pesquisa* 25 (1993).

19. Ana Maria Goldani, "Retratos de família em tempos de crise," *Estudos Feministas*, special issue (1994): 303–35; citation at 309–10.

20. Ibid., 320.

21. Ibid., 309, 320.

22. Alvarez, "Latin American Feminisms," indicates that the power imbalance is one of the main problems of the women's movement today. For internal views of the black women's movements, see Matilde Ribeiro, "Mulheres negras brasileiras: De Bertioga a Beijing," *Estudos Feministas* 3, no. 2 (1995): 446–57, and Luiza Barros, "Nossos feminismos revisitados," *Estudos Feministas* 3, no. 2 (1995): 458–63.

23. Programa das Nações Unídas para o Desenvolvimento (PNUD) and Instituto de Pesquisa Econômica Aplicada (IPEA), *Relatório sobre o desenvolvimento humano no Brasil, 1996* (Brasília: PNUD/IPEA, 1996), 132.

24. Célia Regina Jardim Pinto, "Mulher e política no Brasil: Os impasses do feminismo, enquanto movimento social, face às regras do jogo da democracia representativa," *Estudos Feministas*, special issue (1994): 256–70; citation at 268; my translation.

25. In 1950, the proportion of women in the economic active population was 14.75 percent. This proportion reached 27.4 percent in 1980 and 35 percent in 1990. Between 1980 and 1990, the activity rate (the relation between the number of economically active women and the total of women aged 15 to 65) of married women almost doubled, rising to 38 percent from 20 percent. PNUD-IPEA, *Relatório*, 33. However, the discrimination of women in the labor market continues to be very high. In 1990, the average salary of men in urban Brazil was 6.1 minimum salaries, while women's was 3.4 minimum salaries. White women's average salary was double (4.2 minimum salaries) those of black

women (2.1 minimum salary). Cristina Bruschini, "O trabalho da mulher brasileira nas décadas recentes," *Estudos Feministas*, special issue (1995): 179–99, table 18 of addendum.

26. For the case of Brazil, see Caldeira, "Women, Daily Life, and Politics," and Alvarez, *Engendering Democracy.*

27. Others are human rights organizations and legal reform advocates.

28. Holston and Caldeira, "Democracy, Law, and Justice." The ideas presented in this section rely on the arguments developed in this article as well as on my forthcoming book *City of Walls: Crime, Segregation, and Citizenship in São Paulo* (Berkeley: University of California Press).

29. The civil dimension refers to the rights necessary to individual liberty, to the assertion of equality before the law, and to civil rights in general; the political refers to the right to participate in political organizations, to vote, and to be voted for; the social dimension refers to the rights associated with the welfare state. Marshall makes clear that the process of legitimating those rights is one of intense struggles. T. H. Marshall, "Citizenship and Social Class," in *Class, Citizenship, and Social Development* (1949; New York: Doubleday, 1965).

30. Holston and Caldeira, "Democracy, Law, and Justice," 21.

31. Recent criticisms of Marshall's scheme have cast serious doubts both on his optimistic view of the development of rights that give an impression that citizenship is always expanding and on the universality of the model, even within the restricted universe of Western nations. See, for example, Albert Hirschman, *The Rhetoric of Reaction: Perversity, Futility, Jeopardy* (Cambridge: Harvard University Press, Belknap Press, 1992), and Bryan Turner, "Outline of a Theory of Citizenship," in *Dimensions of Radical Democracy: Pluralism, Citizenship, Community*, ed. Chantal Mouffe (London: Verso, 1992), 33–62.

32. Nonpublished data made available by the Commission of Justice and Peace of the Archdiocese of São Paulo.

33. The April 1997 episode made the Congress pass a law transferring to civil courts the trials of homicides and torture committed by policemen. Although the proposal for this law had been presented to the Congress a long time ago, it had never had the necessary support for approval.

34. A telephone survey conducted by the newspaper *Folha de S. Paulo* after the massacre at the Casa de Detenção found that one-third of the population of São Paulo favored the police action, and a poll by *O Estado de S. Paulo* found that 44 percent of the population supported it. Many people went to the streets to demonstrate in favor of the police and against the defenders of human rights.

35. The analysis that follows is based on Caldeira, *City of Walls.*

36. It should be noted that the people defending human rights were denouncing not only the deplorable conditions of the prisons but a series of abuses committed by the institutions of order, such as arrest without a mandate, torture of suspects—not necessarily criminals—and summary executions. Most of those abuses are committed against people who have not formally been found guilty. All those aspects that only enforce the view of the distortions of the justice system were totally obscured by the emphasis on the "defense of criminals." See also Teresa P. R. Caldeira, "Crime and Individual Rights: Reframing the Question of Violence in Latin America," in *Constructing Democracy: Human Rights, Citizenship, and Society in Latin America*, ed. Elizabeth Jelin and Eric Hershberg (Boulder, Colo.: Westview Press, 1996), 197–211, and *City of Walls.*

37. See Teresa P. R. Caldeira, "Fortified Enclaves: The New Urban Segregation," In *Cities and Citizenship*, ed. James Holson, 303–28, special issue of *Public Culture* 8, no. 2 (1996), for a discussion of how the proliferation of fortified enclaves transforms the character of public life in cities such as São Paulo and Los Angeles.

38. Labor legislation constituted one of the central elements of the Brazilian populist-corporatist state headed by Getúlio Vargas (1930–45 and 1950–54). The rights it established were offered to the workers as "donations" of the dictator. Although formulated in the midst of an authoritarian and corporatist project and although frequently not fully enforced, this legislation had some provisions that might be considered progressive. Since the 1930s it extended women's rights such as paid maternity leave with job security and time off to breast-feed during the working hours. Also during Vargas's rule, women's suffrage was approved in 1932.

39. Cf. Caldeira, "Women, Daily Life, and Politics."

40. See Alvarez, *Engendering Democracy*, esp. chap. 8, for a summary of the relationship of feminist agenda and state policies of family planning and population control.

41. PNUD-IPEA, *Relatório*, 65–67, for the demographic data. For an explanation of the fall in fertility rates, see Vilmar Faria, "Políticas de governo e regulação da fecundidade: Consequências não antecipadas e efeitos perversos," *Ciências Sociais Hoje* (1988): 62–103.

42. Elza Berquó, "Contraception and Caesareans in Brazil: An Example of Bad Reproductive Health Practice in Need of Exemplary Action," *Estudos Feministas* 1, no. 2 (1993): 461–72; citation at 463.

43. Ibid., 464–65. The information on the percentage of young women sterilized is in PNUD-IPEA, *Relatório*, 67.

44. Berquó, "Contraception and Caesareans," 468.

45. The following argument about the unbounded body and the inseparability of notions of individual rights from conceptions of the body is fully developed in Caldeira, *City of Walls*, esp. chap. 8.

46. PNAD is the National Research by Domicile Sample.

47. A version of this proposal appears as "Women's Manifesto against Violence: Proposal for Changes in the Brazilian Penal Code," *Estudos Feministas* 1, no. 1 (1993): 190–91. For a feminist proposal for transformations of the legislation concerning violence within the family, see Silvia Pimentel and Maria Inês Valente Pierro, "Proposta de lei contra a violência familiar," *Estudos Feministas* 1, no. 1 (1993): 169–75.

48. For an account of the practice of violence against women and of the biased trials of violent crime in which the victim is a woman, see Danielle Ardaillon and Guita Debert, *Quando a vítima é mulher: Análise de julgamentos de crimes de estupro, espancamento e homicídio* (Brasília: Conselho Nacional dos Direitos da Mulher, 1988), and Americas Watch Committee, *Criminal Injustice: Violence against Women in Brazil* (New York: Americas Watch Committee, 1991). It is necessary to emphasize that most cases of rape and physical assault of women do not end up either in the official records of the police or in the justice system.

49. It is interesting to note that the editorial of the first issue of *Nós Mulheres*, the first Brazilian newspaper to call itself feminist, found justification for their struggle for equality in the social function of motherhood. This editorial is reproduced in Alvarez, *Engendering Democracy*, 95. The most famous example of women using traditional roles to

legitimate subversive political intervention in Latin America is obviously that of the mothers of the disappeared in Argentina.

50. Cf. Caldeira, "Women, Daily Life, and Politics."

51. For a critique of liberal individualism and a feminist discussion of the question of difference and women's rights, see Zillah R. Eisenstein, *The Female Body and the Law* (Berkeley: University of California Press, 1988).

52. Jennifer Nedelski, "Law, Boundaries, and the Bounded Self," *Representations* 30 (1990): 162–89.

Chapter 5

Female Leadership, Violence, and Citizenship in Peru

MARUJA BARRIG

*P*eru is a unique case in Latin America today. Not only was its military dictatorship of the 1970s (1968–80) free from the regressive and repressive practices of other military governments, to the extent that it made efforts to modernize the country and expand its social democracy, but its current government is also atypical. Two years after his election in April 1992, constitutional president Alberto Fujimori dissolved the Congress and reorganized the judiciary with the support of the armed forces. This move, widely interpreted as a return to authoritarianism, had the sympathy of important sectors of public opinion, who were angry at the politicians and judges for being unrepresentative and corrupt. Pressures from outside Peru influenced the government's decision to call for elections for a constituent assembly. Peru's main political parties did not participate in the elections but at the same time proved to be incapable of organizing a cohesive or significant opposition. As a result, majority control of the assembly belongs to allies of President Fujimori. Under the circumstances, and in contrast to the other countries in this study, Peru can be described as quasi-democratic at best.

A second contrast is provided by Peru's response to structural adjustment policies. In August 1990 the government started a structural adjustment program that, contrary to what had happened in other Latin American countries, was not met with angry, violent, or spontaneous reactions of the population, despite the fact that the Peruvian government did not produce a consistent social program to offset the policy's effects. As a result, almost 7 out of every 10 Peruvians have incomes that fall below the poverty line. Poverty-related diseases increased, among them the cholera epidemic that killed thousands of people in 1991. A third distinguishing characteristic, until 1993, was the strength of a Maoist guerrilla movement, Sendero Luminoso, or Shining Path. Apart from spiraling poverty and cholera, the early 1990s brought Shining Path even closer to the center stage in Peruvian politics.[1] While guerrilla groups from countries in Central America initiated pacification processes to bring armed opposition movements into negotiations for peaceful incorporation,[2] the cadres of Shining Path multiplied and expanded from the southern Andean provinces, the country's poorest. They preached a Marxist fundamentalism and practiced terrorism in most of Peru, including Lima, the capital city. Bridges and electricity pylons were blown up, and social and political leaders were murdered in selective criminal attacks. The government's response was more violence and a counterterrorist policy that amounted to systemic violation of human rights.

The rise of Shining Path had to do with Peru's profound social, economic, and racial fractures. It is not our purpose here to interpret Shining Path in detail. But its development is an important factor in interpreting women's political mobilization over the past decade, which has occurred around two radically different proposals: the collective survival movements of urban poor women on the one hand, and militancy around a leader, Abimael Guzmán, Shining Path's number one, on the other, who demanded that his followers destroy the state to build a new society. In several ways and with different results, both groups of women crossed the threshold into the sphere of vital political decisions, and both have played key roles.

Using women's roles in the democratization process as a frame of reference, I propose a specific reading of the conflicts between personal aspirations and collective projects, between desire and frustration. The first part of this chapter examines how women's popular organizations developed and the tensions that surfaced when each group succeeded, a process that projected individual leaders onto a public stage. The second part reviews the aspirations and frustrations of the group of women who have chosen violence and, in that context, murdered popular leaders. Many Shining Path women militants had sought personal advancement through a college education. But success was denied them by leaders like María Elena Moyano, who was killed by Shining Path in February 1992. Her death was a product of resentment and intolerance; these in turn are important but unexamined features of the politics of depressed and strongly hierarchical societies.

Two analytical approaches I have found helpful are an examination of the way in which female leaders of both groups reconstructed their gender identities and a careful consideration of the process by which citizenship is defined in Peru, where individual and political rights are weak and ill defined compared with the collective social construction of citizens' rights and claims.[3]

FEARING CHANGE

One trait that is specific to Peru in the Latin American context is the massiveness and heterogeneity of its women's movement. Over the past decade, the Peruvian women's movement showed a multiplication of feminist ideas, with high visibility of women's issues in magazines and academic research. Hundreds of specialized nongovernmental organizations (NGOs) were organized, and popular organizations vigorously expanded on the urban fringes. The very size of the women's movement makes it difficult to grasp it fully. Although this analysis looks primarily at the leaders of the female urban popular groups, it should be noted that their roles have been influenced by feminist ideas and by the support and commitment of professionals from NGOs who have specialized in building women's leadership.

The styles and approaches of these female leaders, which appeared by the dozens in the slums and shantytowns of Lima during the past decade, illustrate how popular subjects are constructed in Peru. They show the peculiar combination of practices, symbols, and values of gender construction within the complex process of Peruvian democratization.

Lima's community kitchens appeared in the midst of the economic crisis of the 1980s. Following a long-standing pattern of organization in the shantytowns, these groups administered food donations from the state or from international development agencies. The communal kitchens are an efficient food preparation and distribution system, built by women of the popular sector. They are based on collective buying and have had the backing of parishes and NGOs.

All these groups operate in a similar way: the women work for free, elect a board of directors, organize to take turns at different tasks, make up a weekly menu, shop for food (donations cover only part of the cost), prepare the meals, and sell them to the "members" and their families. In 1991, Lima, a city with a population of seven million, had some seventy-two hundred community kitchens, which prepared close to a million and a half meals a day. According to official calculations, one year later the number of community kitchens had been halved, although the kitchens still serviced 9 percent of the city's inhabitants. This decrease can be attributed both to the exhaustion of that organizational formula and to the violence and intimidation unleashed by Shining Path against the community kitchen leaders. The women leaders of the community kitchens movement, along with the women who headed the Municipal Glass of Milk Program (which was created by the municipal government of Lima in 1984 to distribute a glass of milk a day among children and pregnant and breast-feeding mothers and which has extended to Peru's main cities), became the targets of a terror campaign that succeeded in part because the close ties that once existed between the leaders and their communities had broken down.

In 1986 the leaders of these livelihood organizations began to extend their groups, becoming federated first in neighborhoods, then in districts, and finally at the metropolitan and national levels. By 1989 there were 62 federations of community kitchens in Lima, which grouped hundreds of smaller organizations working in 17 of Lima's 43 districts. The federations were organized in a pyramidal structure and used an assembly-oriented pattern to elect their representatives to the various levels of the federation. The elected representatives became known to others and thus could be elected by virtue of a varied list of attributes: either they had played an outstanding role in the consolidation of the neighborhood by holding posts in the local board, or they had shown a better educational level and a family and economic situation more stable than those of the other neighbors, giving them more free time. The perception that they were different was shared by the leaders themselves, who tended to describe their motivations and actions as a way of "helping the neighborhoods' most needy families."

Although distinguishable from the other women in their communities, these women leaders achieved legitimacy in part by their constant effort to differentiate themselves from the hierarchical style of the male community leaders. These women were "democratic" and not manipulative, they were neutral in disputes among the political parties, and, above all, they had proved that they could "deliver the goods" and meet their constituency's needs. Centralization had made it possible for them to negotiate more successfully for food supplies, for equipment and space for the community kitchens, for health campaigns for the children, and finally for courses, lectures, and educational workshops available in a myriad of subjects at the NGOs, through the central and local government, and in Catholic and other churches. In spite of the fragility and the tensions caused by the novelty of the organizational formula (both for the protagonists of this movement and for its analysts), these women's organizations became a space for women of the shantytowns to bring their interests together in a new and effective way.

As many have noted, the practice of leadership was at the same time a process of self-education. Members and leaders overcame the resistance of their spouses to their participation in extradomestic groups, they learned to work with NGOs, governments, religious organizations, wholesalers, and other "external agents," and they came to express their ideas in groups outside the family circle. "Knowing how to talk" is a symbolic resource as important as education. Women's silence had been rooted in ancient patterns of gender and cultural domination. Garcilaso de la Vega, the author of Peru's most celebrated colonial chronicle, tells the story of his mother, the Inca princess Chhimpu Ocllo, who was handed over as a concubine to a Spanish conquistador in the sixteenth century; she spoke no Spanish, and he spoke no Quechua. After 30 years of "living together," she had to use an interpreter to dictate her last will. It is not hard to imagine the violence of this and other unions; lack of Spanish seems to have put women at a severe disadvantage.[4] Today, researchers Stahr and Vega find that poor women who migrate to the cities come to understand their arrival to modern life through words.[5] They see the capacity to express themselves as a form of power which brings a feeling of personal confidence.

Initial studies of the communal kitchens stressed the parallels between women's work in the kitchens and their customary domestic activities and failed to perceive the dynamic of the process in which these leaders were immersed.[6] Dozens of leaders of these organizations, still sticking to the seemingly narrow agenda of feeding people and meeting their immediate needs, were able to navigate the muddy waters of political clientelism, negotiating on the fringes of pressure and seduction until they became a layer of intermediate leaders, the "horizontal mediators" between the political elite and the social base.[7]

The success of the popular women's organizations can best be illustrated by showing how they attained institutional recognition. After a long period of negotiations with representatives from all the political parties, in 1991 the women leaders managed to push through parliament a bill that granted legal status to the livelihood organizations, entitling them to a 65 percent subsidy for the food rations they distributed. The law could not be implemented because state spending had been cut by the 1990 structural adjustment measures, but it was celebrated as an important political victory and a sign that these shantytown leaders could make their way in the traditionally male and elitist political system.

Paradoxically, the institutionalization of the communal kitchens movement and its success in establishing itself as one of the state's interlocutors revealed a fatal weakness. As the centralization process progressed and the leaders within it defined their roles, a gap emerged between the leaders, who were increasingly dedicated to institutional red tape, and the community women, who were mostly dedicated to the distribution and preparation of food. The anonymity of the tens of thousands of women who made up the social base of the movement contrasted with the growing public visibility of the leaders, who had embarked on a "personal affirmation" process in sharp contrast to the homogenous prostration of the rest.

Stahr and Vega suggest that the tension between modernity and tradition appears among the women of the urban popular sector. This takes the form of resistance to behavior that can be considered a quest for personal change and progress, which they identify as selfishness and individualism and which they see as reproducing a pattern of domination: individual benefits cannot be spread to all of the community and simply privilege the few at the expense of the many. In therapeutic work with poor women, these researchers found that some of the conflicts between leaders and their constituencies stemmed from the latter's fear of change. Change would have meant a break with family and provincial origins and community bases; fear of change was fear of a new world—the urban modern one—into which they had not integrated. These women envied those who had risen above the crowd, demonstrated leadership, experimented with new ways of living and relating to others, and dared to try new types of interpersonal relationships. The evidence is that urban poor women had little tolerance for diversity and individuation, which is not surprising when their survival depended on the affective and instrumental bonds that link members of a family to one another and ensure that neighbors will help one another.[8]

Despite these obstacles, the women leaders we studied did go through a personal affirmation process. On the way they met with two different kinds of tensions: one born out of their condition as shantytown dwellers, and one intimately related to their gender. Leaders frequently feel that to appear to seek power—even legitimate power—will tarnish their image. This is one reason why they constantly describe their activity as a sacrifice made in the name of community service and the defense of life and why they refer to their social base and their organization as their "children" or to their neighborhood or its needs as their "big house."[9] Leaders dealt with their wish for personal change through the image of an amplified motherhood, which they perceived as their only socially legitimate role, yet used this discourse in a public and political way. The more the leaders overcame traditional gender socialization, the more they ran up against the logic of community action. These leaders were and are shantytown dwellers, but their visibility and their public personalities, which produced political results, also produced resentment.

Peruvian researcher Carlos Franco has concluded that the hundreds of thousands of mostly rural Andean migrants, who came to the cities from the 1970s onward, built an alternative, a community of "others" at the fringes of the modernization pattern imposed by the state, a pattern they found inaccessible.[10] The migrants illegally invaded deserted lots to build their shantytowns, and they constructed their houses and basic infrastructure themselves on the basis of community cooperation. In the face of job instability and the rise of the informal sector, they organized as independent workers. Through their cultural, neighborhood, and guild organizations they created participatory formulas different from those proposed by the state.

The state also participated in this process, of course, by tolerating and sometimes even promoting self-help organizations as an efficient way for migrants to provide for themselves the services that the weak public sector could not offer. This reinforced the deep social gaps that, according to Franco, have resulted from the political exclusion of the majority of the Peruvian population and which have generated a particular concept of citizenship. Individual rights tend to be claimed through social organizations: in Peruvian cities the right to property and housing generally arrives through collective and illegal action, such as the massive invasions of vacant state and even private lands. This experience teaches that an individual claim will fare better if promoted through collective action. Franco argues that many civil rights that are conceived of as individual, or "human," rights in Europe or the United States are conceived of and acted on as social claims in Peru. Peruvians experience their individual rights as collective social rights.

The leaders of the livelihood organizations have emerged in this environment. They appear in the shantytowns as a natural presence, as part of the constant renewal of community self-management spaces. Nonetheless, the leaders of these organizations increasingly came to distinguish themselves from those whom they served.

As we will see later on, women continued to nurture one another collectively even when the personal changes brought about by the community kitchen movement clashed with community expectations. In 1992, this distance increased sharply when prominent female leaders entered the public political arena. Until then, the leadership of the women's movement had insisted on publicly rejecting any form of party alliance and had insisted instead on the principle of political autonomy. It could be, as Ruth Cardoso suggests, that this neutrality vis-à-vis party politics was useful in negotiating with public officers as well as in maintaining legitimacy at the grass roots.[11] And it is clear that the tarnished image of the politicians discouraged most forms of association with them. On the other hand, the commitment to autonomy meant that the leaders of the livelihood organizations failed to develop stable relations with "mixed" neighborhood organizations, local city halls and political parties, masculine spaces where women were expected to stay in secondary and instrumental roles.

President Fujimori's April 1992 closing of the Congress in what many have described as an *auto-golpe*, or self-inflicted coup, shattered the political parties' credibility and brought the independent organizations back into the political limelight. Dozens of previously unknown movements and community groups participated in the November 1992 constituent assembly elections and in the January 1993 municipal elections called by the president. Many of these movements invited women leaders of popular organizations to join their lists of candidates, and quite a few accepted. The virtual disappearance of many political cadres from the political scene, the nonparticipation of several important parties in the legislative election, and the social power these female leaders had achieved enhanced their visibility, and they were extensively filmed, photographed, and interviewed by the media. This "promotion" from community leadership to the center of the political arena widened the gap between the women leaders and their social bases.

Shining Path was able to capitalize on the resentments of the women left behind in the neighborhood organizations. Describing the community kitchens' style of self-management as "the worst exploitation," Shining Path labeled the movement's leaders as a "corrupt stratum of leaders" who had to be eliminated. Some women leaders were assassinated, and others were threatened. This produced an abrupt break in the relations between groups and leaders and brought their projects of self-help and civic participation to a virtual halt. Shining Path, which also promised changes and a new society through mass participation, was attacking the popular forms of participation which had arisen from the shantytowns themselves.

SHINING PATH: THE FRUSTRATION OF YOUTH

Shining Path's first revolutionary action—the burning of a ballot box in a small locality in Ayacucho, in the southern Andes, in 1980—was met by indifferent and dismissive responses from the public and from the government authorities. Over the next 13 years, as Shining Path succeeded in posing a serious challenge in both rural and urban areas, it became the subject of scholarly analyses from multiple perspectives. The conflict claimed twenty-five thousand victims and brought Peruvian development to a standstill. Despite calculations that 40 percent of its cadres and half of its Central Committee are women, there are few studies of the role of women in Shining Path. It is women who give the *coup de grâce* to the men who are assassinated, and women leaders are the majority of those murdered in the so-called popular execution.[12]

An analysis of female militancy in Shining Path is an interesting starting point to show the obstacles and limits to the country's democratization process and the contradictory roles women can play within the framework of a fragile democracy. It shows the conflict between two rationales of female public action: that of community leaders, and that of the young *senderistas* who murdered the former in the name of an immutable truth.

Peru's 12 years of military dictatorship (1968–80) did not fit the bureau-

cratic authoritarian mold of disappearances and extrajudicial execution of opponents which characterized the Southern Cone. Some political rights were cur-
tailed and civil rights denied in the name of the military's "Revolution." But it was
a period of economic growth and redistribution and of the expansion of social
citizenship. The military government, which took power in 1968, maintained the
previous government's emphasis on public education, thus reinforcing the "myth
of progress" through education and college attendance which was absorbed by
a growing number of young, low- and middle-class, urban and rural Peruvians.

Several studies show that in the 1960s Peru had one of the largest education
budgets of the countries in the Andean region. This generated high expectations
of personal advancement and upward social mobility. The powerful idea behind
this investment was that professional qualification would wipe out the roots of
discrimination in a society deeply divided along class and racial lines. In the 1970s
the popular imagination turned education into the magic formula that would
open the doors to social respect and to a form of consumerism never seen in the
countryside, to equality in a milieu as restraining and discriminatory as Lima.
Waves of migrants from the Andean regions, looking for better employment and
academic opportunities, caused Lima's population to grow at a disproportionate pace. For some, migration to the capital was the founding gesture of modernity in the country, the quest for a promising future. But it all proved a mirage.[13]

Peru suffers from chronic poverty, acute distributive inequality, and a
deep-seated racism, which operates as a complex mechanism of social control.
In this perspective we can isolate, among many others, two factors that are useful when we consider the striking percentage of women members and leaders in
Shining Path. On the one hand, there is the gap between expectations and reality which has formed a generation of young people searching for social inclusion. On the other hand, the devastating impact of the "dirty war" against
Shining Path and the ensuing violations of human rights in the 1980s touched
women's sensibilities.

As Balbi and Callirgos and Kirk have pointed out, the reopening of the Uni-
versidad San Cristobal de Huamanga in Ayacucho in the late 1950s, and the
prestige it rapidly gained among provincial public universities, became the gate-
way through which the expectations of the young daughters and sons of peasants
and small tradesmen and of their families were filtered. By 1969 one out of three
Huamanga students was a woman. Control of key academic and administrative
jobs at the university allowed Abimael Guzmán and his followers to start developing a discourse specifically aimed at these young female students.[14]

With the simple trade-off of "My sacrifice in exchange for your effort" in
mind,[15] the parents of these and thousands of other lower-class students at Hua-

manga and in various other public universities throughout the country placed their hopes on a college education as the means by which the family could rise. It was a symbolic investment but also an economic one. The mother of a young Ayacucho schoolteacher of peasant origin who was suspected of belonging to Shining Path and assassinated by the police remembers how the family—herself, her husband, and four other children—worked to pay for the dead girl's studies. Her death also ended their dreams: "You will eat well, she used to tell me, I will buy you your dresses. We have invested in her, and now she is dead."[16]

Death, however, was not the only cause of shattered hopes: the long economic crisis of the 1980s increasingly constrained white-collar job opportunities and decreased the number of stable jobs in other fields of activity. By contrast, their subordinated status notwithstanding, more and more women were going into technical and university careers, raising considerably the overall level of qualification of the female workforce. Three out of seven women employed in metropolitan Lima in 1991 had entered or completed a course of higher education, and a similar percentage had completed secondary school. But these improvements had not translated into an increased status in the labor market. According to the Peruvian Ministry of Labor, in that same year in Lima, 35 percent of the women were "independent workers," a grouping that includes the various forms of informal and self-employment. Eleven percent were domestic workers. And if what the market offered in terms of jobs was far below their expectations, corresponding incomes were dramatically worse: 81 percent of women workers in Lima were in fact underemployed and thus insufficiently paid.

A study of persons sentenced in Lima for terrorist crimes in the first six years of the 1980s found that close to 60 percent of the *senderistas* were between 18 and 25 years of age and almost 80 percent were migrants, predominantly from the most impoverished provinces.[17] One out of every four was a college student, and there was a high presence of blue-collar workers and small informal vendors. Of those condemned persons, 86 percent lived with an income below the minimum legal wage. Although their income and their occupation placed them in the popular sector, this contrasted with their high educational level: 36 percent had a college education.

In this group of highly educated convicts, 57 percent of the women had a college education against only 31 percent of the men. And of these women, 10 percent had a professional degree or had completed postgraduate studies, something only 4 percent of the men had done. As the study suggests, by their places of birth, these youth came from a provincial elite, since their families had managed to put them through college, which made them a privileged group in their milieu. Their expectations—defined in terms of a career future—contrasted sharply with their jobs and their meager incomes. This frustration greatly enhanced the appeal of a movement promising structural change through violence.[18]

In their study of women militants, Balbi and Callirgos emphasize the party's message to women as part of a strategy unique to Shining Path: none of the other Peruvian political parties, regardless of their left-right orientation, developed a discourse of gender. Shining Path iconography always shows women close to leader Guzman, even in close-up representations, with a presence greater than that of men. Not only did Shining Path give more visibility and power to women in its ranks than any other political party in Peru, but it also developed specific analyses geared to specific groups of women: housewives, mothers, factory workers, students, and professionals. The message is that women are subordinated in Peruvian society, that capitalism and imperialism are the sources of that oppression; and that "bourgeois" feminism, which "separates the struggle of the feminist movement from that of all the people, . . . stunts the consciousness of women."[19]

The high levels of education found among women *senderistas* correspond to the messages directed to professional women by Shining Path. This message, from *El Diario*, the party's daily newspaper, is typical:

> With every coming year the problem of the formation and performance of professionals in general, and women in particular, becomes worse. This is directly linked to the general crisis of Peruvian society, because an increasingly reactionary State denies them a future. What can women professionals expect from this old system? In a word, nothing. In a regime in which professionals find their hope to improve and serve the people blocked . . . the only way for a professional woman is to play the role which, as an intellectual, history demands from her: participate in the revolution.[20]

In 1992 a home video taken by the police in a raid on a Shining Path safe house showed Abimael Guzmán and members of his Central Committee in one of their political meetings. Men and women stood beside the leader to be filmed. Guzman is surrounded by anxious women, who show disheveled smiles and adolescent excitement at being near him. Kirk and other political analysts could not help comparing the reverent attitude of the video's women with that of the nuns around the pope. As in the case of the nuns, the new faith of the *senderistas* demands their total dedication. Just like the men, in Shining Path women signed the so-called letters of subjection to President Gonzalo. In these letters, militants renounced the past, their families, and their personal ambitions; they put their lives at the service of Guzman and his cause. Kirk interviewed a *senderista* woman in a Lima jail. When asked if she has children, the woman answers, "That is secondary. And where they are is also secondary" (she finally admits she has four children). Question: "What do you feel when you leave your children to join this war?" Answer: "The most important inheritance one can leave for them: a new society. That is what makes us happy."[21]

Women *senderistas* suffered the devaluation common to their gender along with deep racial and social discrimination; they felt that their aspirations to progress were frustrated. One man—Abimael Guzmán, recognized by his followers as the "Guide to Thought" (Pensamiento Guía)—defined these women, valued them, offered them a future of equality and happiness.[22] But Shining Path's appeal went beyond the psychological. "President Gonzalo" gave women in the organization a power that made them the equals of men, one that projected them as weapons of the movement against the external world. If in the past women did not inspire respect, now they caused fear. The cost, however, was very high and contradicted Shining Path's alleged feminism. Shining Path saw the domination of "the family, the clan and religion" as the source of female oppression, but it proposed another submission, to an almighty and infallible man, Guzmán. American sociologist Carol Andreas's sympathetic interview with a woman militant makes the point well. "She insisted that having overall leadership that was dependable, not vacillating, was an inspiration. . . . The vertical leadership of 'El Guía' appears as a welcome relief."[23]

As a *senderista* confessed to researcher Carmen Rosa Balbi, "the Party channeled her hatred." And it may be true, as Hannah Arendt observes, that anger only surfaces when there is a suspicion that conditions may change but they remain the same.[24] This could be a clue to why Shining Path enrolls young people with expectations but without hopes. Sociologist Sinesio Lopez has shown that there is a closer relation between political violence and economic inequality in countries with a middle level of modernization.[25] This process, which breaks up traditional structures and prompts a geographical mobilization of the population, creates expectations it cannot satisfy. Democratization enhances the population's consciousness about rights and increases its desire for participation. But at the same time most people are excluded from an adequate distribution of income in the region. A government survey of the standard of living in Lima revealed that, in 1990, the poorest 10 percent of the population had access to only 1.8 percent of total household consumption, while the richest 10 percent consumed 40 percent. The ruling elites and the government resisted the demands of the excluded. Lopez suggests that this is an explosive combination, and in the case of Peru the hypothesis seems reasonable.

However, another explosive combination exists: the violation of human rights of peasants and the urban poor, committed by the state in the name of a countersubversive war. The appearance of Shining Path was originally down-played and then treated by the government as a criminal problem, not a politi-cal challenge. Two years later, given the frequency and the publicity of Shining Path's actions in the southern Andes—including the murder of government au-thorities—the military responded. Military repression was yet another mistake in the handling of a political phenomenon that was rooted in centuries of social and economic postponement of the legitimate demands of important sectors of the population. Moreover, the way military officers treated suspects of terrorism and the peasants as a whole revealed the deep contempt in which the white (and even the not so white) middle classes hold the Indian and the poor.

It was then, when vast areas were declared under a "state of emergency" (which puts the armed forces in command of a geographical area and suspends basic civil rights), that the extrajudiciary executions began. Common graves, each with the remains of dozens of peasants, were discovered, and there were tortures and forced disappearances. All of this went largely unpunished. A conservative calculation by the Coordinadora Nacional de Derechos Humanos (National Council for Human Rights) put the number of disappeared at 2,785 since 1982. In 1991, and for the fourth year in a row, the United Work Group on Forced Dis-appearances described Peru as the country with the most disappeared in the world.[26] Amnesty International estimated that 85 percent of the abuses against human rights occurred in the emergency zones and were carried out by the armed forces.[27]

Although there is no systematic information on the matter, initial analyses suggest that Shining Path gained new militants in reaction to the human rights abuses committed against brothers, parents, spouses, or, in the case of women, against themselves. A recent report from Americas Watch reveals that, according to Amnesty International and the U.S. State Department, rape of women "can be considered a common practice tolerated—or at least ignored—by officers," and it is "a widespread and routine feature of military incursions into peasant com-munities." The same report states that rape of women is strongly coded in terms of race and class: most were Indians or dark skinned (*cholas*) and poor. Reports on the rape of women during political repression in the Southern Cone countries suggest that women were also being punished for having transgressed their gen-der role: they were under suspicion because they participated in politics and knew how to use a weapon.

In the case of Peru, the rape of women by members of the armed forces also reveals the triple rite of domination over women: they are women, but they are also poor and *cholas*.[28] The testimony of a former marine who had served in Ayacucho, given to Degregori and Lopez, is quite illustrative:

> One day they gave us a *chola* to terminate. So three of us made a stop, and one after the other they went over the poor *chola*. I remember that before they started the guys dressed her nicely with her little dress and all, they really dolled her up. I also remember that the patrol chief did not want us to touch her and I answered him, "You must be out of your god damn mind. We have to get rid of this *chola* and that's it." I remember that she repeated, "I am a virgin, I am a virgin." Get off it, you *chola*. Of course she proved not to be a virgin. Here one learns to be a shit. After that the guys kept her moving like a yo-yo. And later, finally, we terminated her.[29]

Many tortured or raped women lived to tell their story. It is not hard to imagine that accumulated anger pushed them into the desperate Shining Path option and in competition with urban popular leaders.

THE BATTLE FOR LIMA

The female leaders of urban livelihood organizations acted in two spaces that, for different reasons, would become the battlefield in the struggle for hegemony. One was social organization, with a clear inclination toward democratization and services, and the other was local leadership, legitimated by the community and at other levels of the public sphere. Henríquez argues that Shining Path could not tolerate this legitimacy in its battle for Lima.[30] The archipelago of social institutions of various kinds—shopkeepers, small entrepreneurs, community association, female organizations—which was stirring in Peru's largest city and creating a new kind of urban dweller and a different experience of citizenship was a challenge to its ability to consolidate control.

In 1990, when Shining Path declared the beginning of "strategic parity"—the moment when the insurgent forces became the strategic equal of the government's forces—the struggle for control of Lima's geography became decisive. Shining Path escalated its actions in Lima slums and shantytowns in order to eliminate the self-managed organizations that stood in the way of its confrontational logic. The *senderista* strategy was social and territorial control. To accomplish this it took over daily life in several shantytowns. Contrary to what happened in the 1970s in some of the Southern Cone countries, where state violence opened some microsocial spaces of resistance, in Peru the violence *against* civil society was also exerted from *within*, a fact that makes it difficult to put Peru within a comparative context based on the Southern Cone experiences with bureaucratic authoritarianism. After infiltrating *senderistas* as poor and dark skinned as the local population, Shining Path tried to recruit neighborhood leaders. Those who resisted were intimidated and eventually murdered: in all of 1991 and the first months of 1992 Lima saw the murder of more than 40 neighborhood leaders, of whom 10 were women and leaders of livelihood organizations.[31]

Shining Path could not deny that the voluntary work of members and leaders in seven thousand community kitchens prepared and distributed in Lima a million and a half daily food rations, or that a similar number of children benefited from the Municipal Glass of Milk Program, or that, in the midst of generalized poverty that was worsened by the August 1990 adjustment measures, these organizations provided critical services. But Shining Path was able to use the success of the leaders of these programs to promote their political agenda. One of their pamphlets reads,

> Behind the facade of the Glass of Milk and the community kitchens lurks an ideological-political traffic, a direct manipulation of the masses. The aim is to keep an enormous, extremely impoverished mass away from a critical spirit, without the will to fight, unable to think beyond the next daily food ration they get as a "gift." . . . Community kitchens have a strategic importance for the plans of the state and of imperialism.[32]

By attacking the women leaders, Shining Path intended to destroy women who were going beyond their instrumental role of food distributors to enter a process of institutional democracy building. A second aim of Shining Path was to transform the livelihood organizations into "struggle committees" that would give food and refuge to its combatants. Its efforts at recruitment and intimidation followed an established pattern: Shining Path would invite the leader of a livelihood organization to listen to its lectures, to give free food to the *senderistas*, and to participate in violent actions, such as attacking a police station or blocking a road. If the woman refused, she was visited by militants who threatened to kill her. At the same time anonymous flyers were distributed around the neighborhood accusing the leader of having stolen food donations, of corruption, or of being an accomplice of the state or an informer for the armed forces.

In this way Shining Path positioned itself to take advantage of the mistrust, envy, and bickering that the process of centralization and the growing distance between leaders and followers had fostered. At the same time Shining Path sympathizers infiltrated the organization, creating fear and instilling mutual suspicion. The stage was set for the assassination of the leader, a crime to which many neighbors responded with a single phrase: "There must be some reason for it."[33] With its leader dead and suspicions high, the group weakened or broke down.

This pattern was aided by a constellation of supporting factors: the state's indifference to attacks against the women's organizations, the failure on the part of political forces opposed to Shining Path to articulate an alternative explanation of events, and, consequently, the isolation and bewilderment of the neighbors, incapable of organizing their own self-defense at the grassroots level.

Finally, there were the constant threats against the NGO professionals who worked with the women in the neighborhoods. The intimidation of NGO professionals, who were also murdered by Shining Path in the cities and in the countryside, was twice as intense for women's NGOs. Their names, activities, and work areas were constantly publicized in *El Diario*, where they were attacked as "feminist matrons . . . narcotic mattresses . . . instruments of oppression and delay for women that keep them away from the road that the proletariat and the people have charted through popular war."[34] Because nongovernmental organizations played a key role in advising in women's popular organizations, the threats took their toll on organizational activity. Many professionals were prevented from staying permanently in the neighborhoods, and the women were left alone. Under the circumstances, a social vacuum formed around them, deepened by the mistrust that had emerged among members of the community, and a political vacuum was created by the parties' failure to support them and by their lack of physical security.

Leaders of the Glass of Milk Program or the Community Kitchen Commission were under death threats from Shining Path. In 1991, in each of the neighborhoods they came from, Shining Path sympathizers spread rumors and suspicion. Enma Hilario, one of these leaders, escaped miraculously when she was shot at while sleeping at home. She has lived in exile since 1992, and, in view of the risks implied, several of her colleagues have quit their posts or made temporary trips out of the country.

Temporary exile is what María Elena Moyano, deputy mayor of Villa El Salvador (a shantytown district with three hundred thousand inhabitants), lived through shortly before her death in February 1992. A few months earlier Shining Path had accused her of blowing up the warehouse of a committee of community kitchens in the district. These were kitchens she had helped establish when she was president of the Federación Popular de Mujeres de Villa El Salvador (FEPOMUVES; Popular Federation of Women of Villa El Salvador), an institution she had founded which had ten thousand members. In late 1991 Moyano led a march of women under the banner "Against Hunger and Terror." She openly rejected *senderista* efforts to infiltrate Villa El Salvador in public debates and declarations against Shining Path. In 1991 a nationally circulated daily newspaper named her "Person of the Year" for her activism against violence. Although forced to leave her neighborhood and family to live a clandestine existence, the day before she was murdered she led a mobilization of neighbors against a Shining Path initiative of an "armed stoppage" backed by terror.

Moyano had grown up in Villa El Salvador, which was considered the foremost self-managed popular district and had formed in the deserted outskirts of Lima in 1970. Like many young people from her generation, she had been a militant in parties of the new Left and a promoter of grassroots community organizations. She approached feminism without the restraints of other lower-class women. Unlike most of the female popular leaders, who were mostly of Andean origin, over 40 years of age, austere in dress, maternal in political style, and devout Catholics, Moyano was 33 years of age, African Peruvian, attractive, charismatic, and arrogant. She was friendly with the middle-class feminists and wore jeans and leather jackets. She also smoked and liked singing and dancing. In certain ways she was the symbol of a new style of being a popular woman and leader. Her old classmates from the barrio eyed her with suspicion; they felt she was different, that she had taken on upper-class airs. The women in her community felt for her a mixture of admiration and envy, made worse by the proximity of the differences between them. (Stahr and Vega argue that people tolerate lifestyle differences when they see them at a distance, not when they are adopted by people who belong to their milieu.)[35]

This argument is presented to attempt to explain why Moyano's assassins displayed unusual ruthlessness. She was shot in front of her children, in a public ceremony, and then blown up with 11 pounds of dynamite. Moyano's public persona had challenged the racial and social stratification mechanisms that underlie gender domination in Peru. Dark skinned, with humble origins and an incomplete higher education, Moyano's leadership represented a new possibility for citizenship, democratic and empowering yet affirming of her individuality.

As anthropologist Patricia Oliart argues (using myths, stories, and songs from sixteenth-century chronicles to deconstruct the symbolic representations through which women are confined within the limits of their family and social group), the social and sexual controls exerted by men over women are heightened when there is economic, social, and cultural domination of the wider group.[36] One of the forms in which this male control expresses itself is the constant devaluing—in the daily life of the family or in the cultural imaginary—of the personal capacity or physical appearance of women (a recurring insult against wives at home is to call them ugly, useless, or stupid). Stahr and Vega's research found that poor, urban women feel that they embody "ugly, *cholo* aspects" of the oppressed group "that are shameful and should be concealed."[37]

When women from a Cuzco peasant community (in the southern Andes) were asked why they wore no modern clothes, instead of defending the traditional custom, one of them answered in sobs: "If I change my way of dressing they will surely say that out of the dog's crap has risen a *mestiza*." On the other hand, one of the characters in an Andean Carnival party is the *limaca* (from Lima), a young woman who returns from Lima putting on airs and despising the local Quechua speakers. She also wears very tight and bright slacks, sports an arrogant walk, chews gum, and constantly fixes her hair. This representation, along with the derision it aims to provoke, implies a warning to those who might resent this woman's differentiation from the group's norms.[38] It is no coincidence that in Carol Andreas's reconstruction of a play possibly used by Shining Path to "educate" people, there appear "women who gossip and who try to imitate upper-class Peruvians or characters from soap operas [and who] are also ridiculed."[39]

For these and other reasons, the assassination of Moyano was the destruction of a symbol. It was patriarch Guzman who punished her for straying from the norm. And, of course, he used women to do the job. The authorship of the crime was claimed by a Shining Path organization in Villa El Salvador, with the following explanation: "Was she a popular leader? No! Just superficial scum who trafficked with and rode on the backs of our people's hunger. . . . María Elena Moyano was not annihilated for being a 'popular leader,' but because she was a declared and proven agent of imperialism."[40] The other leaders of female popular organizations got the message and froze: Moyano had proclaimed a double challenge, against Shining Path and against the burden of her origin and her gender. For that she was murdered.

CONCLUSION

This is not a text that leads to easy conclusions. Conclusions transmit an aura of objective advice about unlearned lessons which could prove useful in the future. Even today, with President Gonzalo in jail and Shining Path no longer a revolutionary threat, Peru seems trapped in an unresolved past formed by injustice and adversity. An unpaid social debt remains which Peruvians have to service day after day. Recent answers have ranged from the total destruction of the old society and the old state as proposed by Shining Path, to the popular approval of President Fujimori's authoritarian and covertly dictatorial project, promised order, security, and growth. It is paradoxical that the horrors of the dirty countersubversive war that the Southern Cone countries suffered under dictatorial regimes were suffered by Peru under its newfound democracy.

Organizational structures like the communal kitchens and the Glass of

Milk Program gave rise to passionate debate. Some saw in them the promise of democratic, solidarity, and emancipatory space for female groups; others argued that they helped maintain the state's old-style clientelist and authoritarian politics. Perhaps we are nearing the moment when we can take a more balanced view, one that can rescue the personal benefits obtained by the participants and also their human condition, their imperfection.

We need a better understanding of the process through which popular women's groups became social actors and collective subjects. In the neighborhoods, the streets on which they mobilized, and with donor agencies and the Congress, the leaders of these groups performed their role as nourishing mothers well; at the same time, through their acts they won self-confidence and self-esteem. Perhaps they thought that being leaders of organizations could translate into upward social mobility, or at least more visibility. And if so, so what? To what forms of personal fulfillment or prestige could these mestizo shantytown women aspire, with their dark skins, their household and maternal chores, their lack of professional qualifications?

The community kitchens and Glass of Milk not only cushioned the impact of economic depression on poor families, thus defusing the social explosion Shining Path was counting on, but they also proved that from self-managing social practice it was possible to negotiate with the state without being coopted or submerged—a process critical to democratic practice.

But Shining Path was able to capitalize on resentment, on the desire to level downward, which characterizes Peruvian social behavior. Terror interrupted the process though which these women leaders were redefining themselves and their roles in Peruvian society and paralyzed the aspirations of those who could have replaced them.

If we understand citizenship not only as the collective pursuit of social demands but also as a process of individuation which allows us to recognize ourselves in and with others as bearers of individual rights, then we will also understand that Juana Lopez, María Elena Moyano, Bernardina Maldonado, and the many other female popular leaders were murdered by Shining Path in the process of claiming their citizenship.

NOTES

This text is an enlarged and revised version of "Violence and Economic Crisis: The Challenge of the Women's Movement in Peru," a paper prepared for the conference "Women and Political Transitions in South America and Eastern and Central Europe: The Prospects for Democracy," University of California at Berkeley, December 1992. This version benefited from valuable suggestions made by Jane Jaquette and Susan Bourque. My thanks to the dedication of the Centro de Documentacíon de la Mujer, to the DESCO Documentation Center, to Ernesto de la Jara, and to María Ángela Canepa for generously sharing with me important material, and to Jessica McLauchlan, Eduardo Ballon, Carmen Rosa Balbi, and Marga Stahr for their accurate criticisms of the first draft of this chapter. The mistakes are all my own. Mirko Lauer has translated the text from Spanish.

1. The Communist party of Peru, Sendero Luminoso, was until 1980 a small group on the fringe of the kaleidoscopic Peruvian Left. In the 1970s several Marxist-Leninist parties had started a unification process that concluded in the forming of the Frente de Izquierda Unida (IU) in 1980. IU was a legal organization and by 1985 became the country's second electoral force. Shining Path has frequently attacked the progress and the leaders of IU.

2. When this chapter was originally written (October 1993), Abimael Guzmán, serving the first year of a life sentence, had started to exchange messages with Alberto Fujimori, president of Peru, proposing a peace agreement.

3. The importance of social rights in Latin American political culture and the fragility of the notion that citizens are bearers of individual rights have recently been studied by Elizabeth Jelin ("La construccíon de la ciudadanía: Entre la solidaridad y la responsibilidad," working paper, CEDES, Argentina, 1992). They have also prompted interesting comments from Teresa Caldeira—see her chapter in this volume—which coincide with the reflections of Peruvians Jose Carlos Ugaz and Virginia Vargas interviewed by Maruja Barrig (*El aborto en debate: Entrevistas a lideres de opinión*, ed. Maruja Barrig [Lima: SUMBI and the Population Council, 1993], 130–39, 140–49). For Ugaz, Peruvians seem to lack a widespread notion of their "right to have rights" (when a tortured terrorism suspect was asked in jail why he did not denounce the mistreatment, he answered that he did not know that he could not be tortured). For Vargas, the struggle for depenalization of abortion in Peru failed to attract the attention of many feminine sectors who also lacked the notion that they could choose.

4. Max Hernandez, *Memoria del bien perdido: Conflicto, identidad y nostalgia en el Inca Garcilaso de la Vega* (Lima: Instituto de Estudios Peruanos, Biblioteca Peruana de Psicoanálisis, 1993), 35. Also published by the Editorial Siruela for the Quincentennial Commission, Madrid, 1991.

5. Marga Stahr and Marisol Vega, "El conflicto Tradición-Modernidad en mujeres de sectores populares," *Márgenes*, year 2, no. 3 (June 1988).

6. Maruja Barrig, "The Difficult Equilibrium between Bread and Roses: Women's Organizations and the Transition from Dictatorship to Democracy in Peru," in *The Women's Movement in Latin America*, 2d ed., ed. Jane S. Jaquette (Boulder, Colo.: Westview Press, 1993).

7. Narda Henríquez, " ¿Cerrando brechas?" research report, Lima, 1992.

8. Maruja Barrig, *Seis familias en la crisis* (Lima: Asociación Laboral para el Desarrollo, 1994).

9. Patricia Córdova, "Madres y líderes: Mujeres organizadas en Lima," research report, Lima, 1993.

10. Carlos Franco, "Exploraciones en otra modernidad: De la migración a la plebe urbana," in *La otra modernidad* (Lima: CEDEP, 1991), and idem, "Ciudadanía plebeya y organizaciones sociales (Otro camino para otra democracia)," ms., Lima, 1992.

11. Ruth Cardoso, "Popular Movements in the Context of the Consolidation of

Democracy in Brazil," in *The Making of Social Movements in Latin America*, ed. Arturo Escobar and Sonia Alvarez (Boulder, Colo.: Westview Press, 1992).

12. Carmen Rosa Balbi and Juan Carlos Callirgos, "Sendero y la mujer," *Que Hacer*, no. 79 (October 1992); Robin Kirk, "Las mujeres asesinas de Sendero Luminoso," translated into Spanish from *Image* (New York), March 22, 1992.

13. Franco, "Exploraciones en otra modernidad."

14. Balbi and Callirgos, "Sendero y la mujer"; Kirk, "Mujeres asesinas."

15. Gonzalo Portocarrero, "El silencio, la queja y la acción: Respuestas al sufrimiento en la cultura peruana," in *Tiempos de ira y amor* (Lima: DESCO, 1990).

16. Cesar Rodriguez Rabanal et al., "Violencia estructural: Psicoanálisis," APEP, Lima, 1990, 30.

17. Denis Chávez de Paz, *Juventud y terrorismo: Características sociales de los condenados por terrorismo y otros delitos* (Lima: Instituto de Estudios Peruanos, 1993).

18. Ibid, 58.

19. Quoted from the Shining Path newspaper *El Diario* (n.d.) by Balbi and Callirgos, "Sendero y la mujer."

20. From "Women Professionals in the Class Struggle," *El Diario*, September 13, 1991, quoted by Balbi and Callirgos, "Sendero y la mujer."

21. Kirk, "Mujeres asesinas."

22. Matilde Ureta, "Feminidad y violencia," ms., Lima 1993.

23. Carol Andreas, "Women at War," *Fatal Attraction: Peru's Shining Path* 24, no. 4 (1991): 27.

24. Gonzalo Portocarrero, "Violencia estructural: Sociología," APEP, Lima, 1990, 66.

25. Sinesio Lopez, "Perú: Una modernización frustrada (1930–1991)," in *Desde el límite* (Lima: IDS, 1992).

26. Instituto de Defensa Legal (IDL), *Perú hoy: En el oscuro sendero de la guerra* (Lima: IDL, 1992); idem, *Perú, 1992: Posibilidad y riesgo* (Lima: IDL, 1993).

27. Americas Watch, "Terror no contado: Violencia contra mujeres en el conflicto armado peruano," n.d. Spanish translation made in 1992 by the Centro Flora Tristán, Lima.

28. Maruja Barrig, "Recordando a Georgina Gamboa," *Ideele* year 4, no. 53 (July 1993).

29. Carlos Ivan Degregori and Jose Lopez Ricci, "Los hijos de la guerra: Jóvenes andinos y criollos frente a la violencia política," in *Tiempos de ira y amor* (Lima: DESCO, 1990).

30. Narda Henríquez, "Nuevos y viejos liderazgos: Identidad femenina, identidad política," research report, Lima, 1992.

31. Ibid.; Instituto de Defensa Legal (IDL), *Peru, 1992*.

32. "The Untold Story of Mother Courage" (María Elena Moyano), in *El Diario Internacional* (April 1992).

33. Americas Watch, "Terror no contado."

34. "More Hunger and Unemployment on Women," in *El Diario*, November 30, 1991.

35. Stahr and Vega, "El conflicto Tradición-Modernidad."

36. Patricia Oliart, "Dominación social y autoéstima femenina en las clases populares," *Márgenes*, year 4, no. 7 (January 1991).

37. Stahr and Vega, "El conflicto Tradicion-Modernidad," 58.

38. Oliart, "Dominación social," 207.

39. Andreas, "Women at War," 26.

40. In "The Untold Story of Mother Courage."

Chapter Six

Consequences of Economic and Political Changes for Women in Poland

RENATA SIEMIEŃSKA

T he downfall of the Communist system in the late 1980s and early 1990s created the opportunity to move away from the political and economic structures created by Soviet domination of Poland after World War II. The direction of change was clear for the political opposition in Poland and supported in the early 1980s by a mass social movement, Solidarity. The aim of this opposition was to abolish the Communist system and to replace it with a political system that would be a replica of Western European democracy and a market economy similar to those that exist in highly developed Western European countries.

AXES OF INTEGRATION AND DIFFERENTIATION OF SOCIETY UNDER THE COMMUNIST SYSTEM

Repeated challenges to the existing regime, including the economic and political crises of 1956, 1968, 1970, 1976, and the 1980s, and mass participation in what was widely understood as opposition activity created an exceptionally strong dichotomous picture of society in Poland. In the minds of many Poles, society was strongly divided between "us," or average people, and "them," the Communist authorities.[1] Solidarity had about ten million members in the early 1980s, for example. In this situation gender could not become even a relatively strong differentiating factor of attitudes toward women's role in society.

The dominant Catholic religion also played an important role in creating expectations of civil integration within Polish political culture. As Przeworski notes, "A powerful impetus to unanimity is present in countries that have entrenched traditions of organicist views of the nation, often inspired by Catholicism. If the nation is an organism, it is not a body that can breed divisions and conflicts."[2] The Catholic Church has always played a significant role in Polish society, but in the postwar period this role steadily increased for several reasons. The Catholic Church was not only a religious institution but also the only legally existing institution in opposition to the authorities during the entire postwar period. It actively supported the political opposition and, as a national institution, helped to maintain national identity, as more than 90 percent of the population is Catholic. Poles had great confidence in the church at the apogee of its popularity in the early 1980s. In 1980, 94 percent of Poles declared their confidence in the church and 90 percent in Solidarity.[3]

In none of the countries in the region during the last 50 years was the church so consistently and to such a large extent the base for political opposition. Nor was Catholicism such a dominant influence or such an important component of national identity. The role of the Catholic Church as one of the architects of the transition also ensured that it would be in a strong political position once Communist rule gave way. After the fall of the Communist system, the newly created political parties became the partners of the powerful church, with its rigid views and ambitious political aspirations. The past history of the church and its recent success gave it reason to believe that its active participation in forming the new political system and social relations of the new Polish state was totally legitimate. However, because of its involvement in politics, which many people felt was too strong, the popularity of the church decreased in the 1990s. In March 1997, 29 percent of respondents declared that they had strong confidence and 37 percent some confidence in the church.[4] Despite the decrease in its popularity, it is still among the most trusted institutions in Poland. The awareness of the church's role caught many opposition activists between their opposition to Communism and their opposition to the nationalist-religious ideology that had been the only effective political force against Communism.

Organic views of the nation also color perceptions of what is causing Poland's many current problems, as the ideal image of democratic politics and capitalist economics clashes with the much harsher realities. As Przeworski notes, "Those who do not partake in the national spirit can only be those who do not belong: alien to the body of the nation. . . . [This fact] leads each of the political forces to strive for a monopoly in representing the 'national interest.'"[5]

Changes in the Polish socioeconomic and political systems after World War II brought with them changes in the position of women in society and in perceptions of women's status and their aspirations. The centrally planned system created numerous opportunities for the manipulation of women as a new source of labor. Of every 100 married women, 13 worked in nonagricultural jobs in 1950, 42 in 1960, 68 in 1970, and about 74 in 1989.[6] Following World War II, the authorities attempted to increase or decrease the number of women in paid employment in accordance with the country's economic growth rate. Child care facilities (kindergartens, nurseries, and day care for older children) and paid maternity leave were either increased or limited by the state in various periods, depending on the economic goals adopted and available financial means. Nevertheless, the facilities and benefits were taken for granted, and nobody expected that they might be taken away as part of another systemic solution.

The manner in which women were mobilized through social, political, and economic pressure, together with overt propaganda emphasizing gender equality and difficult everyday conditions, created the double burden of family and occupation which was especially hard for women. This duality consequently gave rise to the feeling of having "too much equality."[7]

The limited promotion of women to higher positions in the workplace and in politics gave rise to the feeling among women that there was an inconsistency between their effort, the stress they experienced, and the goals accomplished. On the other hand, many women preferred not to be considered potential candidates for higher positions in order not to be placed in a stressful situation. However, the results of studies conducted in the late 1970s showed that women's unwillingness to accept a promotion was highly exaggerated: the difference between educated men and women in this respect was in fact small.[8] Moreover, this opinion, so often repeated by politicians, was a convenient explanation and justification for the fact that women were and are almost absent in decision-making positions.

A lack of organizations, associations, and action groups created by women to serve as pressure groups aggravated the difficulties women had in articulating and vocalizing their problems under Communism. These groups did not exist because the Communist regime forbade the activities of any organizations or political parties that were not part of the Communist state structure. The women's organizations that did exist served as a bridge between the ruling Communist party, the Polish United Workers' Party, and women. The basic task of these organizations was to facilitate the process of manipulating and mobilizing women in order to better implement the goals formulated by the Communist party.[9]

However, during Communist rule, the status of women changed fundamentally in comparison to their position in pre-Communist Poland. As legislator and organizer of social, economic, and political life, the state tried to shape women's lives to fit the needs and structures of a Communist economy. These changes increased women's independence while creating additional pressures, as women were expected to fulfill their traditional duties in the home and their new roles at work. Women's access to resources, on the individual (education, work) as well as the collective (legislation, infrastructure) level, broadened significantly. Nevertheless, many of the policies adopted then are now no longer implemented; some are even destructive for women. There is also a strong political tendency to cut back or eliminate some policies that benefited women in the past. Male workers are also losing their protection, but, as they do not have the primary responsibility for the home or for replacing lost social services, the effects on men are less severe. Thus, it is extremely important for women to recognize these changes and to work to protect their interests, so that the costs they bear in the transformation are similar to those borne by men and not higher.

The transition period creates special possibilities and special pitfalls. Jaquette, characterizing the specific character of the transitional period from the military dictatorship to democratic government in Latin America, writes, "Transitions are political 'openings' in the broadest sense; there is a general willingness to rethink the bases of social consensus and revise the rules of the game. This gives social movements an extraordinary opportunity to raise new issues and to influence popular expectations."[10]

This fact suggests a very important problem and opportunity for women: women must develop awareness of common interests, create women's organizations and lobbies, and promote political representation that can articulate the interests of women as whole, as well as express their different needs as members of different social groups. As shown later in this chapter, some changes in this direction are taking place. However, political and social developments in the 1990s are very complicated in Poland.

THE ROLE OF THE FAMILY ON THE EVE OF POLITICAL AND ECONOMIC CHANGE

The models of the family and women which were actualized represented a dual attempt: first, to adapt to external pressure, and second, to maintain to as great an extent as possible the traditional model of the family and women in their respective roles. The latter model was especially important for people with less education. As a result, women and other family members lived under constant stress, believing that the functions of the family and its members were not being carried out as they should be. In conflict with the traditional family model, the man was unable to make enough money to meet the family's needs. In going to work, the woman was unable to satisfy the demands traditionally expected from her in the home.

In the mid-1980s, the family model propagated by the church became the subject of criticism, even by the experts from the Bishops' Subcommittee for the Pastorate of Women, because of its exceptionally traditional character.[11] The church was of the opinion that the changes in the family taking place in Poland were unhealthy and pointed to its erosion and deep crisis. Paradoxically, the policy of the Communist state in relation to the family resembled that of the church at certain periods.[12] This resemblance occurred when the policy of forced development broke down and there was fear of unemployment; when demographic predictions of more rapid population increase were unfulfilled and it became a question of convincing women to have more children; and when social disorganization caused by the deepening economic and political crisis mounted. The need for Polish society to improve social and political conditions in the late 1970s led to a growing conviction that women should be free from the necessity of working. One of the factors that strengthened the family and its role in society was the way the Communist system itself functioned. Studies conducted in the 1970s showed that Polish society was a kind of federation of primary groups and that identification of the citizens took place on two levels: at that of primary groups and at the national level.[13] This phenomenon was caused by the inability of the existing system to create effective, institutionalized channels for mutual communication and interaction between society and the authorities. The family was the place of retreat from the pressure of the surrounding world.

In the late seventies there arose a growing conviction among members of various social groups that a situation needed to be created which would allow women, especially those with small children, to stay at home. This conviction was reflected in the demands the Interfactory Strike Committee, the predecessor of Solidarity, made to the government in 1980. These demands focused on creating conditions that would allow women to fulfill their traditional roles better and included a three-year maternity leave and the guarantee of a sufficient number of places in kindergartens and nurseries.[14] In this respect the situation did not change in the 1980s. At the time of the collapse of the Communist system in 1989, there was a prevailing belief in Polish society that freedom, equality, and the satisfaction of needs would be guaranteed automatically by the new democratic system based on a free market economy.[15] Women's issues merged in political discussion with a strong effort from right-wing political opposition parties against the Communist system and the church to convince women to stay at home. Arguments favoring this position varied. The traditional role of women was presented as typical of pre-Communist Polish society and therefore as a means of escaping the model the Communist rulers had imposed on society. Another justification for this argument pointed to the necessary withdrawal of women from the labor market in a situation of a deepening scarcity of jobs in the transforming economy.

At the beginning of the 1990s, these arguments were broadly accepted and appeared attractive to a large part of society. Polish society, like other Central and East European societies, demonstrated a high degree of acceptance of a traditional concept of women's role in society when the political system changed in 1989 and 1990.[16] In 1991, 34 percent of a nationwide sample of the adult population completely agreed and 31 percent partially agreed with the statement that "the best thing for a woman to do is to take care of the home."[17] At the same time, however, 35 percent of the respondents completely or partially disagreed with the statement, indicating that a relatively large group of people did not accept the model. The degree of rejection of the model in Poland was among the highest in the region. The differences among countries showed that the greater the force with which the Communist system had been implemented, the stronger the negation of the role models enforced by the former system.[18]

The majority of Polish families have one or two children. In the last several years, there has been an increase in the number of single-parent families.[19] According to data from 1993, women are the heads of 30 percent of households in Poland.[20] The reasons for this phenomenon are many, including divorce; the death of the spouse, which reflects the greater-than-expected mortality of middle-aged men in the recent past; the fact that the husband is unemployed or cannot work because of poor health; and the fact that the woman did not marry the father of her child.

WOMEN AND FAMILY AFTER THE FALL OF THE COMMUNITY SYSTEM IN 1989

Many people in Poland soon realized that the changes concerning women and the family proposed by the government, some political parties, and the Catholic Church would be negative for women. It also became clear that the introduction of free-market mechanisms made discrimination against women a common phenomenon.

Growing unemployment in Poland, a phenomenon previously unknown in centrally planned economies where unemployment was hidden, revealed that women emerge as less desirable employees if an employer is able to select freely among candidates.[21] Women constituted 55 percent of all the registered unemployed in 1995, an increase from 1991, when they accounted for 51 percent.[22] A clear majority of them are among those who have looked unsuccessfully for work for long periods of time.[23] Older women have great difficulty in finding new jobs. As economies restructure, there is less need for employees with the type and level of education found relatively more often among women than men.[24] The labor market is being restructured as some enterprises disappear and new ones with different profiles and labor needs appear. Privatized enterprises often hire fewer people than the state enterprises they replace. Tasks and positions are re-defined. Previously routine jobs now require more independence and decision making, and longer hours are expected in private enterprises, which usually offer higher pay. For all these reasons, some jobs that were generally filled by women are now sought by men, and men are the preferred applicants.

The generous benefits given to employed mothers under the Communist regime also help explain why new employers prefer men, as they are afraid of the long-term economic costs of employing women. Liberal social security provisions turn out to be dysfunctional for women when employers can choose among potential employees in a market economy with a limited number of jobs and a much higher demand for work. This situation creates a political dilemma for women: should they advocate change in such policies in order to make women more attractive to potential employers? The growing discrimination against women in the labor market and in legislation has made women increasingly aware that they need people or groups to defend their interests.[25] In the fall of 1996, women parliamentarians submitted draft legislation aimed at strengthening equality between women and men.

In the first years of the economic transformation after the fall of the Communist system, real income dropped sharply. Calculated on the basis of household budgets, real income was 27 percent lower in 1993 than in 1988.[26] This drop was close to the overall drop in real income in Central and Eastern Europe (26 percent). It was higher than that in Slovenia, the Czech Republic, and Hungary and lower than that in other countries in the region. In Poland, as in other countries, older women (especially those over 70 years old) more often live in poverty than men.[27]

Fear of losing one's job and the deteriorating material conditions of a large part of society have caused a change in the behavior models of young mothers. In contrast to the situation in the 1980s, young women do not take maternity leave. In 1984, 11.4 percent of mothers continued working after having a baby; in 1991, 27.9 percent did so.[28] This percentage has continued to increase.

As the number of nurseries and kindergartens decreases because neither the enterprises nor the local authorities have the financial means to support them, women's chances of adapting themselves to the expectations of potential employers are much more limited than those of men. And as prices for services rise, it will be increasingly difficult for women to take advantage of them.

Studies have shown that families are already adapting to the changing conditions. A comparison of data from 1988 and 1992 regarding the division of household duties demonstrates that changes have been made. Tasks traditionally perceived as being "women's work"—cooking, washing the dishes, cleaning, doing homework with children—are more frequently being performed by both husbands and wives.[29] These changes undoubtedly result from the higher costs of services provided by specialized institutions; the simultaneous drop in the incomes of many families; and the rise in male underemployment or unemployment. Data for 1984, 1988, and 1992 show that relatives who are not members of the immediate family take care of children more often than before. Many tasks, such as laundry, are also performed at home and not done by specialized businesses. We may speak here of the deinstitutionalization of many family tasks and an increased intergenerational resource flow, which is becoming a necessity for the young and at the same time available due to grandparents' earlier, sometimes forced, retirement. This situation increases the pressures of growing dependencies within one's family. The large-scale restructuring of the economy is causing clear changes on a smaller scale.[30]

WOMEN'S POLITICAL REPRESENTATION IN NEWLY ESTABLISHED DEMOCRATIC INSTITUTIONS

As they were prior to the end of the Communist system, women have been almost absent from all governments created in Poland in the post-Communist period. However, a number of women's organizations were created; there were 75 of these groups in 1995. The majority of them are very small and weak, but some were active during the debate on abortion and also tried to mobilize women before the parliamentary elections.

An absence of democratic elections for more than half a century, the lack of a women's lobby, and Poles' dichotomous vision of society contributed to the prevailing feeling among members of Polish society that men and women have identical interests. The past situation was conducive to the creation of "gender identification" without developing a "gender consciousness" that would enable women to believe in their political competence and motivate them to act.[31] Issues concerning women were considered less important than the primary goal of weakening and dismantling the Communist system.

On the other hand, the history of Polish women's participation in politics differs from that of women in many other societies. Polish women often played an active part in political struggle. They actively helped in the national uprisings directed against Austria, Russia, and Prussia which partitioned Poland in the nineteenth century. They took part in the struggle against German occupation during World War II, and they joined Solidarity in 1980, accounting for one-half of its members. Hence, we may speak of a significant "politicization" of Polish women in extraordinary circumstances, particularly during political crises.

Few women were in political institutions under the Communist system. Moreover, women were less often selected than men according to their political experience and gained less access to political and economic power. They were primarily tokens to show citizens that the elected bodies contained a representation of a variety of social groups. It is therefore justifiable to ask whether these cumulative, specific experiences of millions of Polish women and their almost total absence in top positions in political institutions after the end of Communism have influenced them to have more active political attitudes in today's liberal democratic system.

MEN AND WOMEN AS VOTERS IN PARLIAMENTARY AND PRESIDENTIAL ELECTIONS

According to a study conducted in 1992, men talked about the approaching first free parliamentary elections in 1991 more often than women and were more likely to follow the information presented in the media. The mass media were the most frequently mentioned source of information by women and men; 51 percent of women and 65 percent of men often or very often followed information about the preelection campaign. In the case of men, the second most important source of information was their discussions with acquaintances at work and with family members; half of the male respondents had such conversations frequently or very frequently. Women, on the other hand, spoke much more frequently with family members than with acquaintances at work (44% and 32% respectively of all women interviewed). Talks with neighbors were least often named as a source of information and opinion on the elections and candidates; these were mentioned by 24 percent of men and 18 percent of women.[32]

In their interest in the elections women constituted a more differentiated population than men, as multiple regression analysis (MCA) clearly showed.[33] The respondents' socio-occupational group was the strongest differentiating factor in the case of women as well as men. Other social and demographic variables differed in their influence on men and women. The higher a group's socio-occupational status, the greater its members' interest in the elections. In fact, socio-occupational affiliation differentiated women to a significantly greater extent than it did men. Women in senior-level positions and women professionals were more interested in politics than men in the same categories. In all the remaining categories men showed greater interest. The differences were particularly large between female and male blue-collar workers and farmers. For women, use of the mass media and the frequency of conversations about politics with acquaintances at work were strongly differentiated by their attitudes toward women's participation in politics. Interest in the presidential election in 1995 was higher than in the parliamentary ones. Men and women more frequently, and almost equally often, followed information in the mass media and talked with members of their families.[34] Younger and university educated men and women demonstrated similar interest.

In the 1991 elections men and women voted equally often (the difference was about 1 percentage point), while in 1993 nonvoting among women was higher by 6 percentage points than among men. Older people voted more frequently than younger people in both 1991 and 1993; differences between the age groups were smaller among women than among men. Both younger and older women more frequently abstained from voting than men. Both men and women with a university education voted far more frequently than others, but 91 percent of men with university degrees voted compared to 81 percent of women. In the 1993 elections, people with a higher level of education voted much more frequently. But this time there were no differences in the frequency of voting between women and men with university degrees. Women with less education took part in the elections less frequently than men in the same group. According to respondents' reports in a study conducted after the presidential election in 1995, more than 79 percent of men and 74 percent of women voted.[35]

GENDER DIFFERENCES IN POLITICAL PREFERENCES IN ELECTIONS

In many countries women are inclined to be more conservative than men, as expressed by their tendency to vote for right-wing parties, though as a rule they choose parties with moderate and not extremist orientations. Dogan analyzed the results of women's election behavior in Western Europe over the last 50 years and found that parties that for doctrinal reasons are most favorable toward women's emancipation (e.g., left-wing parties) are at the same time most shunned by women, who vote instead for right-wing parties.[36] Are the patterns observed elsewhere also evident in Poland?

In the 1991 elections, women and men voted identically in the case of most parties and groups. The left-wing character of the post-Communist Social Democracy of the Polish Republic did not diminish its popularity among women, who voted for it just as frequently as men. Voting differences between men and women were statistically insignificant, not exceeding 2 to 4 percentage points. The 1993 elections brought about fundamental changes in the situation. The parties whose representatives were elected to parliament, such as the post-Communist Polish Peasant Party (PPP) and the Union of Democratic Left (UDL), received more votes from men than from women. The PPP received 16 percent of men's votes and 10 percent of women's. The UDL was the choice of 12 percent of men and 10 percent of women. The Labor Union, a social democratic party with Solidarity roots, was more popular among women than men and received 3 percent of men's and 7 percent of women's vote. There were no gender differences in voting for the other three parties that gained seats in the lower chamber of parliament. None of these parties had a Communist past; their political orientation can be characterized as center-right or center-left.

In the presidential elections in 1995 women more often declared that they voted for Lech Wałęsa, the former president who was also the former leader of Solidarity, while men more often voted for Alexander Kwasniewski, the candidate from the post-Communist party, the Social Democracy of Poland. The difference was 5 percent. Thus, women in Poland, as in many other countries, tend to support parties and politicians who do not represent a leftist orientation or are not associated with it in public perceptions.

Some researchers believe that it is enough to know the political preferences of men in order to be able to say how women who are close to these men will vote. Others, including many feminist researchers, believe that women have a vision of politics different from that of men, that individuals' approaches to daily problems are more important for women than abstract political declarations. In Poland, men and women paid attention to the same issues discussed by candidates during the campaign. The program of the political party was a significant determinant for more than half of respondents. Confidence in a given party and its representatives was also important to one-fifth of the female and male voters. Only 1 percent of men and women pointed to the recommendations of the church.

The differences between the interests of women and men in both parliamentary elections were slight, even though the tendency was similar to that described in Western European countries and the United States. Women stated slightly more often that their decision about whether to vote for a candidate was based on the candidate's support for finding jobs for all those wanting to work and ensuring good medical care, equal rights for women and men, care for the elderly, and the right to early abortions. On the other hand, men more often were won over by a candidate's emphasis on the need for privatization and decommunization. In the presidential elections the differences in motives for voting between men and women were also small; men were a little more likely to stress the need for rapid privatization, while women gave more importance to support for the church to influence citizens and state politics. But the main issue in the last presidential elections was whether to support the post-Communist parties already in power in parliament or to support President Lech Wałęsa in order to create some counterbalance to Communist influences. Men's and women's opinions on this issue were similar.[37]

WHO VOTES FOR WOMEN?

In explaining the reasons for the small number of women in elected positions it is often stressed that voters do not trust women and do not vote for them. In Poland, women constituted a small group among candidates put forth in the 1991 and 1993 elections. In 1991, women constituted 5.2 percent of candidates for the Senate and 11.8 percent of candidates for the Sejm. In 1993, women constituted 10 percent of candidates for the Senate (68 women and 616 men) and 13 percent of those elected. In 9 provinces none of the parties whose representatives entered the Senate put forth a single woman candidate. Yet in 18 provinces the average number of votes for women was greater than that for men. In total, the mean number of votes for women (47,112) was greater than the mean number of votes received by men (38,962). In 1997, women constituted 15.7 percent of the total number of candidates to the Sejm and 10.4 percent of those to the Senate. The number of women candidates varied greatly among political parties. Left- and center-oriented parties tended to include more women on their lists of candidates to the lower chamber of parliament (Sejm); for example, women constituted 24.9 percent of the total number of candidates of the Union of Labor, 18.5 percent of the candidates of the Union of Freedom, and 15.1 percent of the candidates of the Alliance of Democratic Left. Right-oriented parties had fewer women on their lists of candidates—for example, Election Action Solidarity, 10.9 percent. The first-mentioned party did not get 5 percent of the total votes and therefore does not have deputies in the parliament. Women constitute 15 percent among deputies elected from the Union of Freedom, 17.6 percent among deputies of the Alliance of Democratic Left, and 10 percent among deputies of the Election Action Solidarity. Among deputies elected from the Polish Peasant Party and the Movement of Rebuilt Poland—the other two parties that have representatives in the Sejm—women are absent while they constituted about 12 percent among candidates of the parties. These results clearly contradict the idea that voters do not want to elect women.

Parties place women on their candidate lists only unwillingly, and even if they do so, they usually place them in lower positions, which diminishes women's chances to be elected at all. The rank orders of candidates on party lists show the order of party preferences and indicate the candidates whom the party would like to be elected. Comparison of women's positions on all party lists separately in each district (mean positions were calculated for women) and calculation of rank orders of women's and men's positions on the same lists after the elections showed that women got on average more votes than men. In other words, women got more support than parties wanted them to get. Thus, the problem for women candidates lies more in the actions of party leaders than in voter resistance.

Analyses carried out after the 1991 and 1993 elections confirmed the patterns discovered earlier.[38] Men, particularly highly educated men in high social positions, tend to be unwilling to vote for women or to have women play a significant role in public life because they see them as competitors. In the case of women, the higher the level of education and social and professional group, the more frequently they support women in nontraditional roles.

THE REPRESENTATION OF WOMEN IN ELECTIVE AND APPOINTED POLITICAL POSITIONS

WOMEN IN PARLIAMENT

The greatest number of women in the unicameral parliament under the Communist regime was 23 percent, in 1980–85.[39] As a result of the elections of 1989, 1991, and 1993, the number of women in parliament declined. In the semifree elected parliament of 1989, in which the Communist party and its allies were guaranteed a certain number of seats as an outcome of the negotiations conducted before the elections, women constituted 13 percent of members of the lower chamber (Sejm) and 6 percent of the higher chamber (Senate). In the first freely elected parliament in 1991 the respective figures were 9 percent and 8 percent. In the parliament elected in 1993, women accounted for 13 percent of members of both houses. After the 1997 elections women's representation decreased from 13 to 12 percent in the Senate but remained approximately the same (12.6%) in the Sejm.

The higher number of women elected in 1993 was due to the victory of left- and center-left-oriented parties and the total defeat of right-wing parties, which had almost no representatives in the parliament. The post-Communist party and the coalition of the post-Communist party and organizations with the same roots (the Democratic Left Alliance) largely replaced parties of Solidarity background, especially those of the Center Right and Right. The results concerning women are again congruent with the findings in Western Europe, as left-oriented parties tend to have more women deputies. The higher number of new female members of the parliament elected in 1993 (64% in the Sejm) was due to the change in its political composition. However, the elected women tended to have been deputies longer than the men. Among deputies to the Sejm, 58 percent of women and 65 percent of men were elected for the first time in 1993, which shows that a basic barrier for women is to be selected by the party machinery. When that hurdle is overcome, there is a relatively greater chance that women candidates will be considered in the next elections. Since the 1989 elections, there has been a tendency for women to be as old as or even older than their male counterparts. The significant age differences between women deputies of the Democratic Union (DU) and other political parties (or coalition of parties) shows that in the DU, which has a pure Solidarity background, numerous women became deputies as the result of the "political capital" gathered in Solidarity underground activity in the eighties. There is a general tendency in the party to select people possessing this type of experience as candidates. An opposite tendency has been evident in the post-Communist parties, which are fighting for new images; they have looked for new people who are not associated, or are less associated, with the old system to get credibility for their new programs.

As in 1989, female deputies were better educated than male deputies in 1993. Of the 60 women deputies, 54 (90%) had university educations, and the rest had secondary educations. Of the 400 men, 307 (77%) had university educations, and the rest had secondary or basic vocational educations. The most numerous professional group among women consisted of teachers and research workers (one-third of the women deputies), as it was before 1989. In contrast to the situation in the earlier period, women farmers or health service workers were extremely rare. A relatively large group consisted of women holding high positions in the state administration (the minister of construction and two women deputies were undersecretaries of state) and trade union leaders (the president of the largest trade union organization, OPZZ [Ogolnopolskie Porozumienie Zwiazkow Zawodowych; National Alliance of Trade Unions], created in the early 1980s as a counterweight to Solidarity), and the vice president of one of the smaller trade unions, the Trade Union of Farmers, Agricultural Circles, and Organizations). Among the women deputies, as among the men deputies, a relatively small group (12% among women and 19% among men) had law degrees. Almost one-third of the men had technical educations, and one-fifth had agricultural educations. Therefore, despite the changes that took place in the demographic and social composition of the Polish parliament, parties and social organizations still tended to nominate and elect women with "womanly" professions. These differences were also reflected in women's own preferences when selecting which committee of the Sejm they wished to join, as well as in men's perceptions of their predispositions regarding parliamentary work.

There were also marked differences in the levels of education of men and women in the Senate; 92 percent of women and 72 percent of men had university degrees. Despite this fact, women were very underrepresented in key parliamentary posts. One woman deputy was vice president of Sejm, and another was vice president of the Senate. Two women deputies chaired Sejm committees (social policy and economic policy, budget and finances). Six performed the functions of deputy chairpersons in the following committees: education, economic system and industry, regulations and deputy matters, social policy, ownership transformations, agriculture and food management. One chaired the Senate committee on science and education.

Institutionalization of a Women's Lobby in the Parliament

The lack of an organized women's lobby in Poland has been most noticeable in the last several years, as different social and political groups tried to have a decisive say in discussions, to secure their position in the new social order, and to redefine women's position in society. To a large extent this situation was the heritage of the entire postwar period, in which no organizations could be created except within a socialist ideological framework.

Initiatives to create a women's lobby began almost immediately after the change brought about by the 1989 elections. The first of these was carried out by the Governmental Office of Family and Women's Affairs, whose head was a deputy minister of the first non-Communist government. The Forum, a gathering of women's groups and other organizations of diverse political orientations, was created in the spring of 1990 to provide opportunities for the representatives of all women's and feminist groups and associations to meet, exchange views, and formulate their platforms regarding the government's stand on women's issues. The idea of the Forum was maintained under a new office appointed by the second post-Communist government. However, the existence of the office became unacceptable to the church and parties connected to it because the woman who headed the new office was clearly against the restrictive antiabortion law. She was fired at the beginning of 1992, and no one was appointed to replace her until the spring of 1995. The office did not conduct any activities to protect women's rights during this period.

Another attempt to create a women's lobby among deputies in parliament was undertaken by women from the Parliamentary Club of the Democratic Left. They organized two conferences, inviting deputies, scientists, and activists from a wide spectrum of women's organizations. The Parliamentary Club of the Democratic Union (rooted originally in Solidarity) undertook a similar initiative to strengthen women's political position in the late spring of 1991. The deputies proposed to establish the Parliamentary Circle of Women Deputies of all political affiliations. Two-thirds of women deputies and senators joined the circle. In the parliament elected in October 1991, one-third of women deputies and senators joined. In the parliament elected in September 1993, two-thirds again joined.[40] Women representing the Democratic Left Alliance and some of the women from the Democratic Union Club are the most active participants in the work of the Women's Parliamentary Group (WPG, initially called the Women's Parliamentary Circle).

Legislative Initiatives of the Women's Parliamentary Group

According to its declaration, the WPG mainly puts forward legislative initiatives intended to protect the interests of women and children, although it does not limit itself to these problems. The group is very active and undertakes various legislative initiatives. The members attempted to change the act regulating the modified method of calculating taxes. According to their proposal, single parents could calculate their income together with one of their children, as do married couples, to obtain a tax reduction. This act was to protect single parents, who are usually single mothers.

During the second term of the National Assembly, the Women's Parliamentary Group put forth an initiative to amend the Family and Guardian's Code, in the name of 10 women deputies and 12 deputies from various parliamentary clubs. The initiative's proposed changes to the code include extending adoption rights to all adults, accelerating the adoption process by withdrawing parental rights in certain situations not previously included in the code, introducing the need for agreement of both parents for adoption, and bringing the regulations of the Polish Family and Guardian's Code into accordance with the requirements of the Convention on the Rights of Children, especially in the case of foreign adoptions. The WPG also took a position opposing the proposed implementation of separation of the Family and Guardian's Code.

The WPG favored simplifying once again the regulations that govern divorce. Until 1990, regional courts could approve divorces. Since that time, as the result of an initiative of the Catholic parties and groups, divorce matters are conducted solely by provincial courts, a higher level of courts, which prolongs the proceedings and hinders divorces. The WPG also suggested that the courts should not examine the reasons for divorce, including whether conjugal life has permanently disintegrated, since this is meddling in personal affairs. The WPG believes that the only argument against granting divorce should be the protection of minors and the prevention of threats to their mental health. At present, the court may also dismiss a summons that is submitted by a person who was the cause of marital disintegration when the other partner opposes divorce and when divorce is not in accordance with the "Principles of Social Life." The WPG also proposes to amend the act regarding the method of collecting alimony, as well as an administrative change, that is, eliminating the regionalization of bailiffs. It is important to introduce changes in this area, as 2.2 million children are being brought up in single-parent families and 9 percent of all persons convicted of crimes in Poland are people convicted for not paying alimony.

The involvement of the WPG in the liberalization of the abortion law deserves separate examination. The fight about the act is an interesting example of the mobilization of various political forces and the relations between parliament and public opinion in a society in which democracy is beginning to appear. From 1956 until 1993, Poland had a liberal abortion act that permitted abortions based on social considerations. It was the woman who made the decision to have an abortion, and a high number of abortions were performed. Some of these were carried out because people, due to lack of knowledge of or access to contraception, or to unwillingness to use it, treated abortion as a form of contraception.

In the spring of 1989 the draft of an act was worked out under the auspices of the episcopate (even though it was supported in other circles, such as the United Peasants' Party), making abortion illegal and advocating prison sentences both for women having abortions and for the doctors performing them. After the 1989 elections, the effects of rapid political and economic changes reduced interest in the issue for some time. However, the antiabortion act became a highly politicized issue and the topic of public discussion preceding the 1990 elections to local governments, the presidential elections in the fall of the same year, and the 1991 parliamentary elections.[41]

After a long struggle in the parliament and actions undertaken by the newly created women's organizations, some of them for, others against the liberal law, a restrictive law was passed at the beginning of 1993 and remained in place until 1996, when it was abolished. However, in the spring of 1997 the Constitutional Tribunal decided that the liberal law was not congruent with the Polish constitution, which emphasizes the protection of individual life, leaving the issue to be discussed again in the newly elected parliament in the fall of 1997. An analysis of the content and course of the discussions and voting outcomes in parliament, briefly outlined here, shows that in 1993 deputies were guided more by inter-parliamentary alliances than by their own electorate (80% of respondents of a national random sample favored a less restrictive law at the time).[42] Furthermore, the church, which had no formal representation in parliament, had a significant influence on the nature of the law.

Women's Parliamentary Group Goes beyond Parliament

The WPG performs an integrative role in the women's community, systematically cooperating with women's organizations across the country and representing diverse political orientations. The goal of the WPG is also to integrate the broadly defined women's community through the involvement of researchers and journalists concerned with women's problems. Thus, in 1992 the WPG created the Consultation Council. The council was concerned with the status of women in the Polish legal system, the position of women in the countryside, unemployment, women's participation in politics, and their images in the media and school textbooks.

The WPG also organizes periodic community meetings, which is significant because from 1992 to the beginning of 1995 no one was appointed plenipotentiary for women's and family issues. The WPG adopted some of the functions of this post, including integrating the women's community; monitoring discrimination against women and unjustified dismissals from television work; informing the public through television of the WPG's position on various issues; determining the situation of children (in collaboration with UNICEF and the Association for the Convention on Children's Rights); monitoring the situation of women in family and public life in the context of the Year of the Family; and preparing for the 1995 Beijing conference on women.

The fact that it is an interparty body creates a number of problems for the WPG. When women from various parliamentary clubs develop a joint position, difficulties result from their divergent interests and tactics. For example, WPG president Barbara Labuda's clearly defined stands on the antiabortion law and other initiatives have long made her the object of attacks from within her Union of Freedom party. Nonetheless, as the above description of women's activity in the parliament demonstrates, women deputies are trying to influence the legislature and to become a visible lobby on both women's and more general issues.

WOMEN IN LOCAL COUNCILS

The results of the elections to local councils in 1990 and 1994 showed that women were again underrepresented in politics in terms of numbers in both urban and rural areas. There are fewer women leaders at the local level than before 1989, when women constituted 22 percent of local council members. In the local council elections held in 1990, women constituted only 15 percent of candidates and 11 percent of elected councilors. In 1994 their number increased; women constituted 17.8 percent of candidates (less in rural communes, more in town communes) and 13.2 percent of those elected. The councilors elected in the last local elections are more educated than those elected four years earlier. In 1990, 44 percent of women and 28 percent of men had higher educations; in 1994, these proportions were 54 percent and 35 percent.

The results of the elections to local councils and parliament show that after a dramatic decrease in women's representation immediately after the change of political system the number of women in elective bodies is slowly increasing. The fluctuations in the levels of women's representation may be related to the crystallization of the new, democratic system with its mechanism for selecting candidates and holding elections. The recently observed patterns tend to be congruent with the thesis that there is a relationship between an increase in political tensions and a decrease in the presence of women in politics, a tendency that was also evident in the Communist system.[43]

As in some other countries, such as Italy and the Scandinavian countries, there are fewer women leaders in Poland at the local level than at higher ones. Women were more likely to be elected in towns and cities than in villages. There are many different explanations for this phenomenon. One emphasizes the persistence of traditional attitudes at the lowest (local) level.[44] Another points to the lower level of education for women than for men in rural areas.

The same types of differences between men and women in terms of age, education, and type of professions which exist among parliamentarians also are found at the local level. Organizational channels (e.g., trade unions) of recruitment play a more significant role for women than for men in local and parliamentary elections, as in many other Western countries.[45]

THE SIGNIFICANCE OF WOMEN'S APPOINTMENTS TO TOP POLITICAL POSITIONS

In the early 1990s, a number of women gained prominent positions in politically important institutions, such as ombudsman; prime minister; presidents of the largest state bank, the Antimonopoly Office, and one of the two biggest trade unions; and head of one of the factions of the party that held power from 1989 to 1993.

These appointments were sometimes a way of solving selection problems when there were too many male candidates. Professor of law Ewa Łętowska, who became the first ombudsman in Polish history when the office was created in 1987, wrote about her appointment in her autobiography in 1992, *A Strong Woman in the Spotlight*: "Nobody knew me and nobody took me seriously. I had no doubts that the function of ombudsman was created as a puppet one, considered decorative.... [The authorities] thought that the position would be decorative one, something that simply exists in a state. The choice of a woman was made because, in the eyes of decision makers, there was a greater chance that she would focus her attention on unimportant things."[46] In reality, during her term Łętowska made the position of ombudsman into an important and influential one. Both she and the position became an important part of public life in Poland. Hanna Suchocka, who was prime minister from 1992 until September 1993, also expressed her surprise when she was informed that she had been considered a candidate for the position following a crisis in the former government. Not all of these women have been advocates of "women's issues." Nonetheless, they are important as visible signs of women's ability to be good leaders.

BUILDING A WOMEN'S LOBBY IN THE POST-COMMUNIST PERIOD OUTSIDE PARLIAMENT

Polish women have little experience with independent organizations. The lack of a women's lobby is an inheritance from the Communist system. The first feminist group was created by students at Warsaw University in the early 1980s and gradually came to include people not associated with the university. The goal of the group was to become acquainted with the ideas of feminist movements in Western countries and raise women's consciousness. In 1986, the association organized an international film review, "Women's Cinema," showing films made by popular women directors and asking some of the directors to discuss their work.

Attempts to broaden the group's membership were not successful. When asked to join, women workers felt that the newly created trade union Solidarity would help them solve their problems, which they saw mainly as enabling them to quit their jobs and stay at home. It was also difficult to recruit women who were professionally successful, as many believed that if someone was really talented and strongly motivated to have a career, she was capable of doing so without belonging to a group. As was the case in Latin America, the imposition of martial law, contrary to what might have been expected, seems to have helped the process of awakening feminist awareness. The creation of new, although illegal, organizations of various kinds contributed to the appearance after the mid-1980s of several feminist groups and associations that were active mainly in large cities and in student and intelligentsia communities.

The announcement of the proposed antiabortion law, officially called the Act for Protecting the Unborn, resulted in the creation of at least a dozen new women's groups and associations that have acted alongside the four women's groups still remaining from the mid-1980s. These associations, which are sometimes informal groups, have different political orientations. Some have clearly left-wing orientations and are connected to the Polish Socialist Party or to the Social Democracy of the Polish Republic (Profemina and the Democratic Union of Women). There are also groups tied to the Episcopate's Sub-Commission on Women's Issues which are not clearly associated with a given political orientation but keep in touch with and sometimes coordinate their activity with organizations with a clear political affiliation, for example, the Movement for Protecting Women in Poznan and Women's Dignity in Bydgoszcz. The abortion issue has promoted communication and cooperation among these organizations. Some organizations plan broader activities, such as undertaking steps to raise the level of sexual education, fighting against discrimination against women, and organizing meetings and seminars. These activities have made the feminist movement more visible in recent years.

The organizations created in academic circles wanted to stimulate studies of the situation of women based on feminist theoretical assumptions. But despite their broadly formulated agendas, the attention of these newly created organizations concentrated mainly on petitions and leaflets and on attempts to use the mass media to oppose the draft of the act on abortion. In the early 1990s members of these groups were less interested in "strategic" gender issues or how to increase the political influence of women. Some women also either joined ecological movements or formed eco-feminist groups with activities and strategies similar to those observed in other European countries.[47] In the beginning, there were no feminist magazines because the women's groups suffered from financial difficulties, small memberships, and rapid turnover in members. Now, a few feminist magazines are published but in small numbers of copies.

Another trend is the creation of many professional organizations that bring together managers and women who own enterprises. These organizations have sprung up spontaneously in different parts of the country and have worked toward creating national-level federations. Many of them assume at the start that they will be highly selective in their membership. They wish to maintain their elite character, for they have as their goal the promotion of women to high positions in enterprises and administration. In addition to locally organized groups, there are others that are Polish branches of international organizations such as the Association of Women with University Education. Organizations of the first type constitute the majority of women's organizations. Some are beginning to develop international connections.

Representatives of the women's organizations prepared their own report for the Beijing conference assessing women's problems in the transition period. The church and members of Catholic organizations took part in writing a third report, which was focused almost exclusively on issues related to abortion.

CONTINUITY OR CHANGE IN THE CONCEPT OF WOMEN'S ROLE IN SOCIETY IN THE 1990S?

The changes that have taken place in the years since the fall of the Communist system have altered the perception of women in both the private and public spheres. The family model accepted by society in the 1970s and 1980s comprised a mixture of traits belonging to the traditional and partnership models, with the former dominating. The new political and economic situation after 1990, when women and men experienced unexpected problems of decreasing standards of living and unemployment, has led to some slow changes in popular attitudes about men's and women's role in family. Studies conducted in 1992 and repeated in 1995 produced almost identical results.[48] They confirmed that Poles continue to value the family very highly (on a 7-point scale, 91.1% of respondents chose 7, the highest value). However, there are some changes in attitudes concerning the concept of the family, with a slow decrease in the number of people who choose the traditional model. The opinion that it is good when the woman takes care of the house and family and the man is the breadwinner was shared by 85 percent of the respondents in 1992 and 79 percent in 1995. An almost equally numerous group believes that it is detrimental to children (72% in 1992 and 1995) when women with small children work professionally. But many fewer (52% in 1992 and 47% in 1995) believe that "a working mother cannot establish just as warm and secure a relationship with her children as a mother who does not work." At a same time, a large and growing number of respondents opt for characteristics that are considered to be traits of the partnership model of the family, in which the rights of both partners are treated in a more equal way. A significant number of respondents (44% in 1992 and 53% in 1995) are convinced that it is not true the woman should be limited to helping her husband pursue his career rather than following her own.[49]

We may wonder, particularly in the context of the last opinion, whether the answer to the question on the role of the man as breadwinner and the woman as the one taking care of the home should not be treated as an expression of the conviction, at least in the case of some respondents, that the man's wages should be high enough so that a woman could choose whether or not to work. It should perhaps be regarded, therefore, as an expression of the dreams of higher living standards which appear throughout Poland's postwar history.

Age and education are factors that strongly affect what family models people find acceptable. There is considerable similarity in the opinions of men and women of the same generation and with the same level of education. Nevertheless, women slightly more frequently than men are in favor of a family model based on partnership. Among women with higher education, the number who accept women's right to their own careers is about three times higher than among less educated women; the difference is slightly less among more and less educated men.[50]

The shift in models of the family as a general, fairly stable trend in recent years is confirmed by a study conducted at the beginning of 1997. The number of respondents who believe that "a woman must have a child in order to be fulfilled" decreased substantially between 1989 (79%) and 1997 (64%), especially among young people.[51] Almost all Poles are convinced that both the husband and wife should support the family financially (46% of respondents strongly agree and 42% agree). As the same study shows, more than half of respondents believe that it will not cause family tensions if a wife's income is higher than her husband's. These findings demonstrate that the image of the family and the concept of men's and women's roles within it are changing in response to the new experiences of the 1990s.

In the 1990s the issue of woman's public roles has become the subject of sharp political debates. Some political parties and the church believe that women should limit themselves to taking care of the household and family. According to others, women should have the right to take an active role in politics. Feminists strongly emphasized the latter opinion. The opinions of Poles are slowly changing in this respect as a result of their experience with decreasing living standards in the early 1990s; growing unemployment, especially among women; the debate concerning the right to abortion and introduction of a restrictive law in 1993; women's visibility as individual leaders; and the increased role of women's organizations in public life. The opinion that women should take care of the home and leave the governing of the country to men was accepted by half the respondents and rejected by the other half in 1995. The number of people rejecting this opinion has steadily increased from 39 percent in 1992 to 48 percent in 1995.[52]

Changes in opinions concerning women's participation in public life are generally parallel among women and men. However, there have sometimes been different directions and dynamics in each of the populations. In the last few years, the number of women who believe that women should play the same role as men in business, industry, and politics has increased; the number of men holding this opinion has decreased slightly. Younger men and those with primary and university educations were less likely to support this view.

Attitudes related to women's participation in politics have been changing in opposite directions in the 1990s in clear reaction to political developments and women's visible participation in them. The fluctuation of opinions has been more pronounced among women than men. Women switched more easily to more favorable attitudes toward women's participation in political life and also more easily withdrew from supporting this opinion. In 1992, 35 percent of male respondents and 44 percent of women in a random national sample did not agree that "men are better suited to politics than women"; in 1993 these proportions were 42 percent of men and 62 percent of women. In 1994, 42 percent of men and 55 percent of women did not agree, and at the end of 1995, 35 percent of men and 39 percent of women refuted this view.[53]

The increase in favorable opinions toward women's participation in politics can be linked to a generally positive opinion about the way in which Hanna Suchocka handled the position of prime minister, especially after the tension-filled period of Olszewski's presence in the office. A survey carried out just before Suchocka's appointment showed that two-thirds of respondents expected that she would be a good prime minister; only 8 percent felt that she would not be. The same number of people considered it good that she was a woman, and 23 percent of the respondents even claimed that a woman was better suited to the top political position than a man. Sixty-eight percent declared that the gender of the prime minister was unimportant.[54]

For years it was difficult to evaluate the popularity of or popular confidence in women politicians because their names were not included on public opinion surveys about political figures. The assumption was that female politicians were not "real" leaders. For many years this was Łętowska's problem. But in a March 1994 survey on the popularity of political figures, the names of three women politicians were included. The women placed well; out of 28 names on the list Professor Zofia Kuratowska (vice-speaker of the Senate, leader of the Liberal Democratic Faction in the governing party (the Democratic Union) until the 1993 elections) placed 5th; Ewa Spychalska (deputy in the parliament, leader of a post-Communist trade union) placed 12th; and Hanna Suchocka (deputy in the parliament, former prime minister, member of the Democratic Union) placed 14th.[55]

Changes in the perception of women as potential politicians depend first of all on respondents' evaluations of women's visibility in the political arena and their performance in carrying out their offices. The public is influenced not by "women's issues" but by the broader political agendas pursued by actual politicians. Popular opinion regarding women's political roles also depends on whether "women's issues" (e.g., abortion, jobs) are the subject of public debate when the polls are being taken.

CONCLUSIONS

Since the mid-1990s women have been increasingly accepted in public roles in Poland. This acceptance has been greater in the economy than in politics. The most important reasons for this situation include the fact that even though there are still too few women in political roles, there has been an increase in the political "visibility" of women. Women leaders were often experienced politicians who were relatively more active and undertook actions beyond the work of parliamentary committees. A women's lobby has been created. It has been institutionalized in the form of the Women's Parliamentary Group, which strengthened it and increased its visibility and effectiveness.

The often voiced opinion that women now have much less influence on decisions concerning them than before the political changes because there are fewer women in parliament is totally incorrect. In order to assess women's power in political office, it is important to asses the role played by parliament. If, as in Communist countries, parliament played a mainly "decorative" role, discussions about women's presence and power there are meaningless. The strength of women's influence depends more on the cohesiveness of women's groups and their dedication to raising issues important for women than on the numbers of women in formal political office.

In the last few years a small number of women have been nominated to important political positions; the first women in Polish history have become prime minister, president of the largest state-owned bank, and head of the antimonopoly office. Although there are not many women at the higher levels of the parties, trade unions, and economic organizations, and even though those who are there are often not particularly interested in women's problems, they are visible, nontoken politicians. This development is new in Poland, and it contradicts the stereotype that women cannot perform such roles.

Several years of stormy debates on the right to abortion, which ended in the restrictive 1993 act, undoubtedly contributed to women's awareness that they have common problems. Their particularly bad situation in the labor market played a similar role.

The deteriorating situation of women on the one hand and their increased "visibility" due to their public activity on the other have brought about a change in the perception of women as political actors among both women and men in the last several years. Let us also hope that the changes in awareness, the means by which the parties elect and list candidates, and voting behaviors will offer women greater opportunity to take part in public life and influence decisions concerning themselves and the rest of Polish society.

NOTES

1. Renata Siemieńska, "Women and Social Movements in Poland," *Women and Politics* 6, no. 4 (1986); Renata Siemieńska, *Plec, zawod, polityka: Kobiety w zyciu publicznym w Polsce* (Warsaw: Institute of Sociology, Warsaw University Press, 1990); Siemieńska, "Polish Women and Polish Politics"; R. Siemieńska, "Women in the Period of Systemic Changes in Poland," paper prepared for the Conference on Equality between Women and Men in a Changing Europe, organized by the Council of Europe, Poznan, Poland, March 31–April 2, 1992, published in *Journal of Women's History* 5, no. 3 (1994): 70–90.

2. Adam Przeworski, *Democracy and the Market* (Cambridge: Cambridge University Press, 1991), 92.

3. Aleksandra Jasinska and Renata Siemieńska, "The Socialist Personality: A Case Study of Poland," *International Journal of Sociology* 12, no. 1 (1983): 5–88.

4. Unpublished data of "World Values Survey 1997"; principal investigator in Poland—R. Siemieńska, fieldwork conducted by Centrum Badania Opinii Spolecznej (CBOS; Social Opinion Research Center).

5. Przeworski, *Democracy and the Market*, 92.

6. Andrzej Kurzynowski, "Aktywność zawodowa kobiet a rodzina," in *Rodziny w Polsce: Ewolucja. Zrnicowanie. Okres Transformacji. Raport Instytutu Pracy i Spraw Socjalnych*, vol. 7 (Warsaw: Instytut Pracy i Spraw Socjalnych, 1995).

7. Renata Siemieńska, "Polish Women and Polish Politics since World War II," *Journal of Women's History* 3, no. 1 (1991): 108–25; Barbara Einhorn, *Cinderella Goes to Market: Citizenship, Gender, and Women's Movements in East Central Europe* (London: Verso, 1993); Nanette Funk and Magda Mueller, eds., *Gender Politics and Post-Communism: Reflections from Eastern Europe and the Former Soviet Union* (New York: Routledge, 1993). Sharon L. Wolchik, "Women in Transition in the Czech and Slovak Republics: The First Three Years," *Journal of Women's History* 5, no. 3 (1994): 100–107; Sharon L. Wolchik and Alfred G. Meyer, eds., *Women, State, and Party in Eastern Europe* (Durham, N.C.: Duke University Press, 1985).

8. Mino Vianello, Renata Siemieńska, Natalia Damian, Eugen Lupri, Renato Coppi, Enzo D'Arcangelo, and Sergio Bolasco, *Gender Inequality: A Comparative Study of Discrimination and Participation* (London: Sage, 1990).

9. Siemieńska, "Polish Women and Polish Politics since World War II."

10. Jane S. Jaquette, introduction to *The Women's Movement in Latin America: Feminism and the Transition to Democracy*, ed. Jane S. Jaquette (Boulder, Colo.: Westview Press, 1991), 13.

11. *Raport o sytuacji kobiet* (Warsaw: Podkomisja Episkopatu do Spraw Duszpasterstwa Kobiet, 1985).

12. Franciszek Adamski, *Socjologia malzenstwa i rodziny* (Warsaw: Panstwowe

Wydawnictwo Naukowe, 1982); Renata Siemieńska, "The Contemporary Dilemma of the Polish Family and Its Genealogy," *European Journal of Women's Studies* 1 (1994): 207–25.

13. Stefan Nowak, "Przekonania i odczucia wspolczesnych Polakow," in *Polakow portret wlasny* (Cracow, 1979).

14. Siemieńska, "Women and Social Movements in Poland," 13–41.

15. Minton F. Goldman, *Revolution and Change in Central and Eastern Europe: Political, Economic, and Social Challenges* (Armonk, N.Y.: M. E. Sharpe, 1997).

16. Renata Siemieńska, "Gendered Perceptions: Women in the Labour Market in Poland," *Women's History Review* 5, no. 4 (1996): 553–66; Renata Siemieńska, *Kobiety: Nowe wyzwania. Starcie przeszlosci z terazniejszoscia* (Warsaw: Warsaw University Press, 1996).

17. Siemieńska, *Kobiety*.

18. Ibid. In 1988 the proportion was 13.6 percent.

19. *Analiza sytuacji rodzin i dzieci w Polsce: Raport 1992* (Warsaw: Polski Komitet UNICEF, 1993).

20. *Aktywność ekonomiczna ludności Polski, Sierpień 1993* (Warsaw: Glówny Urząd Statystyczny, 1993).

21. Maria A. Knothe, "Warsaw as an Employment Market for Women," in *Women: The Past and the New Roles*, ed. R. Siemieńska (Warsaw: Center for Europe, Warsaw University Press, 1995), 92–98.

22. Ewa Lisowska, *Women on the Labour Market in Poland* (Warsaw: Office of the Government Plenipotentiary for Family and Women, 1996).

23. Janusz Witkowski, "Bezrobocie i bezrobotni," in Malgorzata Kalaska, Tadeusz Szumlicz, and Janusz Witkowski, *Aktywnosc zawodowa i bezrobocie w Polsce* (Warsaw: Glówny Urząd Statystyczny, 1992).

24. Zdzislawa Janowska, Jolanta Martini-Fiwek, and Zbigniew Goral, *Bezrobocie kobiet w Polsce* (Warsaw: Friedrich Ebert Stiftung, 1992).

25. Malgorzata Fuszara and Eleonora Zielinska, "Obstacles and Barriers to an Equal Status Act in Poland," in Siemieńska, *Women: The Past and The New Roles*, 92–98.

26. Ibid., 92–98.

27. Branko Milanovic, "Dochod, nierownosci i ubostwo w okresie przeksztalcen w krajach Europy Srodkowej i Wschodniej," *Polityka spoleczna wobec ubostwa: Ujecie porownawcze*, ed. Stanislawa Golinowska (Warsaw: Friedrich Ebert Stiftung–Instytut Pracy i Spraw Socjalnych, 1996), 77–91.

28. *Analiza sytuacji rodzin i dzieci w Polsce: Raport 1992.*

29. *Sytuacja socjalno-bytowa mlodych malzeństw w 1992* (Warsaw: Glówny Urząd Statystyczny, 1992), 28–32.

30. Siemieńska, "Gendered Perceptions," 553–66.

31. Arthur H. Miller, Anne Hildreth, and Grace L. Simmons, "The Mobilization of Gender Group Consciousness," in *The Political Interests of Gender*, ed. K. B. Jones and A. G. Jonasdottir (London: Sage, 1988). Sue Tolleson Rinehart, *Gender Consciousness and Politics* (New York: Routledge, 1992), 132.

32. Renata Siemieńska, "Gender and Political Participation in Democratising Poland," *Polish Political Science Yearbook* 24 (1994): 115–30.

33. Siemieńska, *Kobiety*; Renata Siemieńska, *Plec a wybory: Od wyborow parlamentarnych po wybory prezydenckie* (Warsaw: Warsaw University Press, forthcoming).

34. Siemieńska, *Plec a wybory*.

35. Ibid.

36. Mattei Dogan, "Les Consequences politiques du Vote Feminin: Comment les femmes ont porte les Conservateurs au pouvoir en Europe," *International Political Science Review* 6, no. 3 (1985): 306–16.

37. Siemieńska, *Plec a wybory*.

38. Vianello et al., *Gender Inequality*.

39. Renata Siemieńska, *Plec, zawod, polityka*; Siemieńska, "Polish Women and Polish Politics"; Renata Siemieńska, "Polish Women as the Object and Subject of Politics during and after the Communist Period," in *Women and Politics Worldwide*, ed. Barbara J. Nelson and Najma Chowdhury (New Haven: Yale University Press, 1994), 608–24.

40. Renata Siemieńska, "The Formation of Women's Lobby in the Polish Parliament in Post-Communist Poland," delivered at the Conference of the New Legislatures of Central Europe: Institutionalization of the Democratic Transition, Stiřin Zamek (Czech Republic), August 14–17, 1994.

41. Siemieńska, "Polish Women and Polish Politics."

42. Bogdan Cichomski and Pawel Morawski, *Polish General Social Surveys, 1992–1995* (Warsaw: Institute for Social Studies, University of Warsaw, 1996).

43. Siemieńska, *Plec, zawod, polityka*; Siemieńska, "Polish Women and Polish Politics."

44. Joni Lovenduski and Jill Hills, eds., *The Politics of the Second Electorate: Women and Public Participation* (London: Routledge and Kegan Paul, 1981).

45. Joni Lovenduski, *Women in European Politics: Contemporary Feminism and Public Policy* (Amherst: University of Massachusetts Press, 1986).

46. Ewa Łętowska, *Baba na swieczniku* (Warsaw: BGW, 1992).

47. Lovenduski, *Women in European Politics*.

48. For the 1993 studies, see Siemieńska, "Gender and Political Participation."

49. Cichomski and Morawski, *Polish General Social Surveys*.

50. Siemieńska, "Gender and Political Participation."

51. Siemieńska, *Kobiety*, and unpublished data collected by CBOS for R. Siemieńska as part of World Values Survey conducted in 1997.

52. Cichomski and Morawski, *Polish General Social Surveys*.

53. Siemieńska, *Kobiety*; Siemieńska, *Plec a wybory*.

54. Survey conducted July 15–16, 1992, by OBOP—Public Opinion Research Center.

55. Survey conducted by CBOS, March 1994.

Chapter Seven

Gender and the Politics of Transition in the Czech Republic and Slovakia

SHARON L. WOLCHIK

On November 17, 1989, the foundations of the seemingly stable, hardline Communist system in Czechoslovakia began to crumble. Within 21 days, mass demonstrations by hundreds of thousands of citizens and skillful negotiation by leaders of the newly formed Civic Forum and Public Against Violence brought about the end of Communist rule. The election of Václav Havel capped the victory of the so-called Velvet Revolution and seemed to usher in a new era of democratic political life in Czechoslovakia.

With this step, Czechoslovakia joined other Central and East European states in the transition to post-Communist rule. As in other post-Communist states, the country's new leaders sought to re-create a stable democratic political system, reintroduce a market economy, and rejoin Europe. They made substantial progress in achieving all of these aims very quickly.

However, a little more than three years later, the newly reestablished democratic Czechoslovak federation fell victim to the same problem that had helped to undermine Czechoslovak democracy in the interwar period: ethnic tensions and misunderstandings. Once the constraints on political debate and control of the political agenda by the Communist party were eliminated, unresolved tensions between Czechs and Slovaks and the ambitions of political leaders resulted in the politicization of ethnic issues and the breakup of Czechoslovakia.

The following pages examine women's roles in bringing about these changes and the impact of both the collapse of Communism and the breakup of the federation on women and their political roles. As they illustrate, the end of Communist rule has resulted in many positive changes for women. However, it has also led to new hardships and challenges in many areas. The end of the federation has also had important implications for women, for political and economic develop-

153

ments in the Czech and Slovak Republics that are the successors of the Czechoslovak federation have diverged considerably since the end of the common state.

In both the Communist and post-Communist periods, women's roles and opportunities have been influenced in important ways by the nature of the political system, as well as by underlying social and ethnic factors and popular attitudes and values. As is the case in many other areas of life, women's roles in the Czech and Slovak Republics also continue to be influenced by the legacy of Communism. This legacy has many elements in common with the legacy of Communism elsewhere in the region. However, there are also elements that reflect the particular way the Communist system functioned in Czechoslovakia and the interaction of that system with popular values and attitudes dating from the interwar period.

WOMEN AND THE DOWNFALL OF COMMUNISM IN CZECHOSLOVAKIA: BACKGROUND

Women's roles in bringing about the end of Communism in Czechoslovakia were influenced by the political conditions that prevailed during the last 20 years of Communist rule and by the way in which the Communist system collapsed. They were also influenced by the Communist government's approach to women's issues. In contrast to the situation in Poland and Hungary, where reformist Communist party leaders negotiated themselves out of power in round-table discussions with the opposition over an extended period of time, the old system collapsed very suddenly in Czechoslovakia. This fact in turn influenced the role women played in bringing about the end of the Communist system and in the transition that followed.

The events that brought about the fall of Communism were confined to a very short period of time in Czechoslovakia. However, the dramatic end of Communism was preceded by a less noticed but important process of political change. This process, not often noted by outside observers prior to November 1989, in turn was conditioned by the strategy of rule which prevailed in Czechoslovakia for 20 years after the failed reform effort of 1968 as well as by changes in the Soviet Union under Gorbachev in the late 1980s. Sometimes depicted as an early precursor to Gorbachev's reforms in the Soviet system, the effort to create Socialism with a Human Face in 1968 was a short-lived attempt to develop a form of socialism more suitable to a Western, economically developed society.[1] Although the Warsaw Pact invasion of August 21, 1968, ended the reform effort, the legacy of 1968 dominated political and economic life in Czechoslovakia for most of the remaining 20 years of the Communist era. Under the guise of "normalization," the leadership that replaced that of reformist Communist party leader Alexander Dubček in April 1969 made a concerted effort to turn back the clock and restore strict party control in all areas. Hundreds of thousands of supporters of the reforms lost their jobs and all possibility of participating openly in the political life of the country or in economic decision making. In contrast to the strategy of the Dubček leadership, which attempted to rely on opportunities for genuine participation on the part of citizens to create loyalty to the state, the leadership of Gustáv Husák relied instead on a combination of material incentives and coercion to keep the population in line.

This strategy, which remained in effect for more than 20 years, worked fairly well from the perspective of the regime. Thus, in contrast to the situation in Poland, where periodic upheavals occurred throughout the 1970s and 1980s, or in Hungary, where János Kádár's "goulash communism" led to a marked liberalization of the political climate but also eventually to a great deal of popular disillusionment, in Czechoslovakia "normalization" led to apparent political stability. Bought off by a rising standard of living and reluctant to suffer the fate of those who openly disagreed with the regime, most citizens withdrew from politics to focus on their private lives.

The legacy of 1968 also meant that any discussion of reform was taboo in Czechoslovakia for almost 20 years. Fearful that any loosening of the reins would lead to a repetition of the events of 1968, the Husák leadership did not allow any real examination of economic, social, or political problems. The restoration of tight party control of political life and "normalization" of the mass organizations, which had begun to function as interest groups in 1968, also meant that it was very difficult for citizens to articulate or defend their interests in the political arena.

These policies, together with the reimposition of censorship and efforts to control information, meant that most citizens' political activity was limited to required participation in single-candidate elections and other generally symbolic activities. In these circumstances, women as well as men had little real opportunity to be involved in politics in any meaningful way.

With the exception of a brief period in the mid-1960s, when the official women's organization began articulating women's real problems and serving as an interest group to defend women's interests,[2] women lacked an effective means of getting issues of concern to them onto the political agenda directly. Instead, as with other groups of citizens, issues that had a particular impact on women generally came to the attention of political decision makers only indirectly, through the action of specialist elites or party functionaries. In Slovakia, the journal of the official women's organization, *Slovenka*, raised issues related to problematic aspects of women's situation in the 1970s but did not challenge the official approach to women's issues. Nor were women able to form their own organizations outside the official women's organization.[3]

The activities of Charter 77 were the main exception to this pattern. Founded in 1977 in response to the Helsinki declaration and the regime's prosecution of a young rock group, the Plastic People of the Universe, the charter called on the Czechoslovak government to observe the international agreements it had signed to respect human rights. The charter also came to function as an alternative intellectual community. The immediate impact of the charter and other dissident groups on political life in Czechoslovakia was negligible, though the charter activists and the less well known individuals who engaged in "creative deviance" in Slovakia were to prove extremely important in November 1989 and for the subsequent effort to rebuild a democratic political system.[4] Yet because their numbers were small and they were primarily groups of intellectuals centered in Prague and other cities who failed to establish firm links with other groups of the population, the dissidents had little impact on policy prior to 1989.[5]

Women participated in the activities of Charter 77 and other dissident groups. Twenty-three percent of the original signatories of the charter were women, and one of the three spokespersons for the charter was generally a woman.[6] Women activists were often arrested, and some, including the mother of an infant, were repeatedly incarcerated for their participation in the charter's unauthorized activities.[7] Although the charter's documents seldom addressed women's issues, those that did so reaffirmed women's rights to employment outside the home and other aspects of equality. Most of the women intellectuals active in the charter, however, appear to have shared their male counterparts' concern with human rights issues more broadly defined.[8] Most women who participated in the activities of the less defined circles of nonconformists which operated within the framework of official institutions such as the Club of the Defenders of Nature in Slovakia were not interested in women's issues specifically but rather in the same more general economic, political, and environmental issues that motivated men in these networks.[9] Women also took part in mass pilgrimages in Slovakia and in the 1988 candlelight demonstration in Bratislava that called for religious freedom.

Most women in Czechoslovakia contributed to undermining support for the Communist system less directly than the relatively small numbers of women who were involved in dissident or nonconformist activities. Although women as well as men were required to vote under Communism, the regime in fact tolerated lower levels of political activism on the part of women. Women themselves often explained their lack of interest in party membership or in assuming political functions by reference to their lack of free time and family responsibilities, and party membership was not as uniformly required of women as it was of men to hold comparable economic positions.[10] However, given the considerable personal costs associated with becoming dissidents, most women did not openly oppose the regime or work to change it. Most withdrew from politics or used less direct means to influence political developments.[11]

In addition to withholding support for regime-sponsored initiatives, women also contributed to undermining the regime through their roles within the family. By their actions in the home, women played an important role in socializing the younger generation to values at odds with the official value system of the Communist state. In Slovakia these values included, in many cases, strong religious beliefs. In the more secular Czech Lands, they included the democratic values and traditions of the interwar Czechoslovak republic.[12]

Although little noticed outside the country, there were important changes in political life in Czechoslovakia during the last two years of Communist rule. At the elite level, there was a good deal of turnover in top party bodies between 1987 and 1989. A delayed reaction to Gorbachev's policies in the Soviet Union, these changes were also a response to the increasingly acute economic crisis in Czechoslovakia. The leaders who replaced Gustáv Husák were by no means reformers. However, they were somewhat younger and far less experienced than their predecessors. They were also less personally committed to the policies of "normalization." They therefore vacillated in their responses to increasing challenges from below, a factor that allowed independent activities to increase.[13]

There were also important changes at the mass level. Emboldened by developments in the Soviet Union and other socialist countries, more Czechs and Slovaks began to participate in unauthorized activities. The number of independent groups increased, and young people in particular began to be involved in the activities of the opposition.[14] Although these changes gave women as well as men somewhat greater opportunities to take part in public life, and although the regime was somewhat more tolerant of such activities than during much of the previous 20 years, the cost of such activity was still very high. As Václav Havel's imprisonment in the spring of 1989 for his participation in an unauthorized protest illustrates, the leadership could still punish challenges to its authority very harshly.

Women's participation in political activity prior to the collapse of the Communist system was shaped by the pattern of gender role change that took place in Czechoslovakia under Communism. Although Czechoslovakia differed in many important respects from the other European countries that became Communist after World War II, the political system and strategy of economic development adopted after 1948 were very similar to those in the Soviet Union and elsewhere in Central and Eastern Europe. The approach Communist party leaders took to women's issues and the impact of the broader strategies of economic development and social transformation were also similar. Thus, although the situation of women in the Czech Lands and Slovakia reflected the cultural values and social practices of those areas, the pattern of change in women's roles which took place was very similar to that which occurred in other Communist states.

As I and others have documented in some detail in earlier writings,[15] the institution of a Communist system led to an uneven pattern of gender role change in Czechoslovakia as in other Communist countries. Women's access to education increased dramatically, as did their participation in paid employment outside the home. The importance of these changes should not be overlooked. Although almost all Czech and Slovak women were literate before the establishment of Communism, the expansion of educational access allowed many more women to obtain secondary and higher education. Women also moved into technical studies in large numbers for the first time. Similarly, women's employment became an accepted part of life during the Communist period.

At the same time, many inequalities remained in both areas. In the area of education, most girls and women continued to choose or be channeled into areas traditionally thought appropriate for women or areas, such as medicine, which became feminized. Differences in skills and educational specializations were in turn reflected in the economy, where there was considerable occupational segregation.[16] Women's concentration in low-priority branches of the economy, such as light industry, trade and public catering, education, and medicine, in turn contributed to the fact that women's wages were approximately two-thirds those of men during the Communist era. Women also were far less frequently found in leading economic positions than men, even in those areas of the economy in which they were the majority of the labor force.[17]

There were similar elements of change and inequality in women's political roles and in relations within the family. As the result of the leadership's efforts to mobilize the population, most women as well as men took part in symbolic political activities designed to show support for the regime. Thus, almost all women as well as men voted. Women were well represented in the symbolic, governmental elites at all levels but were seldom found in top positions in the Communist party, the effective political elite. In both the governmental and party elites, women functionaries differed from men in terms of their educational levels and social backgrounds. They were dependent on the party for their positions and, in contrast to many male leaders, did not have strong power bases within the party or state bureaucracies. They thus had little influence on decision making.[18] The regime's effort to force women to participate in mobilized political activities and the overwhelmingly negative image most people held of those few women who were active party functionaries led many women to avoid political activity once it was possible to do so.

Relations within the family were also influenced by Communist rule. Legal changes guaranteed women equal treatment in case of divorce. Continued economic development also led to change in the structure and size of the family. Many men and women came to accept the notion promoted by law that there should be equality within the family. However, there was relatively little change in the division of labor within the home. Despite the increase in women's educational levels and participation in paid employment outside the home, women continued to be responsible for most of the work associated with caring for children and running the household on a daily basis. Women's lack of free time and their continued identification with the family in turn limited their participation in economic decision making and in more demanding political activities.[19]

The nature of the political system after 1968 and the pattern of gender role change that occurred under Communism are both important in understanding women's roles in the collapse of Communism in Czechoslovakia. Prior to the end of Communist rule, most women did not have the opportunity available to women in many Latin American countries to be active in movements that helped them define their interests or allowed them to pressure political leaders to take action.

Large numbers of women nonetheless took part in the mass demonstrations that ended Communism in Czechoslovakia. Several women dissidents, including Daša Havlová and Dana Němcová, were among those beaten by the police during the November 17 demonstrations that served as a catalyst for the Velvet Revolution, and many women joined the growing numbers of citizens who protested police action and, as the demonstrations grew, called ever more vociferously for political change.

Women were also involved in the formation of the Civic Forum in Prague and Public against Violence in Bratislava. Intellectuals such as Němcová, Eda Kriseová, Jiřina Šiklová, and Rita Klimová who had long been active in opposition circles were joined by women students and prominent women in the theater and other arts in the deliberations of Civic Forum in Prague. In Bratislava, Soňa Szomolányi, Zora Bútorová, Iveta Radičová, and Helena Woleková were among the women who took part in the formation of Public against Violence.

With few exceptions, however, women played secondary roles in these organizations. Most women involved in Civic Forum and Public against Violence, as well as in the numerous student organizations that were formed in 1989, were active primarily in service, rather than policy-making or deliberative activities. Certain women, such as Rita Klimová, who became Czechoslovakia's first post-Communist ambassador to Washington; Eda Kriseová, who served as an advisor to President Havel for two years; and Dagmar Burešová, an attorney who later became chair of the Czech National Council, were appointed or elected to important positions after the revolution. However, as the following sections illustrate, most women soon retreated from or were forced to give up the direct exercise of political power.

CENTRAL FEATURES OF THE TRANSITION FROM COMMUNISM IN CZECHOSLOVAKIA

In order to understand women's roles in politics and economic life after the fall of Communism and the impact of the transition on women, it is important to appreciate what the transition from Communism involved in Czechoslovakia. As in other Communist countries, leaders and citizens in post-Communist Czechoslovakia were faced with the need to re-create democratic political institutions and a market economy. They also had to reorient the country's foreign policy and begin to come to terms with the devastating ecological consequences of Communist rule.

In Czechoslovakia, the difficulties involved in the transition were magnified by the way the Communist system had operated for much of the 1970s and 1980s. The tight political control exercised by the regime until the late 1980s, for example, meant that very few citizens had any experience with autonomous political activity or working to defend their own interests. Travel restrictions and the leadership's fear that contact with the West would be dangerous meant that most intellectuals had few contacts with the West or experience there. In the economic realm, the effort to re-create a market economy had to start almost from scratch, as nearly all economic enterprises, including small-scale services and retail outlets, were in state hands in 1989.

The transition from Communist rule, then, involved much more than a simple change of regime. It also involved transformation of property relations and the social structure, as well as a large-scale shift in values, opportunities, and choices for individuals.[20] Increased contact with people and ideas from previously forbidden areas of the world challenged old preconceptions and certainties and introduced new possibilities in many areas. However, in addition to new opportunities, the transition also had economic, social, and psychological costs. The extent of the changes involved is illustrated by the fact that approximately 25 percent of the population changed jobs in the first four years after 1989 in Slovakia, for example.[21] The cost to individuals of living in a situation in which everything from the organization of child care to expectations at the workplace changed very quickly has been considerable. The high level of uncertainty which characterized life in the first few years after the revolution and continues to some extent today, particularly in Slovakia, was reflected in all areas from the workings of political institutions to family life.[22] Similarly, greater openness to other countries exacerbated old social pathologies such as alcoholism and drug abuse and allowed new ones to flourish. Prostitution increased, as did pornography, sex shops, rape, and other violent crimes against women.[23]

It is in this context that women's roles in economic and political life, as well as policies that affect women, must be understood. The nature of transition politics in Czechoslovakia has had an important impact on the level of women's involvement in politics and on the way in which women's issues have been considered by political leaders. Similarly, women's as well as men's choices in the economy have been conditioned by the rapid changes occurring in that sector. Women's efforts to organize on their own behalf have also been shaped by these factors as well as by ideas from other parts of the world.

WOMEN AND THE MOVE TO THE MARKET

As in other Central and Eastern European countries, the transition to a market economy has brought many benefits for women. Once restricted almost exclusively to working for the state, women are now able to establish their own private businesses and work in a wide variety of newly established or newly privatized enterprises. Women are also free to practice their occupations without the ideological and political interference that occurred during the Communist era, develop their skills, and travel abroad for business purposes as well as pleasure. From a consumer's perspective, the shortages that occurred from time to time have vanished, and there is now a much larger range of goods and services available. At the same time, the shift from what in Czechoslovakia was an economy that was almost entirely in state hands to one in which private enterprise predominates has created hardships for many women. Many of these are evident in the workplace. Others result from women's continued responsibility for the care of home and children and the impact of the economic transition on their families.

As is the case for the population as a whole, the impact of the move to the market on women has become increasingly differentiated.[24] Young, well-educated, urban professional women have benefited to a much larger extent than older, less educated, less skilled women who work in manual occupations or reside in rural areas. Marie Čermáková, in a 1995 study of women's labor force and family roles, estimated that the professional and social status of 10 percent of women had markedly improved after 1989. Some women also found that their work had become more interesting. However, many women face a greater work-load and have less job security and less time for their families.[25] Others have experienced greater economic hardship. Elderly and minority women, as well as single mothers, have been particularly hard hit by the impact of economic change.[26] The hardship created by the shift to the market has also been far greater in Slovakia than in the Czech Lands.

Women in both the Czech Lands and Slovakia have been less favorable toward privatization of state enterprises than men since 1989.[27] Despite these reservations, large numbers of women participated in the voucher privatization plan in the Czech Republic and Slovakia.

Women in the Czech Lands and Slovakia also displayed a certain degree of ambivalence about becoming entrepreneurs in the early years after the end of the Communist system. A survey conducted in 1991 for the International Labor Organization found that nearly half of both men and women felt that becoming an entrepreneur was something that was appropriate primarily for men and that women should play only a "helping" role in businesses.[28] Approximately a third of the women surveyed in 1991 wanted to start a private business part-time while continuing to work at their full-time jobs. Women's reluctance to become entrepreneurs is also reflected in the fact that many women who wanted to start private businesses or already worked in such enterprises wanted to be "family helpers" rather than solo owners.[29]

Despite this ambivalence, significant numbers of women have entered the emerging private sector both as employees and as owners. Women constituted 16.6 percent of those employed in the private sector in the Czech Republic in 1990, 35.2 percent in 1991, 35.9 percent in 1992, and 38.1 percent in 1994.[30] In Slovakia, women accounted for 42.1 percent of workers and employees in the private sector in 1989 and 37.7 percent in 1990. This proportion dropped slightly to 35.1 percent in 1991 but increased to 40.3 percent in 1993 and 43.6 percent in the first half of 1995.[31] There has also been an increase in the number of women working in small private enterprises. The proportion of the female labor force employed in small private businesses grew from 3 percent in February 1991 to 12 percent of employed women by early 1992, compared to 15 percent of the total labor force.[32]

The number of women entrepreneurs and employers has also increased. By 1995, 6.6 percent of employed women, compared to 14.2 percent of employed men, were entrepreneurs in the Czech Republic. A far larger proportion of men (9.2%) than women (1.9%) were entrepreneurs with employees; 4.7 percent of employed women and 5 percent of men were solo entrepreneurs.[33] Women in Slovakia accounted for 21.6 percent of entrepreneurs without employees and 19.7 percent of those with employees in 1994.[34]

In reaction to the problems created by the uneven pattern of gender role change that occurred during Communism, many men and women in Czechoslovakia felt that levels of women's employment were too high. In the early period after the end of Communist rule, calls for women to leave the labor force were paralleled by the desire of certain women to stay at home to care for children and family. In practice, of course, this choice was not a realistic one for most women, given the impact of the end of subsidies, the closing of unprofitable enterprises, and growing inflation on family budgets. Survey research conducted in 1995 found that few women or men supported women's total retreat from the labor force. Only 7 percent of Czech women wanted to stay at home permanently; 80 percent of men did not want their wives to do so under any circumstances.[35] As in several other post-Communist countries, women's proportion of the labor force decreased slightly in both the Czech Lands and Slovakia after the end of Communist rule (from 45.5% in 1989 to 43.3% in 1991 in the Czech Republic and from 45.5% in 1989 to 44.3% in 1991 in Slovakia).[36] In the Czech Republic, women's proportion of the labor force began to increase again in 1992 and reached 44.5 percent in 1995.[37] In Slovakia, women accounted for 45.8 percent of the labor force in 1993 and 46.1 percent in mid-1995.[38] Most women continue to be employed full-time.[39]

Although women have not left the labor force voluntarily in large numbers, they have borne the largest share of the new burden of unemployment, as in most other post-Communist countries. In the Czech Republic, where women accounted for 57.4 percent of the unemployed in 1991, 58.0 percent in 1994, and 55.5 percent in 1996,[40] women's levels of unemployment have been consistently higher than their proportion of the labor force. However, because overall levels of unemployment have been very low in the Czech Lands (3.1% in June 1996),[41] few women have lost their jobs there. Women's representation among the unemployed has decreased over time in Slovakia, where women accounted for 52.0 percent of the unemployed in 1991 and 47.5 percent in February 1995.[42] However, given the much higher levels of unemployment in Slovakia in 1994 (13.9% in April 1995 and 12.5% in July 1996), the impact of unemployment has been much greater on women in Slovakia than in the Czech Lands.[43] Thus, although women constitute a larger share of those who are unemployed in the Czech Republic than they do in Slovakia, far more women are unemployed in Slovakia. Unemployment rates were 3.0 for men and 4.5 for women in the Czech Lands in 1993, for example, compared to 13.6 for men and 13.0 for women in Slovakia in early 1994.[44] In addition to constituting a disproportionate share of the unemployed, women have more difficulty than men finding new jobs once they are unemployed.[45]

Those women who continue to be employed face increasingly open discrimination in the workplace. Thirty-five percent of women surveyed in a 1991 study indicated that women workers were the first to be dismissed in their enterprise; 45 percent indicated that they earned less than men who did the same work.[46] The majority of women in both the Czech Republic and Slovakia feel that men have more advantages than women at work.[47] In Slovakia, men are less likely than women to feel that women would receive lower wages than men in the same positions; they are also more likely to feel that men's and women's work is equally valued.[48]

A 1995 study found that men were more likely than women to say that they had experienced discrimination (32.4% of men, 27.1% of women). However, women were far more likely than men to have been discriminated against on the basis of gender (39.2%, compared to 2.5% of men).

More egregiously discriminatory practices, such as demands that women dress in provocative ways or provide sexual favors to clients or customers, appear to be more prevalent in the private sector.[49] Opponents of gender equality now feel that they may openly challenge the principle of women's equality in the workplace; this practice appears to be increasingly prevalent in state firms also.

Women also face new demands in the workplace and new competition from men. There is now greater pressure on women as well as men to increase their skills and knowledge and to work efficiently. The burden that new expectations of better performance create for both men and women is heightened in the case of women because they can no longer routinely use the working day to do errands or attend to family matters, as many did under Communism.[50] Women in many previously "feminized" areas, which had low wages and low prestige under Communism, are also facing new competition from men now that occupations in these areas, such as tourism, banking, and financial management, bring high salaries and opportunities to work for foreign companies or travel abroad. The total number of people employed in the area of tourism in the Czech Republic, for example, nearly doubled between 1989 and 1991; women's proportion of the labor force in that sector dropped from 76.8 percent to 60.6 percent during the same period. Similar trends were evident in banking, where women's share of the labor force decreased slightly (by 1%) at a time when overall employment in this area was rapidly expanding.[51]

As during the Communist era, women continue to receive substantially lower wages than men. Gender was consistently the most important factor in differentiating among groups with different wage levels in research conducted in 1984, 1991, and 1993.[52] Overall, gender-related wage differentials decreased somewhat between 1984 and 1993. Women's average monthly wages were 68.4

percent of men's in 1984; women's average hourly wages were 74.8 percent of men's in 1993 and 76.5 percent of men's in 1994.[53] Among certain categories of workers and employees, gender differences increased between 1984 and 1993. The wages of women with higher specialized education, for example, were 82.96 percent of those of men in 1984 but only 80.47 percent in 1992.[54] In the Czech Republic, the gap began to increase again in the mid-1990s. Women's hourly wages were 73 percent of men's in 1995 and 71.8 percent in 1996.[55] In Slovakia, women's wages were 71 percent of those of men between 1988 and 1993.[56]

The shift to the market has also had an impact on women through their roles in the home. As it is still women who must see that their families have all the necessities of daily life, the burden of stretching the family budget and providing necessities as subsidies are cut and social services decline is a challenge for many women. Certain families, particularly those that have gone into private business or in which family members work for foreign companies, have seen their incomes rise dramatically. But for most families, making ends meet continues to be a daily struggle. Again, this situation is particularly difficult in Slovakia, but it is also true for many families in the relatively prosperous Czech Lands.[57]

Women's roles in this respect have been complicated by the impact of the social and psychological changes that the transition has brought. Because women still perform much of the kin work in both the Czech Lands and Slovakia, as in other societies, much of the responsibility for helping family members who have lost or cannot find jobs, or who are affected by one of the many social pathologies that have increased since the end of Communist rule, falls on women's shoulders.[58] All of these factors limit the time and attention women can give to their economic roles and therefore their ability to take advantage of the positive opportunities the move to the market has created.

WOMEN IN THE TRANSITION: DEMOCRACY FOR ALL?

The end of the Communist party's monopoly of power and the elimination of censorship have had a profound impact on women's opportunities to be active in public life. Since 1989, women as well as men in Czechoslovakia, and in the Czech Republic and Slovakia, have been able to vote in competitive elections and join a multitude of political parties, interest groups, and other voluntary organizations. They have also been able to found new groups and attempt to mobilize others with similar policy preferences and concerns to pressure political leaders to take action on issues of interest to them. In addition, women, as well as men, can run for political office without the need to obtain the Communist party's approval.

As noted earlier, women played an important role in ending Communism in Czechoslovakia. As in other post-Communist states, however, women continued to be marginalized from the direct exercise of political power in the Czech Lands and Slovakia after the end of Communist rule. Women have voted in large numbers, as men have, in the parliamentary elections held since 1989. Yet many women, undoubtedly partly in reaction to being forced to take part in what was essentially meaningless political activity during the Communist era, have little interest in politics beyond the act of voting.[59] Approximately 36 percent of women in the Czech Lands and 44.0 percent in Slovakia surveyed in 1991, for example, indicated that they had never been interested or had ceased to be interested in politics.[60] Fifteen percent of women, compared to 8 percent of men, surveyed in the Czech Republic in 1993 had no interest in politics.[61]

Survey research indicates that both women and men feel that men have advantages over women in the area of politics, as well as in employment. Some 48 percent of women surveyed in the early 1990s, compared to more than 40 percent of the population as a whole, thought that men have greater possibilities in politics than women.[62] However, significant groups of women regard differences in men's and women's social position as an appropriate reflection of men's and women's different "natural" roles.[63] Most women attribute women's lack of representation in political institutions to their lack of preparation to enter politics.[64] A high proportion of a small sample of women in both the Czech Lands and Slovakia surveyed in 1991 felt that they were not able to influence decision making at the federal (88.2% Czech, 92.7% Slovak), republic (84.2% Czech, 88.5% Slovak), or local (52.2% Czech, 54.9% Slovak) levels.[65]

In 1990, Czech and Slovak women were adamantly opposed to any sort of a quota to guarantee representation of women in political posts. However, there has been a good deal of change in this regard. By December 1991, some 70 percent thought that such a law would be useful.[66] Approximately 60 percent of women and 37 percent of men surveyed in Slovakia in 1995 supported a law mandating a certain proportion of women in parliament. Seventy-four percent of women and 58 percent of men thought women's share of deputies in the Slovak National Council should be higher than its current level; 27 percent of women but only 9 percent of men wanted to see women hold between 41 percent and 50 percent of posts.[67]

There have been relatively few significant differences in men's and women's attitudes toward political institutions and leaders. Women, as well as men, had relatively low levels of trust in many political institutions, including the federal parliament, the republic-level parliaments, and local governments in 1991.[68] However, public opinion surveys conducted since the end of Communism have documented certain gender difference in perspectives on issues. Women are more likely than men to feel that their living standards have decreased, for example; they have also been somewhat less supportive than men of privatization of state enterprises and more likely to want to see the state continue to play an important role in ensuring the welfare of individuals and families.[69] A recent study of gender role attitudes in three Central and Eastern European countries indicates that men and women also differ somewhat in terms of their views of desirable gender roles.[70]

The results of a comparative survey that I conducted with Czech and Slovak colleagues in December 1994 were similar. Thus, women surveyed in Slovakia in December 1994 were significantly more likely than men to feel that women had lost as the result of transition (57.5%, compared to 46.7% of men). Women were also less likely than men to feel that the post-1989 system would bring their children a better future than the socialist system and were less sure that capitalism was necessary in the future. Although men and women generally attributed similar degrees of importance to public issues, women were more likely than men to see health issues (86.9% women, 77.59% men), education (67.8% women, 52.7% men), and unemployment (73.0% women, 65.9% men) as very important problems. Women were also more likely (27.3%) than men (16.4%) to see women's situation as an important issue.

Women were less likely than men (22.4% compared to 34.1%) to see the actions of the Communist party before 1989 as very negative. They were also less likely (63% compared to 71% of men) to regard the right to private property as very important and more likely to see the right to a job (82.5% and 75.6%) and social security (88.8% and 78.1%) as very important. There were also important gender differences in levels of political activism. Women were significantly less likely than men to work for a party (8.8% women, 17.7% men), take part in the activities of a group or organization that promoted their interests (31.6% women, 40.9% men), get involved in solving a local problem (35.4% women, 45.2% men), run for office (7.5% women, 13.9% men), or help in an election campaign (14.3% women, 21.7% men). They were also less likely to be members of a party (4.9% women, 11.2% men). Women were more likely to participate in nonpartisan groups or organizations (11.2% women), although their activity levels were still lower than those of men (19.4%).[71]

Women were significantly less likely than men to feel that they understood the political situation in Slovakia completely (7% compared to 13.3%) or rather well (19.1% women, 32.2% men). A far larger number of women felt that they did not understand the situation very well (44.8% of women compared to 35.6% of men) or at all (25.0% of women compared to 16.4% of men). Women were also more likely to indicate that they did not know or had no opinion on many questions. Significantly more women than men felt that it was better not to discuss politics with anyone (24.4% compared to 16.0%). Finally, women's sense of political efficacy was much lower than that of men. Far fewer women felt that they knew how to defend themselves against an action by their local government which threatened their interests (8.2% compared to 16.6% of men), for example. Almost twice as many women as men (22.1% compared to 12.6%) felt strongly that they did not know how to do so.

Women also continued to play a small role among political elites in post-Communist Czechoslovakia. Women's proportion of deputies in the federal legislature decreased from 23 percent to 16 percent in the last decade and a half of Communism to 10.7 percent as the result of the June 1990 elections. In June 1992, 26 women accounted for 8.7 percent of the deputies elected to the federal parliament. As during the Communist period, women fared somewhat better at lower levels of the political system. Women accounted for 13.5 percent of deputies to the Czech National Council in June 1990, when Dagmar Burešová served as chair, and 10 percent in June 1992. In Slovakia, women constituted 9.3 percent of deputies to the Slovak National Council elected in June 1990 and 11.5 percent of those elected in June 1992.[72]

Women's representation in the Czech and Slovak parliaments, which became national parliaments after the split of the country in 1993, has continued to be somewhat higher than the level of their representation in the federal parliament prior to 1993. Women accounted for 15 percent of legislators elected to the lower house of the Czech parliament in June 1996. Nine women (of 81 members) were elected to the newly established upper house, the Senate (11.1%), in November 1996.[73] There were no women among the members of the Czech government formed in 1996. In December 1996, Vlasta Parkanová became minister of justice after her predecessor, Jan Kaldová, resigned. Women's representation in the Slovak parliament increased to 14 percent as the result of the September/October 1994 elections.[74] There were three women in the Slovak government formed in 1994 (one of the three deputy prime ministers, the minister of education, and the minister of social welfare).[75] Zdenka Kramplová was appointed foreign minister in June 1997. Women's representation has been somewhat higher at lower levels in both the Czech and Slovak Republics. However, differences in their levels of representation at the republic and local levels were not great. Women accounted for 16.7 percent of members of local councils in the Czech Republic in 1990 and 17.9 percent in 1994. Five percent of mayors were women in that year.[76] From 10 percent to 30 percent of local council members are women in Slovakia.[77]

As in several other post-Communist states, the largest proportion of women deputies were members of left-of-center parties in both the Czech Lands and Slovakia in the elections held immediately after the end of Communist rule. In the Czech Republic, women accounted for 21.9 percent of deputies of the Communist party in 1990, for example, compared to 14 percent of all deputies in the Czech National Council.[78] Women accounted for 4 percent of the deputies of Public against Violence in the Slovak National Council elected in 1990 and 10 percent of the deputies of the Christian Democratic movement.[79] This tendency has continued in Slovakia, where women constituted 15.4 percent of candidates in the 1994 elections.[80] Women accounted for 13 of 61 (21.3%) deputies belonging to Vladimír Mečiar's left-of-center Movement for a Democratic Slovakia; 2 of 9 (22.2%) of those of the Slovak National Party, and 16.7 percent of those elected by the left coalition, Common Choice (3 of 18).[81] However, it has not been as clear a trend in the Czech Republic. Most women deputies elected in June 1992 (16) belonged to Václav Klaus's right-of-center Civic Democratic Party. In the 1996 elections, women constituted the highest proportion of deputies among those elected on the lists of the extreme right-wing Republican Party (5 of 9, or 27.7%), the Communist party (5 of 18, or 22.7%), and the Social Democrats (11 of 61, or 18%). The largest number of women deputies were members of the Social Democratic Party.[82]

As I have noted before, the decrease in the numbers of women in parliament in and of itself does not indicate a decrease in their political influence.[83] Because most of the women selected to run for parliament during the Communist era were party functionaries who also differed markedly from their male counterparts in terms of their social backgrounds and educational levels, they had higher turnover and little influence on political decision making.[84] Although there are currently fewer women in positions of political leadership, those women who are in such positions have educational and occupational backgrounds that are similar to those of their male colleagues.[85] Although this fact does not guarantee that they have the skills needed to be effective legislators, they are clearly not at such a disadvantage as the collective farm women and ordinary workers who were their predecessors during the Communist era. All the women deputies and senators in the Czech parliament for whom information is available (29) have higher educations. Five have medical degrees, 7 have higher law degrees, and 4 have Ph.D.'s.[86] Women parliamentarians in Slovakia include 2 scientists, 2 lawyers, a doctor, a psychologist, an economist, 2 university teachers, 2 journalists, an engineer, an entrepreneur, 3 state officials, and a high school teacher.[87] At the same time, given the small number of women deputies, as well as their dependence on party structures to get elected and the reaction against many aspects of the gender role changes that occurred under Communism, there has been very little room for women deputies to raise issues of particular concern to women. Many women leaders also reject the notion that they have a special responsibility for women.[88]

WOMEN'S ORGANIZATIONS AND PARTICIPA-
TION IN VOLUNTARY ORGANIZATIONS

As the section above has indicated, many women continue to have serious reservations about becoming active in "politics as usual" or official political organizations in the Czech Lands and Slovakia. Many also continue to view feminism as a dirty word and reject participation in women's groups.[89] The very bad image of the official women's organizations in both the Czech Lands and Slovakia has also been a barrier to organizing women to work on their own behalf, as the close links between these organizations and their subordination to the Communist party discredited them in the eyes of most women. As in the case of party membership, many women are hesitant to become members of any organization, now that such membership is not obligatory.

In many other countries, women have tended to prefer to participate in social movements and other nonpartisan community organizations more than in structured, hierarchical political parties. This trend was evident in Czechoslovakia in the period immediately after November 1989, when women took part in the activities of the Civic Forum and Public against Violence in large numbers but were less likely than men to join the structured political parties that developed later. Approximately 5 percent of women surveyed in the Czech Republic and 3.5 percent in Slovakia were members of a political party in the early 1990s. However, women continue to be very active in the burgeoning nonprofit sector and account for approximately 70 percent of the members of nongovernmental organizations in the Czech Lands.[90] Approximately 9 percent of women surveyed in the Czech Lands and 4 percent in Slovakia in 1991 participated regularly in the work of an interest group or social movement. An additional 20 percent in both regions participated somewhat in the work of these organizations.[91] Women surveyed in 1994 were also more likely to indicate that they participated in or in the future would participate in nonpartisan rather than partisan political groups.[92]

With the repluralization of political life after 1989, women founded many new women's groups. In 1991, there were 27 new women's organizations in the Czech Lands and 9 in Slovakia in addition to the successors of the official women's organizations.[93] By 1994, there were some 34 women's organizations in the Czech Lands. These ranged from the Association of Women Entrepreneurs to the Movement of the Czechoslovak Family, an organization for housewives, and included groups based on religious, charitable, professional, and political grounds. They also included groups devoted to the interests of single mothers and two lesbian groups, as well as a group of people who provide paid sexual services.[94] Most of these groups have few members and are centered in the larger cities. Few of these groups have links to political parties or leaders, and most have very little influence on political developments.[95]

Many women's groups, particularly those established soon after 1989, explicitly renounce any connection to feminism, preferring instead to focus on women's maternal roles and interests or on professional issues. Many also deny that they are political groups at all. Nonetheless, many of these groups, such as the Prague Mothers, sponsor events for women which deal with political topics.[96] They also provide information for women concerning public policies and issues, such as social welfare provisions, regulations concerning children's allowances, and ecological issues. A newsletter of the Prague Mothers circulated in late 1993, for example, contained a reprint of a "Small Guide to Democracy" and discussions of the war in Bosnia and environmental issues as well as information on programs at a number of mother's centers and upcoming activities of the group.[97] Although these groups do not view themselves as political, they serve an important function. By bringing women together to share their experiences, they provide a forum for discussion which may lead to action to articulate and defend women's interests. The demonstration by young mothers in the early 1990s in which they pushed their infants in carriages down the main streets of Prague to protest contamination of the food supply is a case in point.

There are also women's groups that are more specifically geared to political activity, such as those affiliated with political parties, and several groups that identify themselves as explicitly feminist. Most political parties have established groups for women. Other groups, such as the nonpartisan Nova Humanita, which has worked with women parliamentarians and organized efforts to lobby legislators,[98] and the Movement for Equality of Women in Bohemia and Moravia, as well the short-lived Political Party of Women and Mothers of Czechoslovakia, have also focused explicitly on political issues.[99]

Efforts to foster cooperation or coordination among the various women's groups have not been able to overcome the differences that divide these groups along religious and political lines. Most of the newly established groups, for example, will not cooperate with the women's organizations that are the successor of the old official women's organizations. Women's groups affiliated with particular political parties also find it difficult to cooperate with one another. Groups that share the same general political orientation have begun to cooperate, however. Democratic Alternative, founded in 1993, for example, brings together women organized in groups with a center-right orientation, including nonpartisan women's groups such as Nova Humanita, Zonta, the Prague Mothers, and women's groups affiliated with center-right parties.[100]

In 1991, women intellectuals centered around Dr. Jiřina Šiklová, a sociologist and former dissident who founded the new Faculty of Social Work at Charles University, established the Center for Gender Studies with support from the Network of East-West Women. Based for the first three years in Dr. Šiklová's living room, the center sponsored a variety of lectures, seminars, and discussion groups for women. It also organized a number of women's publications and strives to open more discussion about issues of concern to women, including rape and other violence against women, and gender roles in society at large.

Intellectuals affiliated with the center have been instrumental in instituting women's studies courses at universities in Prague and Olomouc and in introducing gender issues into the research agendas and publications of social science institutions.[101] In 1994, the center moved to its own quarters, where it continues to loan books from its sizeable collection and to organize a variety of events for women, including language courses, discussions, and workshops.[102]

In November 1993, ProFem, the Central European Consultation Center for Women's Projects, was established in Prague with support from the Frauen-Anstiftung to advise nonprofit women's groups and individuals about fundraising and financing. The center has also organized workshops and seminars on self-employment for women and self-defense techniques.[103] The foundation supported the creation of the Education and Information Center for Women (ASPEKT) in Bratislava in 1994. Based on a group of women intellectuals who had been meeting informally for a year and a half, the group has organized seminars and workshops on issues such as beauty, motherhood, feminism of various types, and witches. In 1995, the group focused on women's writing and feminist literature, women and power, and reality and myth in discussions of women's nature.[104]

Women intellectuals in Bratislava have introduced women's studies materials into university courses and promoted more public discussion of women's issues.[105] They have also organized training courses for women leaders and activists.[106]

The importance of outside funds in supporting the actions of women's groups is evident in the efforts of women formerly involved in the Guardians of

Nature to organize a new, independent women's group in Slovakia. Research funded by the European Union found that many women, particularly outside Bratislava, missed the opportunity that the old women's organization had provided for them to meet with other women. In the words of a participant in a focus group organized to examine women's needs and concerns, "To the extent that politics didn't enter into it, [the old women's organization] was good. We had a good time. It's necessary to open the door and go out into another world for a little bit. Obviously, it is important to devote oneself to the children, but women also have a right to do something to fulfill themselves." In the words of another, "If only there were a social meeting place, where women could sit down a bit, have a bit of social life . . . that you could go there, have a coffee, talk with others, get some advice. We don't have this."[107]

A decision was therefore made to begin a new grassroots women's organization. At the founding conference of this group, held in June 1995, approximately 30 women from all regions of Slovakia met for three days to discuss their ideas concerning women's situation and the kinds of activities a women's organization could undertake. A follow-up conference was held in October 1995. Members of the organization have begun initiatives, such as a Mother's Center in Košiče, which address women's everyday needs.[108]

Women have also established a number of publications devoted to publishing works by and about women. These include *Žena-91*, the country's first feminist journal; *One Eye Open*, a literary review that also includes essays on themes related to feminism and women's situation; *Wicca*, a feminist "fanzin"; and *Promluv*, the journal of the lesbian women's organization. In Slovakia, women's organizations affiliated with various political currents including the Christian Democratic Movement and Social Democracy have publications for women. The explicitly feminist journal *Aspekt* publishes writings on a variety of feminist themes and has quickly become known in intellectual circles in both Slovakia and the Czech Lands.

Although the circulation of these journals is not large, they demonstrate the lively and ongoing interest of an important minority of Czech and Slovak women in issues related to women's status and feminism. This interest has also been reflected in a far-reaching debate about the nature and meaning of feminism in recent years. One of the continuing themes in this debate concerns the relevance of foreign experience with feminism and the specificity of the Czech and Slovak situations. Debate has also centered on the impact of the Communist experience on women's perceptions and choices and on whether feminism is desirable in the Czech Republic, and if so, what kind.[109]

THE END OF CZECHOSLOVAKIA: DIFFERENT PATHS FOR CZECH AND SLOVAK WOMEN?

In January 1993, the Czechoslovak federation ended and was replaced by two independent states, the Czech Republic and the Slovak Republic. This event reflected the impact of a variety of factors ranging from cultural and historical influences to repercussions of the move to a market economy in the two regions and the influence of political leaders. It also reflected the particular characteristics of the politics of transition in Czechoslovakia and the fact that ethnic issues eventually were unable to be resolved within the framework of the common state. Political leaders, particularly Vladimír Mečiar, currently prime minister of Slovakia, played a large role in politicizing ethnic issues in post-Communist Czechoslovakia. Most Czechs and Slovaks continued to indicate that they opposed the breakup while it was occurring and afterward. However, the inability of their leaders to agree on a constitutional division of power between the federal and republic governments or the proper course of economic reform was paralleled by significant differences in the political and economic preferences of ordinary citizens in the two regions.[110]

Political and economic developments have taken different courses in the Czech Republic and Slovakia since the breakup of the federation. In Slovakia, independence has been accompanied by a good deal of political turmoil at the elite level. Vladimír Mečiar, elected prime minister as the result of the victory of his party in the June 1992 elections, remains the pivotal political figure in the country. With the exception of March to December 1994, when a coalition government that included representatives of parties ranging from the Party of the Democratic Left to the right-of-center Christian Democrats held office, Mečiar's political style has dominated Slovak politics. As a result, political life has been characterized by conflict and instability. Mečiar's early conflict with supporters of his own party and the Slovak National Party, his sometimes coalition partner between June 1992 and March 1993, was paralleled by his conflict with Michal Kováč, president of Slovakia, and led to Mečiar's ouster by a vote of no confidence in March 1994. Although his party won the most votes in the early parliamentary elections of September/October 1994, Mečiar was unable to form a government until December. Conflict between the current government, which is a coalition of Mečiar's Movement for a Democratic Slovakia, the Peasants' Party of Slovakia, the Slovak National Party, and the left-wing Association of Slovak Workers, and his opponents, as well as then President Kováč, continues. Relations between Slovaks and the six-hundred-thousand-strong Hungarian minority have also become strained once again.[111]

The performance of Slovakia's economy began to improve in 1994. However, levels of unemployment are still much higher, and the proportion of the population which continues to experience largely hardship as the result of the change to the market is much greater, than in the Czech Republic.[112]

The impact of these differences is evident in women's lives and opportunities in the two countries at present. Women in Slovakia continue to face more difficult economic circumstances than those in the Czech Republic, a fact that influences their perspectives on political issues. Women in Slovakia tend to be less supportive of the move to the market than women in the Czech Republic, for example. Although there do not appear to have been strong gender differences in the September/October 1994 Slovak elections, most women as well as men supported left-of-center parties. As the result of the personnel policies adopted by Vladimír Mečiar's government, sizeable numbers of women who do not share his political views have lost their jobs. Larger numbers feel the impact of the Slovak government's efforts to control the press and change the educational system to reflect its views. Opposition to the government is still possible, and women as well as men continue to participate in a wide variety of nonprofit groups as well as opposition parties. Women activists are also engaged in a number of efforts to found new organizations and increase the amount of attention given to gender issues in public discussion and debate. At the same time, the cost of speaking out in opposition to the government's policies has increased, a factor that may induce women to remain out of the political sphere.

In the Czech Republic, economic developments have been among the most favorable in the post-Communist world. Unemployment rates remain low, and relatively few women have been affected by the loss of their jobs. Increasing inflation and the change to a needs-based social welfare system, including pensions and other social welfare payments, however, are likely to increase the economic difficulties many families face in the near future. Politically, the center-right coalition of Václav Klaus was very stable until the mid 1990s, and President Václav Havel continues to enjoy considerable public support. However, the Social Democratic Party's strength increased significantly in mid-1995. Václav Klaus was once again chosen as prime minister after the 1996 parliamentary elections but had to form a minority government. Balance of payments and other financial problems in the spring of 1997 and a significant degree of corruption among economic officials led to Klaus's resignation in late 1997. However, although political life has become more fluid, the fundamentals of a democratic system are not in question. Those who oppose the government's policies may raise issues publicly and organize opposition without suffering negative consequences.

Satisfaction with political institutions is higher than in Slovakia, but most people also focus primarily on their private lives and on economic issues.

Neither the Czech nor the Slovak government has shown any interest in concerted action to remedy gender inequalities or address women's issues. Just as in the early years after the fall of Communism, political leaders in both the Czech Republic and Slovakia continue to find other issues more important. To some extent these issues overlap in the two countries; there are also issues particular to each, such as the question of relations with the Hungarian minority in Slovakia and the status of the Roma in the Czech Republic, which occupy the attention of political leaders.

CONCLUSION

It is still too early to assess the long-term impact of the differing economic and political conditions in the Czech Republic and Slovakia on women's situation and on the way in which women's issues will be dealt with by the political system. As time passes, it is likely that the different paths chosen by Czech and Slovak leaders will be reflected in greater differences in opportunities and different problems for women in the two societies. However, at present, although the political and economic climate in which they operate differs, the situation of Czech and Slovak women continues to be similar in many respects. In both societies, some women have gained from the changes since 1989, but many have experienced largely negative impacts. In both societies women continue to be marginalized from politics. Given the small numbers of women in political office, the lack of legitimacy of raising women's issues, and the preoccupation of male leaders with other problems, it is very difficult to get issues of special concern to women onto the political agenda in either country, a fact that is true of social issues more broadly. Since 1993, there has been more attention to the latter, especially in the Czech Republic, as the furor over the division of the state died down and leaders came to focus on more routine issues. However, many of the changes in social policy being enacted in the name of economic necessity will be costly for many women. In Slovakia, the political leadership and the democratic opposition are still embroiled in a high level of conflict. Polarization along political lines appears to be increasing, and the process of defining a form of Slovak statehood which will be compatible with democratic political values is still under way.

Finally, in both societies, relatively few women are willing to put the time and energy needed into organizing on their own behalf. Whether this is a result of the resurgence of traditional values, the legacy of the past, or the day-to-day demands of living in the new economic and social orders that are emerging, there is still relatively little support for the idea that women should organize to articulate and defend their interests.

At the same time, it is important to keep in mind the positive changes that have occurred. Although small in numbers, women activists have succeeded in getting gender or women's studies courses incorporated into the curriculum at several major universities in both the Czech Republic and Slovakia. They have also succeeded, through their publications, seminars, workshops, and public actions, in increasing awareness and public debate about gender issues. Economic and demographic developments will contribute to this process. Greater experience with the workings of a market economy and the increasingly open discrimination that the shift to the market has allowed will in all likelihood mobilize larger groups of women to organize to defend their rights. Generational change will also increase support for efforts to promote gender equality, as younger, better-educated women (and men) are more likely to favor more egalitarian gender roles.[113]

Continued exposure to outside ideas and influences can also be expected to contribute to greater activism on the part of women. Outside events and processes, such as the UN Beijing conference and the desire of Czech and Slovak leaders to be admitted as full members of the European Union, may also induce political leaders to take action on issues that affect women. However, it is important to remember that considerable gender inequality persists in the countries of the European Union and in the United States. In both cases, there is a lack of readiness to view discrimination against women in the same light as policies that discriminate on the basis of ethnicity. Recent statements by high U.S. officials including Secretary of State Madeleine Albright to the effect that women's rights are human rights reflect a change in perspective on this issue. However, this change has yet to be reflected concretely in U.S. policy toward the region.

In any case, as the experiences of Czech and Slovak women to date illustrate, outside influences, while important, are clearly secondary. As Jiřina Šiklová argued, "Feminism is the product of a political culture of a particular country and of a particular social system. That's why the feminism of the post-communist state is certain to be of a different hue than West European feminism. Each wave of feminism, wherever and whenever it appears, casts a new light on various symbols. It uses it own political diction and is confronted with various adversaries, political traditions, means of expression, and solutions specific to its culture."[114] The responses of Czech and Slovak women to the challenges and opportunities created by the fall of Communism in 1989, then, will be shaped primarily by their own actions and ideas. They will also be shaped by the legacy of Czechoslovakia's Communist past and by the nature of the transition.

NOTES

I would like to thank the International Research and Exchanges Board, the MacArthur Foundation, the East European Program of the Woodrow Wilson International Center for Scholars, and the Institute for European, Russian, and Eurasian Studies and Elliott School of International Relations of the George Washington University for their generous support of the research on which this chapter is based. I would also like to thank Nancy L. Meyers, Spencer Smith, Igor Prochazka, and Zsuzsa Csergo for their assistance.

1. See H. Gordon Skilling, *Czechoslovakia's Interrupted Revolution* (Princeton: Princeton University Press, 1976), for a comprehensive analysis of the reform effort.

2. See Hilda Scott, *Does Socialism Liberate Women?* (Boston: Beacon Press, 1974); Barbara Jancar, *Women under Communism* (Baltimore: Johns Hopkins University Press, 1978); Sharon L. Wolchik, "The Status of Women in a Socialist Order: Czechoslovakia, 1948–1978," *Slavic Review* 38, no. 4 (1979): 583–603.

3. See Sharon Wolchik, "The Scientific-Technological Revolution and the Role of Specialist Elites in Policy-making in Czechoslovakia," in *Domestic Policy in Eastern Europe in the 1980s: Trends and Prospects*, ed. Michael J. Sodaro and Sharon L. Wolchik (New York: St. Martin's Press, 1983); see also Sharon L. Wolchik, "Women's Issues in Czechoslovakia in the Communist and Postcommunist Periods," in *Women and Politics Worldwide*, ed. Barbara J. Nelson and Najma Chowdhury (New Haven: Yale University Press, 1994).

4. The term is Martin Bútora's; interview with Martin Bútora, Bratislava, March 1990.

5. See H. Gordon Skilling, *Charter 77 and Human Rights in Czechoslovakia* (Boston: Allen and Unwin, 1981), for an analysis of the charter's activities.

6. See Barbara Jancar, "Women in the Opposition in Poland and Czechoslovakia in the 1970s," in *Women, State, and Party in Eastern Europe*, ed. Sharon L. Wolchik and Alfred G. Meyer (Durham, N.C.: Duke University Press, 1985), 171.

7. Interview with Dana Němcová, Prague, June 1990.

8. See Jancar, "Women in the Opposition"; also, interview with Jiřina Šiklová, Prague, March 1991; interview with Helena Klimová, Prague, April 1991; interview with Dana Nemcová, Prague, June 1991.

9. Interviews with Soňa Szomolányi and Zora Bútorová, Bratislava, 1991.

10. See Sharon L. Wolchik, "Women and the State in Eastern Europe and the Soviet Union," in *Women, Development, and the State*, ed. Sue Ellen Charlton, Jana Everett, and Kathleen Staudt (Albany: State University of New York Press, 1989).

11. A case of the latter is the impact women's (and men's) decisions to limit the number of children had on the adoption of pronatalist population policies in the 1970s. Although it is clear that the decision to have or forgo having children was influenced by other factors, the failure of young couples to produce the desired number of children was a primary factor that led to the adoption of measures that, although controversial from the perspective of gender equality, brought immediate benefits for many young families. See Sharon L. Wolchik, "Demography, Political Reform, and Women's Issues in Czechoslovakia," in *Women, Power, and Political Systems*, ed. Margherita Rendel (London: Croom Helm Publishers, 1981), and Sharon L. Wolchik, *Czechoslovakia in Transition: Politics, Economics, and Society* (London: Pinter Publishers, 1991), chap. 2.

12. Research conducted in the 1980s found that religious belief and practice were more widespread in Slovakia than in the Czech Lands. In 1984, for example, 71.6 percent of children in Slovakia were baptized, compared to only 31.2 percent in the Czech Lands (Wolchik, *Czechoslovakia in Transition*, 214–15). Differences in value orientations were also evident in Czech and Slovak evaluations of the interwar period. Czechs viewed the interwar period, which exemplified traditions of political pluralism, much more favorably than most Slovaks (ibid., 111–12).

13. See Wolchik, *Czechoslovakia in Transition*, 129.

14. Ibid, chap. 2.

15. See Scott, *Does Socialism Liberate Women?*; Jancar, *Women under Communism*; Alena Heitlinger, *Women and State Socialism: Sex Inequality in the Soviet Union and Czechoslovakia* (Montreal: McGill-Queen's University Press, 1979); Wolchik and Meyer, *Women, State, and Party*; Wolchik, "Status of Women in a Socialist Order"; Sharon L. Wolchik, "Ideology and Equality: The Status of Women in Eastern and Western Europe," in *Comparative Political Studies* 13, no. 4 (1981); Wolchik, "Demography, Political Reform, and Women's Issues"; and Marie Čermáková, "Gender, společnost, a pracovní trh," *Sociologický časopis* 31, no. 1 (1995): 16.

16. See Sharon L. Wolchik, "Gender Issues during Transition," in *East-Central European Economies in Transition: Study Papers Submitted to the Joint Economic Committee. Congress of the United States* (Washington, D.C.: GPO, 1994), 147–70; Liba Paukert, "The Changing Economic Status of Women in the Period of Transition to a Market Economy System: The Case of the Czech and Slovak Republics after 1989," in *Democratic Reform and the Position of Women in Transitional Economies*, ed. Valerie M. Moghadam (New York: Oxford University Press, 1993), 248–79; and Čermáková, "Gender, společnost a pracovní trh," 13–14.

17. See Čermáková, "Gender, společnost a pracovní trh," and Wolchik, "Gender Issues during Transition," for references to further studies that document these trends.

18. Wolchik, "Status of Women in a Socialist Order"; Sharon L. Wolchik, "Women and the Politics of Transition in the Czech and Slovak Republics," in *Women in the Politics of Postcommunist Eastern Europe*, ed. Marilyn Rueschemeyer (Armonk, N.Y.: M. E. Sharpe, 1994), 3–28.

19. See Wolchik, *Czechoslovakia in Transition*, 201.

20. See Valerie Bunce, "Should Transitologists Be Grounded?" *Slavic Review* 54, no. 1 (1995): 111–27.

21. See Ján Bunčák and Valentina Harmadyová, "Transformacia sociálnej struktury," *Sociológia* 5, nos. 4–5 (1993).

22. See Valerie Bunce and Maria Csanádi, "Uncertainty in the Transition: Postcommunism in Hungary," in *East European Politics and Societies* 7, no. 2 (1993); see also Wolchik, "Women and the Politics of Transition in Central and Eastern Europe," in Moghadam, *Democratic Reform and the Position of Women*, 29–47, and Hana Havelková, "Family and Gender between Public and Private Realm," *Czech Sociological Review* 4, no. 1 (1996): 77–78.

23. See Hana Malinová, "Prostitutky všech zemí, spojte se!" *Prostor*, April 9, 1992, 13, and Ľudmila Mistriková, "Prejavy intolerancia a násilia voči ženám v SR," *Sociológia* 27, nos. 5–6 (1995): 399–405.

24. See Marie Čermáková, Lumír Gatnar, Irena Hradecká, Hana Mařlková, and

Hermenegilda Symůnková, "Sociální postavení rodiny jako základního činitele adresata sociální pomoc," in *Výzkumní zpráva* (Prague: Sociologickýústav AVCR, 1993), 12–15.

25. Marie Čermáková, "Rodina a zameštnané ženy," *Data & Fakta* 1 (January 1996): 4.

26. See Pavel Machonín and Milan Tuček, "Geneze nové sociální struktury v České republice a její sociálni akteři," *Sociologický časopis* 30, no. 3 (1994): 285–305, and Jiřina Šiklová, "Elderly Women—Second Class Citizens?" in *Bodies of Bread and Butter: Reconfiguring Women's Lives in the Post-Communist Czech Republic*, ed. Susanna Trnka with Laura Busheikin (Prague: Prague Gender Studies Centre, 1993), 63–68.

27. See Mary E. MacIntosh and Dina Smeltz, "Women on the Verge: Gender Role Attitudes and the Transition in Central and East Europe," manuscript, in MacIntosh's possession at Gallup, Inc., Princeton, N.J.; Wolchik, *Czechoslovakia in Transition*, chap. 2; and James R. Millar and Sharon L. Wolchik, "Introduction: The Social Legacies and the Aftermath of Communism," in *The Social Legacy of Communism*, ed. Millar and Wolchik (Washington, D.C.: Woodrow Wilson Center Press, 1994), 1–28. See also Zora Bútorová et al., *Ona a on na Slovensku* (Bratislava: Focus, 1996), 114–17.

28. See Paukert, "Changing Economic Status of Women," 275.

29. Ibid., 274–75.

30. Čermáková, "Gender, společnost a pracovní trh," 18.

31. Bútorová et al., *Ona a on na Slovensku*, 86.

32. Paukert, "Changing Economic Status of Women," 274.

33. Marie Čermáková, "Process of Developing Pro-women Policies in the Czech Republic," manuscript, Institute of Sociology, Czech Academy of Sciences, Prague, table 3.

34. Bútorová, *Ona a on na Slovensku*, 89.

35. Čermáková, "Process of Developing Pro-women Policies," 10.

36. For a discussion of the German case, see Dr. Ute Kretzschmer, "East Germany: Women and Employment under Change," paper presented at the conference "Can They Build a State without Us?: Women and German Unification," at Goethe House, New York, April 1993; see Wolchik, "Gender Issues during Transition," 151–52, for an overview.

37. Wolchik, "Gender Issues during Transition," 151, and Čermáková, "Process of Developing Pro-women Policies," table 1 and p. 11.

38. Bútorová, *Ona a on na Slovensku*, 86.

39. Marie Čermáková, "The Social and Economic Status of Women in Czechoslovakia before the Partition," in *Gains and Losses: Women and Transition in Eastern and Central Europe* (Bucharest: Metropol, 1994), 23, and "Process of Developing Pro-women Policies," 10.

40. *Czech the News: Newsletter of the Czech Republic* 3, no. 8 (1995): 8. For 1996, Eva Munk, "Unemployment Rate Remains Low—Perhaps Too Low for Employees," *Prague Post*, March 13–19, 1996, 18.

41. Munk, "Unemployment Rate Remains Low," 18.

42. Tlačová agentúra Slovenskej Republiky report, "Roznava, Trebisov, Rimavska Sobota, and Svidnik Have the Highest Rates of Unemployment," *Bratislava SME* (March 20, 1995): 3, reported as "Slight Dip in Unemployment Rate in Feb" in *FBIS-EEU-95-059*, March 28, 1995, 4.

43. "Report of Oxford Analytica," Oxford-based International Research Group, and "Slovakia: Unemployment Rate Rises to 12.5 percent in July," *FBIS-EEU-96-175-S*, Sep-

tember 3, 1996. See Wolchik, "Gender Issues during Transition," for a discussion of some of the problems involved in assessing labor force statistics in the region at present.

44. *World Labor Report, 1993* (Geneva: ILO, 1993); Paukert, "Changing Economic Status of Women," 249; information received from Liba Paukert, July 1994.

45. See Jacqueline Heinen, "The Reintegration into Work of Unemployed Women: Issues and Policies," in *Unemployment in Transition Countries: Transient or Persistent?* (Paris: Center for Cooperation with the Economies in Transition, OECD, 1994), 315.

46. See Čermáková, "Social and Economic Status of Women," 23.

47. Čermáková, "Process of Developing Pro-women Policies," 16–18, and Bútorová, *Ona a on na Slovensku,* 92–93.

48. Bútorová, *Ona a on na Slovensku,* 90–92.

49. See Paukert, "Changing Economic Status of Women," 259, 171. See also "Magistrat mesta Brna přijme právnika (muže)," *Lidové noviny,* April 12, 1993, 1.

50. See Paukert, "Changing Economic Status of Women," 261.

51. *Statistická ročenka České a Slovenské Federativní Republiky 1990* (Prague: SNTL–Nakladatelství technické literatury, 1990), 1902; *Statistická ročenka České Republiky 1993* (Prague: Český statistický uřad, 1993), 197. See also Paukert, "Changing Economic Status of Women," 263–68, and Wolchik, "Gender Issues during Transition," 163–64.

52. Machonín and Tuček, "Geneze nové sociální struktury v České republice," 293.

53. Čermáková, "Gender, společnost a pracovní trh," 18–19.

54. Machonín and Tuček, "Geneze nové sociální struktury v České republice," 294; see also Marie Čermáková, "Sociální postavení ženy v Československé společnosti," in *Každodenosť ženského světa: Problemy a pristupy* (Bratislava: Slovenská sociologická společnost pri SAV, sekcia ženy a rodiny, 1991), 5–6.

55. Čermáková, "Process of Developing Pro-women Policies," 15.

56. "The National Report on the Status of Women in the Slovak Republic to the Fourth UN Conference on Women in Beijing," Ministry of Foreign Affairs of the Slovak Republic, Bratislava; Centre for Strategic Studies of the Slovak Republic, February 1995, 11.

57. See Petr Matějů and B. Řeháková, "Od nespravedlivé rovnosti ke spravedlivé nerovnosti? Percepce sociálních nerovností a sociální spravedlnosti v současném Československu," *Sociologický časopis* 28, no. 3 (1992): 293–318, and Jiří Večerník, "Smeny v prijmové nerovnosti v letech 1988–1992," *Sociologický časopis* 28, no. 5 (1992): 666–84; see also Wolchik, "Gender Issues during Transition."

58. See Bunce and Csanádi, "Uncertainty in the Transition," and Wolchik, "The Politics of Transition in Central Europe," *Problems of Post-Communism* 42, no. 1 (1995): 35–40; see also Millar and Wolchik, "Introduction: The Social Legacies and the Aftermath of Communism." See also Hana Havelková, "Ignored but Assumed: Family and Gender between Public and Private Realm," *Czech Sociological Review* 4, no. 1 (1996): 77–78.

59. Marie Čermáková and Hana Navarová, "Ženy a volby 1990," manuscript, Sociology Institute, Prague.

60. Marie Čermáková and Lumír Gatnar, "Ženy v sociálni struktuře, 1991, Výzkum pracovních a životních podmínek žen v České republice a Slovenské republiky," Sociologický ústav ČSAV, Prague, 1992, 37. See also Čermaková and Navarová, "Ženy a volby 1990," and Bútorová, *Ona a on na Slovensku,* 150–52.

61. Cited in "Place des femmes dan les pays d'Europe Centrale" (Prague: STEM, 1993), 9.

62. Čermáková and Gatnar, "Ženy v sociální struktuře," 68–69.

63. "Place des femmes dans les pays d'Europe Centrale," 3.

64. Čermáková and Gatnar, "Ženy v sociální struktuře," 72.

65. Marie Čermáková, "Women in Czechoslovakia and Their Reflection of Human Rights," manuscript, Institute of Sociology, Czechoslovak Academy of Sciences, Prague, 1991, 4–5.

66. Čermáková, "Social and Economic Status of Women," 25.

67. Bútorová, *Ona a on na Slovensku*, 156–57. The Social Democratic Party proposed a quota for women as part of its 1996 election campaign.

68. See Wolchik, *Czechoslovakia in Transition*, chap. 2; Čermáková and Gatnar, "Ženy v sociální struktuře," 34.

69. See Wolchik, "Women and the Politics of Transition in the Czech and Slovak Republics," for a more detailed discussion of these differences. See also Bútorová, *Ona a on na Slovensku*, 114–17, for the results of surveys that confirm these finds.

70. MacIntosh and Smeltz, "Women on the Verge." See also Marie Čermáková, "Ženy a muži na trhu práce I.," *Data & Fakta* 6 (June 1996): 3, 4; Čermáková, "Ženy a muži na trhu práce II.," *Data & Fakta* 7 (September 1996): 1–4; and Bútorová, *Ona a on na Slovensku*, chap. 1.

71. All data are from Sharon L. Wolchik, Zora Bútorová, and Jan Hartl, "Citizen Attitudes and Political Values," data files. Only those differences that were statistically significant are reported.

72. Wolchik, "Women and the Politics of Transition in the Czech and Slovak Republics," 8.

73. Data taken from www.volby.cz.

74. Data taken from the Official Homepage of the Slovak Government (www. slovakia.eu.net), May 5, 1997.

75. "Meciar, Luptak, Slova Propose New Cabinet," in *FBIS-EEU-94-238*, December 12, 1994, 11.

76. Čermáková, "Process of Developing Pro-women Policies," 21.

77. Data from Slovak representatives to the UN Commission on the Status of Women, as reported in Naŝé slova (www.ns9704), March 1997.

78. Jindřiška Syllová, "Česká národní rada v roce 1990: Analýza složení a činnosti," *Sociologický časopis* 28, no. 2 (1992): 241–42.

79. Danica Siváková, "Slovenská národná rada: Analýza štruktúry a činnosti v roku 1990," *Sociologický časopis* 28, no. 2 (1992): 250.

80. "National Report on the Status of Women in the Slovak Republic," 12.

81. List of deputies as reprinted in *Aktivita* 1, no. 8 (October 1994): 3–4. See also data taken from the Official Homepage of the Slovak Government (www.slovakia.eu.net) May 5, 1997.

82. Information taken from the Election Server of the Central Electoral Commission (www.volby.cz), including data compiled by the Czech Statistical Office (accessed May 1997).

83. Wolchik, "Women and the Politics of Transition in the Czech and Slovak Republics" and "Women and the Politics of Transition in Central and Eastern Europe."

84. See Wolchik, "Status of Women in a Socialist Order" and "Ideology and Equality."

85. Wolchik, "Women and the Politics of Transition in the Czech and Slovak Republics," 8.

86. Information taken from the Election Server of the Central Electoral Commission (www.volby.cz), including data compiled by the Czech Statistical Office (accessed May 1997).

87. Data taken from the Official Homepage of the Slovak Government (www.slovakia.eu.net), May 5, 1997.

88. Marie Čermáková and Sharon Wolchik, data set from interviews with men and women leaders, Prague and Bratislava, 1995–96.

89. See Bútorová, *Ona a on na Slovensku*, 163–70, for information on popular attitudes toward feminism in Slovakia.

90. Čermáková et al., "Ženy v sociální struktuře," 37.

91. Ibid., 38.

92. Wolchik, Bútorová, and Hartl, "Citizen Attitudes and Political Values."

93. See Ol'ga Plávková, "The Present Trends in Creating a Women's Movement in Slovakia: Civil Society Approach," in *Každennosť ženského sveta: Problémy a prístupy* (Bratislava: Slovenska sociologická společnost, pri SAV, sekcia ženy a rodiny, 1991), 29–38, for an early analysis of women's organizations in Slovakia after 1989.

94. *Alty a soprany* (Prague: Gender Studies, 1994).

95. See Čermáková, "Social and Economic Status of Women," 24, for an analysis that concurs with this evaluation.

96. Sharon L. Wolchik, "Women's Roles in the Downfall of Communism in Central and Eastern Europe," Fourth World Conference of Slavic Studies, Harrogate, England, July 1990.

97. *Zpravodaj Pražských matek* 3, no. 10 (December 1993). Also, "Pražské matky," *Aspekt*, no. 1 (1994): 99.

98. Interview with Martina Holubová, Prague, March 1991.

99. See Alena Heitlinger, "The Impact of the Transition from Communism on the Status of Women in the Czech and Slovak Republics," in *Gender Politics and Post-Communism: Reflections from Eastern Europe and the Former Soviet Union*, ed. Nanette Funk and Magda Mueller (New York: Routledge, 1883), 95–108, for a discussion of this political party.

100. jas, "Ani feministky, ani 'kabrehelky," *Lidové noviny*, June 8, 1993, 1, 2.

101. See, for example, the January 1995 issue of *Sociologický časopis*, which is devoted to gender issues.

102. See Jána Hradilková, "The Discipline of Gender Studies," *One Eye Open* 1, no. 1 (1993): 39–41, for a brief account of the center's founding.

103. Marie Lienau, "proFem," in *Prelude: New Women's Initiatives in Central and Eastern Europe and Turkey* (Prague: Frauen-Anstiftung, 1994).

104. Jana Cviková, "Education and Information Center for Women: Aspekt in Bratislava," in *Prelude: New Women's Initiatives in Central and Eastern Europe and Turkey.*

105. See *Filozofický časopis* 40, no. 5 (1992), and *Slovenské pohľady na literatúru a umenie*, no. 11 (1991).

106. Interviews with Dagmira Šimunková and Anna Okhrulicová, Bratislava, April and June 1995; interviews with Ol'ga Plávková and Etela Farkašová, Bratislava, June 1992.

107. Quoted in Tatiana Rosová, "Ženy na Slovensku," *ASPEKT* (1993): 115.

108. Conference proceedings, Bratislava, June 9–11, 1995, and interview with Katarina Farkašová, Bratislava, December 1996.

109. There is no space in this chapter for a detailed discussion of the various understandings of and views about feminism of women's activists in the Czech and Slovak Republics. For examples of different perspectives, see Jiřina Šiklová, "Are Women in Central and Eastern Europe Conservative?" in Funk and Mueller, *Gender Politics and Post-Communism*, 74–83; Eva Hauserová, "Images from the Life of an Emancipated Woman," *One Eye Open* 1, no. 1 (1993): 31–38; and Havelková, "Family and Gender."

110. See Sharon L. Wolchik, "The Politics of Ethnicity in Post-Communist Czechoslovakia," in *East European Politics and Societies* 8, no. 1 (1994); see also Jiři Musil, ed., *The End of Czechoslovakia* (Budapest: Central European University Press, 1995), and Martin Bútora and Zora Bútorová, "The Identity Challenges of the Newly Born State," *Social Research* 60, no. 4 (1993): 705–36.

111. See Janusz Bugajski, *Ethnic Politics in Eastern Europe: A Guide to Nationality Policies, Organizations, and Parties* (Armonk, N.Y.: M. E. Sharpe, 1994), chap. 11, and Sharon L. Wolchik, "The Origins and Development of Slovak Nationalism," manuscript, Institute for European, Russian, and Eurasian Studies, George Washington University, Washington, D.C., 1995.

112. "Slovak Economic Monitor: Slovak Economy Turns Around Thanks to Impressive Trade Performance," in *PlanEcon Report*, September 9, 1994.

113. See MacIntosh and Smeltz, "Women on the Verge." Čermáková notes that although younger women often give voice to views concerning gender roles which reflect traditional expectations, such as those giving primacy to the family over work, many are in fact choosing to marry later and have fewer children, thus engaging in nontraditional behavior in practice.

114. Šiklová, "Are Women in Central and Eastern Europe Conservative?" 80.

Chapter Eight

Women and Democratization

Some Notes on Recent Changes in Hungary

JULIA SZALAI

hen the future of women in the post-Communist societies of Central and Eastern Europe comes up for consideration, most Western feminists express skepticism, disappointment, and worry. The words of Barbara Einhorn probably reflect the feelings of many of those who, for decades, compassionately watched and supported the struggles against Soviet-type totalitarianism yet are increasingly disillusioned by the actual developments since the collapse of the old rule:

> Where have all the women gone? This may be a frivolous question: they haven't evaporated after all. But what has evaporated, it seems, along with the euphoria and the optimism, the hopes and dreams . . . , is the energy and potential for change on the part of women themselves. Gone too are both the much-vaunted economic independence and the resultant self-confidence of forty years of official commitment to a policy of "emancipation" for women. . . . Will the need to shed labor push women out of the labor force and back into primary responsibility for the family? There are some signs that women themselves may accept this relegation with a sign of relief. What does this imply for our own views on what it means to be liberated? Women's role is very much in question in the current transition period in East Central Europe.[1]

The reasoning is clear: however important it might be from an economic perspective, the turn from "state socialism" to capitalism will destroy the relative advantages that women enjoyed under the old regime and will inevitably lead to a degradation of their situation. Thus, the women of Central and Eastern Europe soon will face all the problems and conflicts known and discussed by the rich feminist literature of the last two or three decades in the West.

Surprisingly enough, authors from the region seem to be deaf to these warnings. They (better to say we) feel some confusion and embarrassment while listening to these gloomy forecasts. Is that because of a lack of feminist tradition in this part of the world and, consequently, our short-sighted neglect of unrecognized dangers? Or is it because we have a different understanding of the main currents of our post-1989 history? Perhaps both factors play some role. In any case, both explanations for the divergent evaluations prompt a series of further questions.

This chapter offers an alternative interpretation of women's reactions to the ongoing changes. I also hope to contribute to a better understanding of some of the deep-rooted political and sociological reasons for the lack of interest in mainstream feminism in Central and Eastern Europe.

The chapter first presents a historical overview of how women coped with their forced "emancipation" from above, which created unbearable circumstances in their daily lives. It illustrates the political functions of the family under Communism and argues that for many, this core institution of "private" life has long been the only secure form of self-protection against oppression from above. In other words, withdrawal to the private sphere was the only secure way of preserving a certain degree of safety and autonomy. The major roots of the communication gap between women in the East and West probably lie here, that is, in their entirely disparate experiences in the decisive domains of work outside the household and family life.

This brief historical outline, based on evidence drawn from the past decades of Hungarian society, is followed by an analysis of some of the consequences of the politicized functions of the family in the current post-Communist period. I apply a broadened concept of political participation to analyze some trends in post-1989 political life. The changing patterns of female employment and the increased role of women in local politics are discussed as alternative means of expressing civil interest in a society in which suspicion toward the "official" channels of political decision making is widespread and is reinforced by people's day-to-day experience. The empirical evidence for gradual democratic development from below is drawn from a brief overview of women's increased participation in community-based politics and in the ongoing reform of local social policy.

SILENT POLITICAL OPPOSITION
AND THE EROSION OF COMMUNISM

Political analysts of the events of 1989–90 face substantial difficulties in applying conventional concepts of political theory to the collapse of Communism in Hungary. Systemic changes in the structure of political power were not preceded by any revolutionary struggles or even by clamorous mass demonstrations, strikes, or other symptoms of massive political dissatisfaction. After 40 years of unbroken centralized one-party rule, a series of peaceful negotiations between the Communist party and the most influential dissident groups led the way to a multiparty-based parliamentary democracy. However, a reformist approach also fails to give an adequate theoretical framework. It is true that important economic reforms had been introduced throughout the 1980s, but the clear political intention of these was to prolong the monopoly of political control of the Communist party over society. Thus, the reforms were aimed at preventing rather than assisting any "dangerous" modifications of the political system.

If neither the concept of revolution nor that of gradual reforms can be applied when interpreting the events of 1989–90, how can one explain the radical turn from a totalitarian to a democratic political order? The response has to be found in historical analysis of the preceding decades, which cannot be understood without a brief overview of the lasting sociopolitical impact of the 1956 revolution. The 33 years of Kádárism (the politics of János Kádár, head of the Hungarian Socialist Workers' Party between 1956 and 1988) were characterized by continuous attempts to resolve an unresolvable political paradox: the perfection of totalitarianism through its day-to-day questioning. This paradox is the key to the peculiarity of Hungarian socialism and also to the surprisingly peaceful character of its disappearance by the end of the 1980s.

To make this statement clear, one has to look at the politically driven innovation of Kádárism, particularly its attempt to consolidate the relationship between the ruling party and the defeated society, which was in silent, though full and lasting, opposition to it. By claiming to recast the fundamental rights to personal freedom, national independence, and multiparty-based democracy, the revolution of 1956 was the first and, until recently, the only radical grassroots critique of and real threat to the openly totalitarian way of governance in the Soviet-type societies of Central and Eastern Europe. The unanimous nationwide refusal of any forms of "blissful" oppression in the name of the sanctified goals of the "collective" was unquestionable. Although the victory of civil society lasted for only two weeks and the power base of the totalitarian reign was successfully reconstructed by Hungarian and Soviet military forces, the messages of the revolution never could be forgotten.

The effort to create a delicate balance between subordination and permissiveness on the part of those in power held true also for the first grandiose actions to stabilize Communist rule. Among these the most important was the campaign intended to accomplish the "socialist social revolution" through the full collectivization of agriculture between 1958 and 1963. Although the abolition of privately owned land was part of the Communist program to extend the all-embracing control of the party-state over each member of society, and although it was implemented by the "classical" methods of forced expropriation and compulsion, there were surprising concessions built into the process in Hungary: all the members of the newly organized cooperatives were permitted to withhold a small plot (at most one acre) for private cultivation.

This concession to "private ownership" turned out to be crucial for later social developments. The privately controlled plots slowly became the foundation of the second economy, which played a critical role in the rapid modernization and material progress of the country, as well as in the gradual emergence of alternative, "private" pathways for promotion, prestige, and success. Thus, the incremental expansion of the informal economy served as a base for increasing independence from the formally regulated, "collective" domain of social life. This growing independence gradually reduced the scope of interventions in the name of absolute control from above. After all, the process resulted in a substantial weakening of the actual power of the Communist party and an ultimate erosion of its totalitarian efforts. Although this fact was not openly spelled out until the very last days of the regime, people were always aware that their private actions were alien—even in opposition—to the system.

The silent though obvious political meaning of their daily exodus to devote the greater bulk of their energy and time to privately designed goals and activities was clearly expressed in thousands of different forms, including the distinct language of verbal and symbolic communication in their formal, as opposed to their informal, settings.[2] At the same time, these clear distinctions and rigid demarcation lines between the "public," which belongs to "them," and the "private," which is "ours," helped both the rulers and the ruled to administer the principally unmanageable, above-indicated political paradox.

It is important to emphasize that the consolidation of the 1960s did not lead to any fundamental changes in the functioning of the socialist system. The centralization of power, anonymous (party-)state ownership of most property, paramilitary way of administering economic and social life from the top, and direct intervention in everyday production and distribution continued to determine the scope of "independent" institutional actions, as well as the established framework of personal life.

Innovation—and the key to the success of Kádárism—lay in the actual content and the everyday meaning of the fragile compromise between the party and society. The essence of this compromise was a tacit acceptance and even a gradual expansion of the space for individual autonomy, based on the ideological and practical "rehabilitation" of the only institution that was legitimately independent of direct political control: the family.

Nobody could foresee the extent of the change which these apparently minor political concessions induced in the everyday life of the country. The regained freedom for privacy, in an exchange for the unreserved fulfillment of one's duties in the socialist domain, activated tremendous capacity. Given the deeply rooted motivations of the material, cultural, and symbolic pursuit of "Europeanism" in broad layers of Hungarian society, a great and increasing number of families were able to combine their compulsory participation in formal "socialist" institutions with a working out of alternative cultural patterns, values, skills, and routes for social mobility based largely on their restricted independence in the second economy.

Participation in informal productive activities geared toward individually chosen goals slowly developed into a vast social movement. Families began to organize their internal division of roles, education, and training for their children, their decisions about jobs that could or could not be accepted by their members, and priorities in spending money and time according to a rationale that was clearly driven by their personal concept of modernity, although this concept was often in contradiction to the officially declared expectations of the authorities. These diverging aspirations and expectations became the grounds for bargaining. Bosses had to accept the seasonal dictates of small-scale agricultural production in designing production plans for their firms. Otherwise they risked losing their workers, who could easily move to another workplace amid the chronic labor shortage in socialist industries. For their part, the bosses found that the threat to withdraw the tacit permission to spend working time on informal rather than official activities was the most effective way to punish "undeserving" behavior in the workplace. Thus, people were continuously disciplined to observe the expected "socialist" norms. The coexistence and mutual adjustment of the two distinct spheres of life had to be taken by all the partners as the basic guiding principle in the delicate day-to-day political game.

Given their traditional key functions in the family, women played an outstanding role here. They not only shared the massive workload required to combine gainful activities in the two spheres of the economy but also became the organizers and managers of the difficult tasks that families faced in coordinating contradictory rules, principles, goals, and duties. The otherwise patriarchal division of roles turned into a source of relative freedom: women gained somewhat more space and an acceptable "excuse" to withdraw from time to time from the formal segments of production. Slowly, these "excuses" for temporary withdrawal from compulsory employment became semilegalized through a series of new employment regulations. The most important was the introduction of the child care grant, a job-protected social security benefit facilitating home care for the child in the first three years of life. Due to its success and popularity, the first step was shortly followed by others pointing in the same direction.[3] For example, centrally administered job contracts started to incorporate extra paid sick leave to take care of sick schoolchildren or other family members; regulations on early retirement were gradually eased; and various forms of part-time employment were introduced for those living on pensions.[4] In all these cases, the ties to the formal segment of social life were maintained. Open and definite withdrawal was politically unacceptable and would have conflicted also with the macroeconomic need for an unlimited pool of easily available labor, but the possibilities for putting one's energy temporarily into the private side were greatly expanded, and the right to do so was tacitly acknowledged.

True, the easing of full-fledged compulsory participation in the "socialist" arena was gender- and age-biased: it applied mainly to women and elderly male workers. It is also true that while these concessions somewhat liberated them from direct control over their daily lives, they became the formal excuse for promoting women more slowly, paying them less, and providing them with fewer channels for occupational mobility. At the same time, however, the performance of the family enterprises run under the administration of these "liberated" family members became a source of self-esteem and prestige. Each tree on the plot, each brick in the newly built family house, each piece of modern equipment in the garden or the home justified their efforts and the advancement of their families. They could never have achieved so much had they relied exclusively on formal work and the earnings derived from it.

Besides being proof of material progress, the increase of private consumption had another significance: it expressed alternative notions about modernization, induced and realized alternative taste (opposing the cultural patterns dictated by the authorities in control of the public realm), created a scope for alternative socialization of children, and helped people to acquire forms of alternative knowledge which they could never get in the officially run educational institutions.

This evolution of alternative concepts of living proved to be crucial politically, economically, socially, and culturally alike. First of all, it gradually undermined the very premise of the delicate compromise, which was designed to prevent alternative communities from emerging to challenge the omnipotence of control from above. There were two competing political drives that continuously clashed throughout the entire period of Kádárism. On the one hand, the totalitarian principle required the maintenance of as much direct intervention by the party-state as possible; on the other hand, the pursuit of post-1956 consolidation dictated efforts to promote an increase in living standards through the liberalization of family-based production. But the latter goal could not be met according to the guiding principles of the former: a modern society could not be confined within the four walls of the home.

Leaving aside the political implications for a moment, the plain technical realities of everyday life contradicted any such attempts. Given the unchanged conditions of low and rigidly controlled wages, compulsory full-time jobs in state-run workplaces, and the prevention of private capital accumulation, people had neither the financial resources nor the time to fulfil the tasks of the "officially permitted" home-based production. The only resource at their disposal was well-organized cooperation within their informal networks. However, this cooperation could not be restricted to one's own family and kin. The incorporation of a wide range of skills, knowledge, and qualifications was a natural development. It was governed by the efficient rules of personal favors and obligations among neighbors, workmates, friends, colleagues, and other companions in competition with the control that the state exhibited over these relations. There were deep-rooted patterns to be mobilized in these rapidly evolving secondary structures of interpersonal relations: the quickly developing new forms of work exchange evolved from the well-elaborated and purposefully revitalized peasant culture of Hungarian society.[5]

Traditional mechanisms for saving capital and substituting labor for cash flow turned out to have great potential and proved to be flexible enough to absorb people's newly acquired experiences with modern industrial techniques and services. Standards of productivity rapidly exceeded those in various industries of the formal economy, giving rise to further expansion. By the mid-1980s, three-quarters of households were already engaged in some form of informal production and collected substantial income from it. Thus, it is not an exaggeration to say that participation in the family-based economy gradually became the organizing principle of everyday life, which substantially reduced people's defenselessness against the official authorities and efficiently counteracted attempts at political intervention from above.

In addition to the political and economic implications, these developments had significant cultural impacts. The latter became especially important for women, the main organizers of the complicated family enterprise. Contrary to the widely expressed concern that women were losing the advantages of "socialist emancipation," the lengthy stay at home on child care leave and other occasional temporary returns to family duties did not imprison them in the household. Rather, these periods of withdrawal from their mostly dull, rigid, humiliating, and exhausting formal work facilitated a substantial accumulation of capacities and knowledge.[6]

In addition to the primary purpose of their home stay, for example, to care for children or the sick, women started to use their "liberated" time to help the ongoing family business. By doing so, they slowly acquired a wide range of new skills and became experts in market-oriented management in a formally "nonmarket" economy. While at home, they learned the complicated bookkeeping of work exchange and money spending, became experts in stretching the limited financial resources that had to cover both daily consumption and long-term investments in the small-scale business (thereby acquiring substantial marketable knowledge in acquisition and banking), learned to negotiate with the various authorities (thus developing skills in bargaining and administration), and, above all, developed a whole range of personal and consulting services for others in a similar situation. As subsequent time-budget surveys show, both the rates of participation and the average time devoted to these types of market-related services grew among women across the social spectrum. Moreover, the respective figures indicate great uniformity across classical sociological dimensions such as educational level, occupational status, and the urban-versus-rural character of settlement.[7]

These newly accumulated skills and knowledge gradually spilled over into the formal sphere as well. Women returning from child care leave and taking their children to the state-run kindergartens had to face a significant drop in standards: both the physical conditions and the educational spirit were far below the level of the self-organized child care facilities in the community. After a while the authorities could not contain the informal pressure of parents' groups. Squeezed between earnest claims from below and permanent financial restrictions from above, they had to open the doors of day care centers to the massive voluntary work of parents, who in turn gradually began to shape the life of these institutions according to the higher, modernized standards of private homes. They began to supplement the low budget of kindergartens by equipping them with high-quality tools, toys, and supplies; organized assistance to take the children to nearby swimming pools; and offered labor and financial help to enlarge the buildings.[8]

Informal modernization slowly reached schools and other public services—the rise of community control could no longer be restrained. Neighborhoods started to mobilize the available informal network of expertise to build an extra room for gymnastics in the rundown nearby primary school for maintaining the "private" norms of leisure; they figured out ways to organize extra language courses and raised the necessary resources from donations or at their workplaces; they formed commissions to negotiate with the local educational authorities about improving the quality of day care after teaching hours and organized the necessary staff.[9]

Similar examples can also be drawn from health care, where the discrepancies between "public" and "private" standards were probably even greater. Rundown state-administered hospitals struggling with chronic shortages of resources and personnel had to tolerate the presence of relatives in the wards, who gradually organized themselves into a group of caretakers. These spontaneously formed pressure groups began to negotiate standards for meals, claimed the right to choose the place and form of treatment, and demanded the use of Western medicine, which they offered to "import" while away on holidays.[10]

In short, the higher norms introduced from private homes progressively filtered into even the most strictly controlled institutions and services. In this way, the initially rigid borderline between the state-dominated "public" and the individually controlled "private" spheres slowly blurred, and the latter, imperceptibly at first, began to regulate the former. As the result of their expertise in home-run services, women became the major activists in this great voluntary movement. Their involvement crossed the social divisions of age, education, occupation, income, and type of settlement. The forms of women's participation were naturally colored by these factors, but the underlying values and motivations showed a great deal of uniformity. It is important to emphasize that despite the clear political implications, the ongoing struggle to draw the state-run domain under informal control did not take the form of open political conflict: the arguments were merely "pragmatic" on both sides. However, the consequences were of basic political importance. These spontaneous arrangements gradually eroded exclusive state control over fundamental spheres of people's lives and slowly produced full-fledged community-based alternatives.

On the basis of these developments, one can state that the transition toward an alternative system began several decades prior to the withering away of Communism. The systemic changes of 1989–90 were the completion rather than the start of a massive transformation; they opened the route to establish an adequate political framework for the social and economic conversion of Hungarian society which had already been accomplished.

ECONOMIC AND POLITICAL DEVELOPMENTS IN WOMEN'S LIVES AFTER 1989

Women's participation in the silent social movement of dismantling the old system at its base in Hungary left a deep imprint on the changes in their economic and social situation after 1989. In contrast to the situation in most of the post-Communist countries of the region, in Hungary, open marketization has not led to a dramatic worsening of women's conditions. In fact, the lasting economic crisis has tended to work more to the detriment of men. The stability of the positions they once had achieved, the unquestioned prestige of their former occupational status, and the regularity and the security of their "deserved" higher earnings seem to have vanished rapidly with the devaluation of "socialist" accomplishments. And although economic restructuring has hit large numbers of female jobs (especially unskilled and semiskilled jobs in state-run firms in industry), both self-reported and registered unemployment has been consistently lower among women than men.

The 1990 census registered a self-reported unemployment rate of 10.3 percent for men, for example, but only 1.7 percent among women. Unemployment has increased significantly since then and has affected increasing numbers of both sexes. Nevertheless, these gender differences seem to persist: while the proportion of registered unemployed was 12.7 percent in the male workforce in early 1995, it remained somewhat below 10 percent among women.[11] Given the worsening opportunities for gainful employment, one would expect a significant rise in the ratio of housewives. However, such an increase has not occurred. In fact, the opposite tendency has been observed in the last few years. The already low rate of women aged 14–55 who were housewives in 1989 (4.4%) fell to 3.5 percent by 1994.[12]

If they are neither at work nor in the household, where are the great masses of semiskilled and unskilled female laborers of yesterday? The answer is that they are making more intense use of the long-elaborated channels for partial withdrawal from employment and purposefully "converting" earlier accumulated marketable skills. Women's "secondary status" in socialist employment seems to have become a definite advantage in the post-Communist period. As a result of their earlier experiences outlined above, women have more numerous channels than men through which to find at least temporary solutions to prevent the withering away of income security and to preserve their relative gains, including access to a wide range of free public services, loans from banks, and housing subsidies.

Sporadic statistical evidence confirms these statements. Women are choosing, at steadily increasing rates, to exit from employment through the "traditional" schemes of social security. Despite a substantial decrease in annual birthrates between 1990 and 1995, the proportion of those on child care leave rose from 4.1 percent to 4.7 percent of the total labor force as more women have used this pathway to avoid dismissals. The so-called nursing fee paid since 1989 for long-term home care for sick or elderly people has similar functions: it has been used by more than a hundred thousand middle-aged women, who see in it a chance to convert "customary" unpaid family duties into "ordinary" respected occupations, thus providing regular contributions to the family budget and simultaneously safeguarding personal financial independence. The list continues: the number of those drawing disability benefits from social security 5 to 10 years before becoming eligible for old-age pensions grew by 31 percent between 1989 and 1992; the ratio of those covered by the numerous new firm-based early retirement schemes increased by 70 percent between 1990 and 1992. Taking all forms of early exit from the labor force together, the number of women making use of these possibilities increased by 90 percent between 1989 and 1995; the respective ratio among men was 43 percent.[13] In short, one can say that, by using the "old" and "customary" techniques of retreat, women were able to attenuate the negative effects of dismissals and avoid the rather poor and vague programs that have been developed to address unemployment.

Although the massive claims represented by these figures indicate perhaps unsustainable obligations for the government and have some role in the continuous increase of the state budget deficit (and thus in the acceleration of inflation), they also demonstrate women's long-practiced and lively skills of self-protection. People are well aware that anything is better than going on the dole. And the accumulated experience of the past few years confirms their evaluation. Booming chronic unemployment, poor and underdeveloped retraining schemes, and the bankruptcy of most of the large state-run firms have shattered hopes for getting back to work through ordinary channels. At the same time, the private segment of the economy is not yet strong and large enough to provide a substitute for all. In this situation any means to prolong at least some loose ties with state-run institutions to secure income and to maintain the sense of "full social membership" seems to be the most "rational" tactic for survival. Thanks to their long practice in these techniques, women appear to enjoy a significant advantage.

The purposeful conversion of previously accumulated knowledge and skills also helps women in today's conditions. Even though overall unemployment is increasing, it is accompanied by a great demand for labor in those areas in which socialist economic policy chronically neglected investments and development. The poor quality of public infrastructure and the serious underdevelopment of services seem to be among the most severe obstacles to a smooth structural adjustment in the current phase of economic transformation. Investment in these spheres is expanding even amid the overall chronic shortage of capital. At the same time, these are the areas in which women had gained a great deal of experience in the decade-long development and expansion of small-scale informal production. Their never-registered "qualifications" are easily mobilizable and adaptable, opening for them relatively favorable employment opportunities in new segments of the market.

The impact of previously accumulated experiences and their conversion to "ordinary" gainful work have played the greatest role in the rapid expansion of the service sector. Between 1980 and 1994, the share of this sector in overall employment rose from 40 percent to 60 percent. This development was due to a large extent to the appearance of industries and occupations that did not exist before 1990. Activities like acting as agents for domestic and foreign firms, financial planning, advertising, tax consulting, and working in employment offices have all been induced by needs that the turn toward open marketization has brought about. Further, a vast new area of employment has been opened in public and social services. The decentralization of public administration, health care, welfare assistance, and educational services has led to an increased need for nurses, home health care providers, and social workers.[14]

True, such employment is rarely secure and stable. But since women are customarily regarded as "secondary earners" within the family, they can more easily accept even those part-time forms of gainful employment which would be unacceptable to men. In addition, their long-established routine in home-based management and administration helps them to find the most flexible and "rational" combinations of various partial jobs. Clerical work in the morning, cleaning in the afternoon, a few hours of paid phone service for a lawyer while cooking the meal for the family, and baby-sitting in the evening are frequent combinations of gainful activities of younger and elderly women nowadays, who often see the only difference between the past and present as getting paid something for doing what they used to do for a long time free of charge. Data from a countrywide representative time-budget survey conducted in 1993 indicate that many women combine a main job with various partial jobs. Although the concrete content of the combined activities differs in different socioeconomic surroundings (more agricultural work in rural settings; more work in personal services in urban ones, for example), the amount of time devoted to them does not show any systematic differences in the various age groups or according to occupation or level of education.[15]

All in all, the home-based female strategies of adaptation and the family-bound forms of women's self-protection have remained relevant despite the collapse of the political regime that inspired their evolution several decades ago. This is perhaps the main reason why Hungarian women show little interest in responding to the call of the few feminist groups that have recently emerged. Although associations with the aim of organizing efficient pressure groups in defense of women's interests were formed by small numbers of devoted and militant professional women in all the university centers and in other towns, most such initiatives have failed.

Several factors explain this failure. Perhaps the lack of a tradition of feminist discourse has to be mentioned in the first place. Claiming distinct rights for women is generally seen as an expression of hostility toward the family in Hungary. It implies the act of breaking apart. When spelling out certain social, economic, and political problems that are specifically bound to women's positions, feminists are frequently blamed in the mass media for undermining the role of the family in defending its members and general social cohesion. Even the recent public debate on the legal regulations of abortion was put into a family framework, where a woman's right to control her body and way of living hardly ever came up for consideration.

A second reason for the low interest in women's issues might be the absence of a tradition of feminist movements. Although such movements were rather important at the turn of the century, later historical developments, including the victory of right-wing political parties and the emergence of strong anti-Semitism in the 1920s, which was followed by a fascist takeover and Hungary's shameful participation in World War II, swept them away. Thus, the postwar generations of women had nothing on which to build. Further, Communist propaganda concerning women's emancipation compromised the remnants of the tradition. The patterns of employment, schooling, and child care which were imposed during the Communist period made the widely claimed goals of feminism subject to general hatred.

The general distrust of political movements also affects attitudes toward feminist groups. The widespread conviction of Hungarians that the only efficient way to achieve one's goals is through individual bargains seemed to be challenged by the colorful movements of the late 1980s. However, most of these movements soon disintegrated as the result of unresolvable internal conflicts and rapid bureaucratization, which gave rise to suspicion and reinforced the truth of the old wisdom "you simply can't trust outsiders." As public opinion polls show repeatedly, contemporary Hungarians are generally disinterested in politics, and people look at all sorts of political activists with a great deal of skepticism.[16]

As a result of these factors, the militancy of feminist initiatives has decreased since 1990, and most feminist groups have dissolved or have become nonpoliticized discussion clubs. The few exceptions are those that provide services for women in need. Shelters for battered or homeless women are functioning in a great number of localities, for example. The newly created association NANE (Women Together with Women against Violence) organizes counseling and legal advice in Budapest and in several other cities. The Hungarian Women's Association, the reformed offspring of the old Communist organization, the National Council of Hungarian Women, runs a great variety of special courses for women through its well-established and well-preserved network. Although these groupings generally hide their feminist orientation and put the emphasis on the pragmatic side of their activities, they often still face the threat of isolation in the hostile political climate around them.

Nor do women appear to be attracted to the more classical forms of political participation, at least as indicated by their serious underrepresentation in party politics. According to the usual standards of measuring political representation, women really seem to have "disappeared" from the core of decision making. In the last elections under socialism in 1985, women won 27 percent of parliamentary seats and 21 percent of positions in local governments. The free elections in 1990 reduced female representation to 7.3 percent in parliament and 16 percent at the local level. These figures rose to about 11 percent and nearly 20 percent, respectively, in 1994. It has to be noted, however, that even in the much liberalized political climate of 1985 the attainable ratios of designated groups (women, youth, blue-collar workers, ethnic minorities, and the like) were centrally prescribed and strictly administered by the local committees of the Communist party. No attempt was made to reflect a "true" representation of any of the target groups. Rather, the candidates were chosen either because of their expressed loyalty to the party or because they were expected to play some "buffer role" in the community, transmitting dictates from above in a "smooth" and acceptable manner.[17]

These statistics have to be interpreted, however, with some caution. One has to take into account the markedly different previous experiences that have shaped current differences in men's and women's attitudes toward party politics. Because of the alternative pathways of social mobility discussed above, participation in formal politics, which served as a prerequisite for promotion in the hierarchy, was seen as less "compulsory" for women than for men in the old regime. Women gained some prestige and were looked upon with some jealousy because they had the freedom to say "no" to the dubious invitation to party membership which men could not refuse without risking their position. While women always had the "good excuse" of their multiple family obligations to avoid an unpleasant and humiliating political dialogue with the boss of the local Communist party organization, men's attempts to refuse often led to open political confrontation. This situation created nearly irresolvable dilemmas: either a moral price had to be paid, or long-term disadvantages had to be faced. Both options entailed a great deal of frustration, concluding frequently in severe conflicts even within the private sphere.

These frustrations played an important role in the characteristic male re-actions to the collapse of Communism. The rapid emergence of the new parties promised to correct unjustly broken careers. Within a short time, party politics became an arena in which men's needs could be met. Thousands of previously nonexistent posts were opened, offering dignified and responsible positions to a great number of well-educated, politically motivated men who earlier could not find acceptable forums to realize their ideas. This same situation, however, reinforced women's skepticism toward party politics. While they often support husbands in their acceptance of long-deserved positions offered on the basis of political loyalty during past "hard times," most women would probably never even think of a similar course for themselves. To women, the newly formed par-ties are not the embodiments of diverse social, economic, and political interests or alternative visions of social development. Rather, they are currently instru-mental channels for correcting certain "masculine" patterns of occupational mobility, and women seek professional advancement elsewhere. When asked about their motivations, women would generally emphasize the negative as-pects of daily politics: it is too time consuming and cannot be combined easily with their family duties; the political arena is too competitive and full of harsh actions and is thus alien to the socially accepted norms of female behavior; there is too much hierarchy and authority within the parties, and these would threaten personal independence; direct participation in politics would require women to give up the "feminine" way of negotiation and would lead to solitude in social life.

Women's abstention from full-time political careers does not indicate a lack of interest in politics, however. Although women refuse to fill posts in the political arena, they express definite opinions about the formation of the power structure. This fact is clearly expressed by their voting behavior. Both in 1990 and 1994, when high proportions of the electorate voted in the parliamentary elec-tions (more than 60% in both cases), women participated at a rate equal to that of men regardless of age, occupation, or place of dwelling. Regularly conducted public opinion polls do not indicate any decline in women's willingness to main-tain their political influence in such indirect ways. Immediately after the systemic changes of 1989–90, women seemed to favor those political groups that had ex-pressed some commitment to pronounced reforms in social policy.[18] However, quarterly opinion polls conducted after the 1994 elections indicate that posi-tioning on the liberal-conservative political axis does not show gender-based party preferences anymore. At present, women's voting behavior and political options seem to be rather similar to those of their husbands or men with simi-lar sociodemographic backgrounds.[19]

Besides making their views known, women's political participation is concentrated in areas outside the formalized spheres of party politics. Tens of thousands of freshly organized associations, local-level chambers, and single-issue nongovernmental organizations (NGOs) seem to rely heavily on women's work. Women also hold many jobs that cross party lines in various committees of the local governments. Women's contrasting experiences in the formal and informal settings seem to bear fruit here: they make good use of their accumulated knowledge in mobilizing the "sleeping" potential of local communities.

Despite women's low representation in elected political bodies, they participate intensely in the professional administration of local governments. We found in our recent countrywide survey that women represent 34 percent of the nonelected part-time members of the local social policy commissions; their proportion is more than 50 percent in every fifth such board. A comparison of per capita social spending by local governments shows significantly higher standards where women are the majority in the decision-making bodies. Their presence safeguards a sufficient level of expenditures on the modernization of local child care facilities, day centers, and homes for the elderly. Similarly, welfare assistance reaches more of the needy and gives them more efficient support in those communities in which women determine the orientation of local politics.[20] These socially "sensitive" political bodies are also usually more open to civil initiatives, thus inviting an even larger circle of women into the shaping of community life.[21]

True, these decentralized experiences have not yet been translated into powerful representation on the national level. It is also true that the low rates of female participation in leading positions in the arena of national decision making may create tensions in the long run. However, women themselves seem to be aware of these dangers and react accordingly when necessary. Otherwise "silent" masses of women played an active role in passage of a liberal new law on abortion in June 1993, for example. Their immense protests against any restrictions helped divert the initially strong conservative drives of the 1990–94 government and have contributed to a significant rise of state spending on much-neglected counseling and preventive services ever since. Women's open support for the new free trade unions in their fights against dismissals and the success of repeated massive strikes of railway workers, nurses, and teachers are other instances of women's intense political participation.

All these examples point in the same direction: no, women have not evaporated. However, they express their presence and political will in ways that are different from those of men—or of their sisters in long-established Western democracies. Whether these marked differences will persist or disappear remains open, but overall pessimism is certainly unwarranted.

NOTES

1. Barbara Einhorn, "Where Have All the Women Gone?" *Feminist Review* (London), no. 39 (1991): 16–36.

2. See, e.g., Tibor Kuczi and Ágnes Vajda, "Privatizáció és második gazdaság," *Holmi* (Budapest) 4, no. 1 (1992): 85–118; László Gábor and Júlia Szalai, "Az én ötvenhatom, a te ötvenhatod, az ő ötvenhatjuk," *2000* (Budapest), no. 1 (1994): 11–21.

3. Six years after the introduction of the child care grant in 1973, three-quarters of young mothers already made use of it for at least a part of the three-year period. This rate increased to nearly 90 percent by 1986. See *A gyermekgondozási díj igénybevétele és hatásai* (Budapest: CSO, 1988).

4. The scope of this chapter does not allow me to discuss at length the multifaceted advantages and the concurrent negative side effects of these developments. While they assisted the combination of formal and informal labor force participation on the individual level, they also facilitated a more flexible and effective employment policy in socialist firms; furthermore, they proved to be useful in substituting central investments for a great variety of state-run services in child and health care, in construction, and so on. The dubious outcome of the latter aspect was an unstoppable degradation of public infrastructure, a significant increase in inequalities in standards of and access to various services, and an unnoticed, gradual "conversion" of the actual functions of social security. The last development resulted in a serious devaluation of benefits in cash, impoverishing those who lacked alternative resources and depended exclusively on central redistribution. For a detailed discussion, see Julia Szalai, "Hungary: Exit from State Economy," in *Time for Retirement*, ed. Martin Kohli et al. (New York: Cambridge University Press, 1991), 324–64, and Eva Orosz and Julia Szalai, "Social Policy in Hungary," in *The New Eastern Europe*, ed. Bob Deacon et al. (London: Sage, 1992), 144–66.

5. The historical roots, their purposeful modern adaptation, and the internal structure of work exchange are discussed exhaustively in Endre Sík, "Munkacsere Tiszaigaron," *Szociológia* (Budapest) 3, no. 1 (1981): 7–18.

6. Compulsory employment of women meant in effect their incorporation into the least-qualified segments of the economy. Although their educational levels rose continuously, the quality of the work they had to do within the socialist workplaces remained very poor, both in physical conditions and in content. This situation is reflected in the fact that, according to census data, unqualified blue- and white-collar workers represented 48 percent of the female labor force even in 1990, while the respective figure for men had dropped to 27 percent by that time.

7. See *Időgazdálkodás és munkatevékenységek* (Budapest: CSO and Institute of Sociology–HAS, 1989), and *A magyar társadalom életmódjának változásai az 1976–77. évi és az 1986–87. évi idömérlegfelvételek alapján* (Budapest: CSO and Institute of Sociology–HAS, 1990).

8. See the case studies done as part of a countrywide investigation on the functioning of public kindergartens in 1978–80 (manuscript, Department of Sociology, ELTE, Budapest, 1980). For a summary, see Júlia Szalai, "Mire kell az óvoda és kinek?" in *Nők és férfiak*, ed. Katalin Koncz (Budapest: MNOT-Kossuth, 1985), 196–212.

9. See the series of case studies produced by a team of sociologists between 1978 and 1990 about changes in the functioning of locally run public institutions in various set-

tlements of Veszprém, Somogy, and Heves Counties and in Budapest. For a summary of the main findings, see Gábor Vági, *Magunk, uraim* (Budapest: Gondolat, 1991).

10. See, e.g., Éva Orosz, *Egészségügyi rendszerek és reformtörekvések* (Budapest: PTI, 1992).

11. See Teréz Laky, *A munkaerõpiac keresletét és kínálatát alakító folyamatok* (Budapest: Labor Research Institute, 1996).

12. The categorization applied in labor statistics measures the size of the potential labor force by the number of those who fall between the age limits of compulsory primary education and retirement. In the case of women, pensions can be drawn from the age of 55. See *A nemzetgazdaság munkaerõmérlege, 1994. január 1.* (Budapest: CSO, 1994), and *A munkanélküliség és a foglalkoztatottság alakulása* (Budapest: CSO, 1994).

13. See Laky, *A munkaerõpiac keresletét és kínálatát alakító folyamatok.*

14. For a detailed discussion of these new developments, see János Tímár, "A foglalkoztatás és a munkanélküliség sajátosságai a posztszocialista országokban," *Közgazdasági Szemle* (Budapest), nos. 7–8 (1994): 633–47, and Judit Ványai and Erzsébet Viszt, "A szolgáltatások növekvõ szerepe," *Közgazdasági Szemle* (Budapest), nos. 7–8 (1995): 777–87.

15. See *A magyar társadalom életmódjának változásai az 1976–77., az 1986–87. és az 1993. évi életmód-idõmérleg felvételek alapján. I. A Társadalmi idõ felhasználása* (Budapest: CSO, 1994).

16. For a detailed discussion of the causes beyond the lack of interest in feminism, see Mária Neményi, "Miért nincs Magyarországon nõmozgalom?" in *Férfiuralom,* ed. Miklós Hadas (Budapest: Replika Kör, 1994), 235–45.

17. For a detailed discussion, see Ágnes Vajda, "Nõk a politikai színfalak nögött?" *Magyar Nõk Lapja* (Budapest), no. 7 (1992): 23–26; István Sebestény, "Az 1994-es magyar parlamenti választások képviselõjelöltjeinek társadalmi jellemzõi," in *Magyarország politikai évkönyve, 1995,* ed. Sándor Kurtán et al. (Budapest: Hungarian Center of the Foundation for Democracy Studies, 1995), 419–34; and János Bocz, "Helyi hatalmi elit, polgármesterek és önkormányzati képviselõk, 1994," in *Magyarország politikai évkönyve, 1996,* ed. Sándor Kurtán et al. (Budapest: Hungarian Center of the Foundation for Democracy Studies, 1996), 485–514.

18. For more details in relation to the elections of 1990, see Eva Fodor, "The Gender Gap in the Hungarian Elections of 1990," manuscript, Department of Sociology, University of California at Los Angeles, 1992.

19. I am grateful to Endre Hann for the verbal communication of these conclusions based on as yet unpublished data and analyses of the regular public opinion surveys run by the MEDIAN Public Opinion Research Center.

20. The survey was done in 1993–94 by the Department of Social Policy of the Institute of Sociology, Hungarian Academy of Sciences. For a summary of the main results, see Júlia Szalai, "A helyi önkormányzatok szociálpolitikájáról," in *Az államtalanítás dilemmái: Szociálpolitikai kényszerek és választások,* ed. Edit Landau et al. (Budapest: Active Society Foundation, 1995), 240–60.

21. See Ágnes Vajda: "Alapítványok, egyesületek és kormányzati intézmények," in *Az államtalanítás dilemmái,* 127–56.

Chapter Nine

Women in Bulgaria

Changes in Employment and Political Involvement

DOBRINKA KOSTOVA

*T*he transitions from Communist totalitarianism to democratic political systems in Central and Eastern Europe shared several common characteristics. These included large-scale popular demonstrations demanding the decommunization of society and parliamentary elections to ratify the political breakthrough that had already occurred.

Individualism and the market are generally idealized in post-Communist societies. The dark side of this process is the fact that governments, step by step, are withdrawing protection from the weaker groups in society rather than exposing all groups to competition. Loss of protection; expectations derived from gender symbolism inherited from the Communist era, which proclaimed equal gender opportunities; and women's efforts to decrease the negative effects of the economic crisis on their families divide women. Under socialism, women's issues were a part of the total program for social equality. In the transition, confronting the economic crisis, women separate the private and public realms, thereby emphasizing their roles as members of families rather than as political participants in their own right.

In this connection, women's participation in the process of democratization will depend on their ability to create a female identity and to form their own organizations. During the transition the focus of women's groups has shifted from family issues to women's economic rights, but groups rarely debate and define issues. Rather, they place demands on governments for relief.

In the first years of the transition women's political participation was weakened by a lack of sensitivity to gender issues. Although women's problems do not appear significant now to many people, they will surely become central as the new democratic and legal systems take hold. However, if women's problems are

203

ignored in constructing the legal framework of the new political system, women will have greater difficulty confronting the long-term consequences of their exclusion later. Due to their different historical and cultural traditions, these processes have differed in the former Communist countries. The aim of this chapter is to provide a more comprehensive analysis of the political, economic, and social involvement of Bulgarian women in the period of transition. It is still too early to be sure of the pattern of future development, so many of the trends described below may change as the process continues.

THE TRANSITION IN BULGARIA

In Bulgaria decommunization took place slowly. The roundtable discussions in the spring of 1990 were held against the background of raging nationalist passions. The Bulgarian Socialist Party, formerly the Bulgarian Communist Party, succeeded in partially consolidating itself, and its main opposition, the Union of Democratic Forces, missed the chance to oust the Communist system by a single act of popular indignation. The main actors were not two directly opposed forces but rather were linked by various common goals and by their participation in a political game that aimed to avoid bloodshed. That goal was widely and repeatedly articulated by both groups and carried Bulgaria through the roundtable discussions, four general elections, the presidential elections, and the formation of several different governments.

In the economic realm there is general agreement that economic development now requires privatization and marketization, which means a decrease in the size of the labor force. Women constitute the group that can be eliminated from public employment with least conflict. Supporters of this approach, mainly representatives of the Democratic Party and some Christian groups, use populist arguments such as the heavy burden on women, who are expected to work and perform their domestic duties, as well as data on the low birthrate in Bulgaria to defend the position that women should focus their energies primarily on their roles in the home.[1] In this difficult time the family is seen as a unit that has to absorb the shortcomings and risks of the transformation period. According to this view, the problems of the individual members of the family are to become invisible.

Ideologically, the beginning of the transformation in Bulgaria idealized the years before Communist rule. There was an attempt to erase the socialist period. With respect to women's status and roles, this process entailed a devaluation of the legislation enacted during the socialist period and the refusal to acknowledge that some of its elements could be used to make the transition smoother and more acceptable for women.

The victory of the Bulgarian Socialist Party in the 1994 parliamentary elections and the formation of a socialist government did not lead to positive changes for women. Focused primarily on efforts to improve the country's poor economic situation, the government was incapable of seriously addressing any social problems and thus could not make women's problems a top social priority.

The new government that came to power in 1997 represents a coalition of democratic forces. It is devoting its efforts to the democratization of political life and the marketization and privatization of the economy. For the first time since 1989, a government has shown a strong will to make political and economic changes in Bulgaria. In this regard the development of women's rights is now more likely to follow a model more typical of Western countries.

THE TRANSFORMATIONS OF WOMEN'S STATUS

In the second half of this century, which saw the emergence and development of socialism in Central and Eastern Europe, the status of Bulgarian women underwent dynamic changes. In 1946, 79.2 percent of all women of working age were engaged in some branch of production, making up 45.0 percent of the economically active population. However, only a quarter of women of working age were employed in the public sphere.[2] Women's high levels of labor force participation were due to the fact that, at that time, Bulgaria was a backward agrarian country with agriculture based on small farms, a small handicraft industry, and very low levels of real industrial production. A large proportion of working women were peasant women, who constituted more than half of the working peasant population.

The structure of women's employment changed dramatically during the socialist period. Working women were no longer concentrated primarily in the category of women peasants. A study conducted in the early 1980s found that most employed women were workers, followed by employees without special qualifications. In third place were women specialists with secondary specialized and some higher education, and in fourth place, peasant women.[3] Women professionals and managers were in fifth and sixth place before craftswomen.

Women workers were found in significant numbers in all branches of industry. At the end of the 1980s the largest concentration of women workers was found in the machine-building and the metal-processing industries and in electronics. In the 1970s women were concentrated in the food-beverage-tobacco-perfume and textile industries. At the end of the 1980s these branches were in third and fourth place.

Women's participation in the various branches of industry since the end of

Communist rule reflects a certain demasculinization in the majority of industrial branches. In 1991 women constituted 45.8 percent of all employees in the productive sphere.[4] In 1995 they accounted for 47.1 percent of those employed in the country.[5] Building and transport, sectors of the economy in which most of the work was not mechanized, continued to have predominantly male labor forces.

During the Communist era, women workers held lower ranks and had lower qualifications than male workers, although they did not have less education.[6] This difference reflected the fact that women were working in light industry, where a good part of production was still based on muscular strength. Women workers were also trained only for more simplified production operations at that time. But the criteria used to evaluate the complexity and heaviness of a certain type of work, on the basis of which workers were classified, also contributed, as they were not precise enough and unfairly allocated a number of production activities in those branches of the economy which were feminized to the status of less qualified labor. The main reason for this pattern was the persistent belief that women's employment was less significant than men's. Since women workers had lower qualifications, their incomes were correspondingly lower than those of male workers.

This tendency continues in the 1990s. In September 1994, for example, women's salaries were lower than the average salaries in both the state and private sectors.[7] The salaries of women are 12.1 percent lower than the average in the state sector of the economy and 8.5 percent in private firms.[8] These data should be seen as tendencies rather than as exact figures. After 1990, statistical publications no longer report data on the salaries of men and women. Such data are published for individuals and households but not reported separately by gender. Data for the private sector are also not very reliable, as the salaries reported in the private sector are kept low to lower taxes. Moreover, employees in many private firms receive additional income in other forms, such as food, gasoline, cars, and rent payments.

Women's educational levels increased dramatically under Communism. By 1991, 182,305 Bulgarian women had a university education, 15 times the number in 1946.[9] During the same period, the number of men with university education increased less than 10 times. The relative share of women with university, college, and specialized education among the economically active population was 56.3 percent in 1991. In the same year 380,253 women had specialized secondary education, 17 times the number in 1946.[10] The number of economically active men with secondary specialized education increased only 9 times during this period. Women with higher education continued to enter the professional fields open to them and also entered jobs previously considered men's domain.

Table 9.1

WOMEN'S AVERAGE SALARIES IN JULY 1990 (IN BULGARIAN LEVA)

Branch	All Economically Active	Women
Industry	346	295
Agriculture	338	276
Transport	391	306
Trade	283	268
Communications	332	315
Science	349	314
Education	296	285
University	371	343
Culture	279	259
Health	336	325
Management	368	333
Textiles	323	304
Electronics	333	295
Food	306	272
Average Salary	337	291

Source: *Zaeti I dohodi prez 1990* (Sofia: National Statistics Press, 1991), 80.

In 1946, women were found in 10 professional categories; by 1991 they were found in more than 50 professional categories. In 1946 most women intellectuals were teachers, but in 1990 there was no preponderant profession.[11]

Despite these changes, women professionals do not have incomes that equal those of men in the same professional group (see table 9.1). The higher incomes of men can be explained in part by their larger share of managerial jobs and positions requiring engineering or technical specialties, in which, as a rule, larger bonuses are given. Differences between men's and women's incomes were very large among white-collar workers. These differences result in part from the fact that women were engaged in office work, which brought lower salaries, whereas male employees in this category often worked for the security and police services, jobs that brought higher incomes.

During the Communist period, Bulgarian women also entered managerial positions. Women held 32.0 percent of such positions by 1990, primarily in the feminized spheres. Women also held more managerial positions at lower levels. In 1990, only 12.6 percent of higher management posts were held by women, compared to 17.5 percent at the lower levels.[12] There was no substantial difference between the educational levels of men and women managers.[13] Thus, women's access to managerial status was not a process that recognized women's equality. Women increased their participation in managerial positions, but at a lower rate than their overall professional advancement. Women's share in managerial jobs did not correspond to their employment levels or to their level of educational and professional training.

The explanation for these inequalities can be found in the persistence of traditional prejudices about women's capabilities. The concept of a good manager was identified with the "manly" man. Under these circumstances it was more difficult for women to assert themselves. The character of managerial work was another factor. Managers had to perform many different functions inside and outside the firm, leaving no time for their families. The model of the self-denunciatory manager was idealized and elevated to the norm. If ambitious men were able to forget that they were also fathers, sons, and husbands, the majority of ambitious and capable women were neither able nor inclined to do the same.

Full employment of women during the Communist period was possible because of the active protection of the state. Legislation provided special protection for pregnant women, and firms could not refuse to hire a woman because of her pregnancy. In addition, pregnant women, mothers with children under eight months of age, and wives whose husbands were doing their regular military service enjoyed special protection against dismissal in case of changes in work conditions.[14] Even when the firm had to be shut down, a pregnant woman could not be fired. The parent organization was obliged to transfer her to another appropriate job with the same salary.[15] However, the structural changes in the economy since 1989 have made these policies impossible to implement, and in 1992 they were deleted from the Labor Code.[16]

One of the achievements of social policy for women during the Communist period was legislation providing maternity leave. Women were granted leave for pregnancy and motherhood according to the number of the children they had. Thus, women received 120 calendar days for the first child, 150 days for the second, 180 days for the third, and 120 days for the fourth and every subsequent child.[17] Working women received the equivalent of 100 percent of their gross salaries while on pregnancy and child care leave. Women were also given leave for rearing children: six months for a first child, seven months for a second, eight months for a third, and six months for a fourth and every subsequent child.[18] Such leaves were paid at the minimum wage.[19]

Families also received and continue to receive monthly child allowances. Leaves for up to 60 days for taking care of a sick child could be used by either the father or the mother of the child. The law also included a number of special regulations for unmarried or single mothers, for mothers who were studying, and for mothers whose husbands were performing their military service. Bulgarian legislation acknowledges motherhood in computing the length of labor service.

According to the Pension Law, those women who have reared five or more children to the age of eight have the right to retire after 15 years of employment and at the age of 40 or 50 years, depending on the type of work.[20]

Under socialism, full female involvement in the labor force subordinated the other roles of women. Maternity leave and child allowances were given to working women at the workplace. The high level of employment of women during the reproductive years led to many role conflicts, which were resolved most often in favor of women's employment. These policies created many demographic and labor force problems. The unfavorable demographic situation has been exacerbated by Bulgaria's deep economic crisis, resulting in a negative birthrate since 1990.[21]

DEMOCRATIZATION AND WOMEN'S EMPLOYMENT

As noted above, under Communism women gained recognition for their productive activity. Communism insisted that both genders were equal and important, an ideological position that was reinforced in practice by the industrialization of the country, which increased the demand for labor. This situation had several important consequences for women. The first was that gender problems were understood within the framework of inequalities existing in the broader society. Discrimination on the grounds of gender was to be resolved predominantly by means of "emancipation" through employment. This "solution" put strong pressures on women to enter the labor force; it also neglected the self-determination and autonomy of women. Further, despite the egalitarian laws, there was a gap between written principles and the real quality of women's lives.

The mechanism for defining and solving women's problems under socialism was directed from above and imposed on the groups below. That policy fostered passivity on the part of women and their organizations. Because of their experiences during the Communist period, women continue to expect policy to be made in their favor. However, they are not accustomed to working to achieve policies favorable to them.

The transition to an economic system based on the rules of the market has produced changes in male/female employment ratios and in the state's protection of labor. It has also altered the structure of women's employment. The initial steps toward a market economy show that women owned 145 (1.7%) of the private firms established in 1989. In 1990, the percentage of such firms increased to 5.5 percent.[22] A survey conducted in 1990 of 350 economic leaders found that women who start businesses of their own do so first of all to be independent. They rank professional interest in the field and the desire to make good incomes second and third in their motivations.[23] The majority (50.0%) of women's business firms are in services; 20.0 percent are in the manufacturing sphere, predominantly in light industry, and the rest are found in education and consulting. Data from the second stage of the same empirical survey carried out in 1994 show that women's involvement in private business has increased.[24] As a whole women leaders account for a fifth of all leaders and deputy leaders in private and state firms.[25] When those who are self-employed are added, women constitute 32.2 percent of all those who are employers and self-employed in the economy.[26]

These patterns are part of a larger shift of women to the private sector. In 1995 women employees constituted 49.6 percent of the labor force in the state and 43.4 percent in the private sector.[27] Nonetheless, only a third of all working women have moved from state to private firms as employees.[28] The main reason for this trend is the slow process of privatization of state enterprises in Bulgaria. In addition, many women fear moving to the private sector. These fears reflect the risks connected with the undeveloped health and insurance legislation for the private sector. Very often working hours are longer than the recommendations of the Labor Code, although the longer working day also brings higher incomes. The balance of interests between private owners on the one hand and women workers and employees on the other is very fragile and can have unfavorable consequences for women's health and family responsibilities in the long term. The large number of women who are employed on temporary or honorary contracts in private firms also face job uncertainty. Despite these negative effects, the private sector remains the only serious alternative to the collapsing state enterprises and the enormous reduction of the labor force associated with it.

The first stage of the economic reform in Bulgaria produced a large supply of labor but a lack of corresponding demand. The deep economic crisis after 1989 created a sharp contradiction between the state's financial and economic capabilities and public expectations. The negative effect was felt predominantly in employment and in the decrease in child care facilities, pensions, and social services.[29] Since the beginning of the 1990s, Bulgaria has experienced a deep crisis in employment. At the beginning of the process it was not a restructuring of the economy which led to the massive layoffs of people but the collapse of employment relations regulated by the state with the end of Communist rule. Subsequently the coincidence of a deep economic crisis and efforts to re-create a market economy led to the economic crisis that is reflected in unemployment in all branches of the economy.

In the 1990s, the importance of the basic sectors of the economy changed. The portion of agriculture in the gross domestic product (GDP) was 15.3 percent in 1991 but 12.6 percent in 1994. Industry accounted for 39.4 percent of GDP in

1991 and 35.7 percent in 1994. The service sector has expanded markedly, from 45.3 percent to 51.7 percent.[30] The private sector accounted for 34.6 percent of the gross domestic product in agriculture in 1991 and 79 percent in 1994. The private sector's contribution to GDP increased from 5.8 percent in 1991 to 18 percent in 1994 in industry and from 8.2 percent in 1991 to 27 percent in 1994 in the service sector.[31] By 1994, the private sector accounted for 33.3 percent of GDP. However, its portion of the gross domestic product is still low in comparison with that of the Czech Republic, Poland, and Hungary.[32] Bulgaria's deep economic crisis is not due to change in the significance of the major sectors of the economy within the GDP but to the enormous decline in total production in the country, which fell by about a fourth in the period between 1989 and 1994.[33]

Changes in thinking about employment have also contributed to high rates of unemployment. The old view that it was necessary for everyone to be employed despite their personal abilities and the economic needs of enterprises collapsed with the transition to a free market. The hidden unemployment that existed under socialism has become real unemployment for many women.

As table 9.2 illustrates, women have experienced higher levels of unemployment since the beginning of the transition. Women previously employed in branches of the economy most closely connected to trade with the former Council on Mutual Economic Assistance (CMEA) countries and particularly with the former Soviet Union have been especially hard hit.[34]

Women from the whole spectrum of economic activities have been affected by unemployment in Bulgaria. The number of employed women has decreased in all areas. The tradition established during socialism of permanent and oblig-

Table 9.2

YEARLY CHANGE IN THE UNEMPLOYED IN BULGARIA, BY GENDER

Year	Registered Unemployemnt	% of Unemployed Women
1991	205,950	54.8
1992	280,075	53.4
1993	626,141	52.3
1994	488,442	54.3
1995	423,773	55.6

Source: National Employment Office of the Ministry of Labor and Social Affairs, *Informatsionen bjuletin* (Sofia: National Employment Office Press, January–December 1992); *Socialno I ikonomichesko razvitie na Bulgaria, 1990–1994* (Sofia: National Statistics Press, 1995), 17; *National Statistics, 1995* (Sofia: Nacionalen statisticheski institut, 1995), 67. *National Statistics, 1996* (Sofia: Nacionalen statisticheski institut, 1996), 71.

atory employment of all women has created a very strong employment habit among Bulgarian women. For 75 percent of the 596 unemployed women studied in a sociological survey conducted in 1995, being unemployed was the worst thing in their lives.[35]

Unemployment has a strong effect on women's position in society, family relations, and women's life satisfaction. To women who for decades have considered their job as one of their most important roles in society, the loss of paid employment leads to serious distress. Their lack of experience in the new situation leads to a loss of flexibility and security. Unemployment and insecurity in society give rise to severely negative reactions among some women, including deep depression or illegal activity. The latter manifests itself in an increase in women's criminality and prostitution.[36]

Further, there is a strong tendency for unemployed women to associate with other unemployed people.[37] This tendency toward social isolation leads to economic deprivation and to the relative atomization of the women concerned. As a consequence, unemployment is associated with high levels of psychological distress. The example of Bulgarian women suggests that the combination of high sustained unemployment and weak welfare provisions imposes very high social and psychological costs on those without work.

WOMEN'S POLITICAL LIFE— TRADITIONS AND NEW APPROACHES

Under socialism women as well as men were required to be members of political organizations, which meant that a great majority of women were involved in at least one organization. When the first sociological research on women's activity took place in 1969, only 6.7 percent of all working women were not members of any organization. In the 1980s women constituted 50.5 percent of the members of the Fatherland Front, 50.0 percent of the members of the Communist youth organization, 46.4 percent of trade union members, and 27.6 percent of the members of the Bulgarian Communist Party.[38]

A time-budget study of the population conducted in 1976–77 indicated that women's political involvement in leading positions increased over time. During this period 25.3 percent of working women held leadership positions in political organizations. There were no substantial differences between men and women, as 32.4 percent of the men also held leading positions.[39] A survey conducted in the 1980s found that only 8.1 percent of women were not members of political organizations. The data also reveal that 35.4 percent of women held leadership positions and 41.7 percent had been active in politics at some period of their life. These levels did not differ substantially from those of men. Forty-seven percent of men were active members in 1980s, and 49.9 percent were active at some periods of their life. Of the men who were surveyed, 7.7 percent were not members of any organization.[40]

Women held responsible positions in all political organizations, but they were most active in the trade unions, the Fatherland Front, and the Communist youth organization. Among men this order was slightly different. For them the first priority was the Bulgarian Communist Party, followed by the Fatherland Front and the trade unions. Although women were represented in the managing bodies of many public organizations (see table 9.3), they played a limited role in the leadership of the Communist Party. As in many other societies, Bulgarian women had more influence in the decision-making process in local political organizations than in national political institutions, in which their participation was determined by quotas.[41] This difference was particularly noticeable in the Communist Party, where women were approximately five times more numerous among local than national officials (see table 9.3).

Table 9.3
WOMEN'S PARTICIPATION IN THE LEADERSHIP OF THE TRADE UNIONS (1980),
THE COMMUNIST YOUTH ORGANIZATION (1980), THE FATHERLAND FRONT
(1979), AND THE COMMUNIST PARTY (1980) (IN %)

Organization	Local	Central
Trade unions	52.2	42.4
Communist youth organization	51.7	38.4
Fatherland Front	47.1	41.1
Communist Party	25.0	5.6

Source: R. Gancheva, M. Vidova, and N. Abadzieva, *Sto waprosa I otgowora za bulgarskite zheni* (Sofia: Sofia Press, 1983), app.

Women's equal political involvement was never a priority during the Communist period. Communist leaders emphasized women's full-time employment rather than their political participation. The relatively large share of women who participated in the political life of socialist society was simply the result of the socialist value system and the image it aspired to create. Many of the women in the National Assembly, for example, were weavers, seamstresses, heroes of socialist labor, and women with low-status jobs. The fact that these women did not have the experience to be taken seriously in important decision making was exactly the reason they were chosen.[42] In general, political women were often satisfied with the roles of performers or mediators of other people's ideas. Such roles meant less responsibility and uncertainty for them.

Women were already overburdened with employment and family duties. So why did they take on the burdens of political activity? One reason was that political involvement was a way to be better informed about what was going on in society. Another was that such activity increased one's chances for promotion. Women, like men, exploited these possibilities, although fewer women than men did so. Political behavior during the Communist period was generally adaptive rather than rebellious in Bulgaria.

Both men and women perceived this political reality in quite similar ways. A survey of 2,959 women conducted in 1975 by the Institute of Sociology of the Bulgarian Academy of Sciences revealed that 58.6 percent of women and 59.9 percent of men thought that women should be engaged in political work. A negative answer was given by 10.5 percent of the men and 5.2 percent of the women. The rest thought that political participation should depend on women's personal inclinations.[43]

Since the 1989 events official data about parties' membership are not published, probably because of the weakness of party organizations during the first years of the transition. In their public speeches, party officials often exaggerate their organizations' membership in order to increase popular support.

Women's political representation depends to a large degree on the structure of the political system and the political culture of the population. As the multiparty political structure emerges, elections become an important mechanism for political activity and influence. In the four parliamentary elections since 1989, different electoral methods were used. In 1990 proportional and majority representation were used. In 1991, 1994, and 1997 a proportional system was used. A proportional representation system can promote the election of women if they are sufficiently high on the party lists. However, under the list system, women's representation may clash with the necessity of meeting different ethnic, age, and other representational claims. By contrast, when elections are held using a majority system, the preferences, and prejudices, of voters are the decisive factor.

Men's and women's representation in leadership in the transition period in Bulgaria differs significantly from what it was in socialist period. The results of survey research[44] and the outcomes of the parliamentary elections in 1990, 1991, 1994, and 1997 show a decrease in the proportion of elected women. In the last Communist parliament (1989), the portion of women was 20.8 percent. In the National Assemblies elected in 1990, 1991, and 1994, women's representation varied from 8.8 percent to 13.8 percent (see tables 9.4 and 9.5.) In 1997, it decreased to 11.3 percent. The explanation of why women's representation in leadership is so low despite the fact that women are as interested in politics as men[45] lies both in structural factors and in women's limited political visibility.

Table 9.4

CANDIDATES FOR PARLIAMENT BY POLITICAL PARTY, 1990 (IN %)

Party	BSP[a]	BANU[b]	MFR[c]	UDF[d]	Others
Men	89.3	91.4	90.3	92.2	85.8
Women	10.7	8.6	9.7	7.8	14.2

Source: N. Naidenov, P. Stoyanova, and D. Kostova, *Politicheska borba 1990* (Political Campaign 1990), Sociological Survey (Sofia: Institute for Trade Union and Social Science Research Press, 1991).

[a] Bulgarian Socialist Party (former Communist Party).
[b] Bulgarian Agrarian National Union (a political organization that existed before socialism and along with the Communist Party under socialism).
[c] Movement for Freedom and Rights (anti-Communist organization to defend minority ethnic groups).
[d] Union of Democratic Forces (anti-Communist coalition, including 16 organizations).

As tables 9.4 and 9.5 show, the proportion of women candidates has been larger than the proportions of parliamentary seats they have received. There are several reasons for this. One is that a number of parties did not win seats in parliament. The number of women candidates was greater in nonparliamentary parties than in the parties that were successful in securing seats in parliament, such as the Union of Democratic Forces, the Movement for Freedom and Rights, the Bulgarian Agrarian National Union, and the Bulgarian Socialist Party (see table 9.4). Another reason is the fact that men, not women, are given the highest positions on the proportional lists of the parties, which means that women rarely have a realistic probability of being elected.

Table 9.5

WOMEN IN POLITICS (IN %)

Parliaments	Last Communist	GNA[a]	1991	1994	1997
Men	79.3	91.2	86.2	87.1	88.8
Women	20.8	8.8	13.8	12.9	11.3

Source: *State Gazette*, June 1990, October 1991, December 1994, April 1997, May 1997. N. Naidenov, P. Stoyanova, and D. Kostova, *Politicheska borba 1990,* Sociological Survey (Sofia: Institute for Trade Union and Social Science Research Press, 1991).

[a] Great National Assembly, 1990.

Women candidates did not have strategies and programs different from those proposed by the party they represented. Observations and analyses done in half of the voting districts during the parliamentary campaigns of 1990 and 1991 and in the presidential election of 1992 revealed that the candidates represented their party programs and did not develop "women's" positions.[46]

The mechanisms for selecting party candidates differ among the parties and in different types of elections. At the beginning of the process of democratization, the candidates of the Union of Democratic Forces (UDF) were chosen by the movement's national coordinating council. In the 1991, 1994, and the last parliamentary elections in 1997, representatives from the local councils played a greater role in the selection process. The Bulgarian Socialist Party (BSP) and the Movement for Freedom and Rights (MFR) also applied this approach.

For the second, third, and fourth parliamentary elections, proportional representation required voting for a list rather than for a definite person. Thus, candidates who were well known to the voters were more likely to bring votes to the party, and men were often chosen because they were better known, especially those who had visible roles in the opposition. The well-known faces from parliamentary and television discussions were particularly desirable candidates, but there were few politically visible women among them.

Despite the low overall share of women's involvement in political institutions, the degree of women's representation in the various parties differs. Women's participation is greater in the parties of the Left than those of the Right (see tables 9.4 and 9.5). To some extent this difference reflects the ideological commitment to formal equality by the leftist parties and the less egalitarian "liberal" approach taken by the rest of the parties.

However, in the parliamentary elections of 1997, the coalition of democratic forces had the most significant participation of women. It appears that women's participation is a function of the number of seats the political force gets in the parliament. This can be shown with the data for women's parliamentary representation from the Bulgarian Socialist Party in the election of 1997. Women accounted for only 8.6 percent, which reflects the fact that women are put in secondary places in the regional lists and that their election depends on the population's overall levels of support for the political force.

The decrease in women's representation in political institutions in Bulgaria cannot be seen as discrimination against women. The levels of women's representation in governmental positions could not be sustained after the abolition of quotas for their representation. The shift toward lower levels of women's political representation is a result not only of the abolition of quotas but of the past experiences under a legal framework that gave women security but also created passivity and inertia. Today there is little awareness on the part of women of the need to defend their current rights or take action to prevent legal changes that will be difficult to reverse. The women's organizations and associations are not very active in this area. They are oriented either to cultural or economic interests and neglect the legal representation of women's interests. Most women who are in politics do not give priority to women's problems.

Women's issues have a tendency to be considered secondary, unimportant, and partial. It is never the right time to put them before decision-making bodies. Women argue that they are using a tactical approach, but this hesitation is a mistake. If women lose their legal rights now, it will take years to reestablish them. Such an outcome may serve to make women more active in the long run, but the costs will be high.

In the period of transition and beyond, the involvement of women in politics is essential to defend their interests. The tradition of the Communist period, which merged social equality and gender issues, has to be overcome. Women need rights that take into account the distinctiveness of their position. The evidence left by the Communist regime has proved that the neglect of this reality leads to cynicism and to the dissatisfaction and overburdening of women.

The gap between the proclaimed and the realized, between the public and the private, between the written and the thought under socialism was very wide. With respect to that it is important now to analyze the degree of continuity or change in women's roles in Communist and post-Communist societies. Concretely, women must define their interests to support the changes. They must also discuss the question of the possibility of a shift of power between men and women, and how to exploit the transformation in order to benefit from it.

There have been two main tendencies in this regard. The first one can be termed the trend of reversibility. It involves the desire to erase the socialist period and allow the society to return to the values that existed before World War II. An emphasis is put on the family. In that way the role of women is perceived as that of good mother and wife. The second alternative is to try to preserve the status of women under socialism. This strategy means to conserve some of the privileges of state socialism, primarily with its guaranteed employment and the extensive social security system. In reality the transition is characterized by the simultaneous existence of newly emerging and old structures, of state protectionism, and economic and social freedoms. This situation deepens the duality of social realities, making the transformation slow and difficult. In this respect the significant participation of Bulgarian women in the transition will depend on their ability to create their female identity and be active in specific organizations that take this identity into account.

There are three types of women's groups working to keep gender issues alive in Bulgaria. The first consists of groups that were part of the socialist women's organizations, such as the Democratic Union of Women, or institutions that were reestablished after the end of Communism, such as the Bulgarian Union of University Women or groups such as the Women's Christian Society and the Bulgarian Women's Business Club. These groups promote feminist ideas and activities to defend their members' interests. All of them deal with the particular problems of their members and negotiate between themselves with difficulty. However, all of these organizations are led by women intellectuals whose role in the transition is crucial. They could empower women in the process of transformation with a strategy during the period when the legal and institutional grounds of a new social order are being built. However, their activity to date is characterized by discussions rather than by a change of gender paradigms.

There are also a number of women's organizations such as Women against the Abolition of Free Medicine for Children and small charity groups that, although small and weak, have been formed to fulfill specific tasks. These groups focus on practical rather than strategic aims.

Women also participate in political parties and at the elite level as decision makers. The major problem with the long-term strategy in the transition is the qualitative rather than the quantitative representation of women. To avoid a further increase in social divisions, women politicians do not stress women's rights. Nor do they foresee that women's rights may need greater protection in the future. Still approaching women's issues with a Marxist perspective, many politicians feel that women already have rights and that the right to work guarantees equality to women. It is difficult to expect that this approach will alter the old Communist paradigm for women. In the new conditions it simply leads to a decrease in the protections women had under Communism. This situation will probably have the effect of making the spontaneous activity of women's groups more organized. Now women's groups are fragmented, and solidarity among them is difficult to achieve. They represent the interests and needs of women from different social groups and defend different political programs and views. However, the "period of silence" on gender issues, which has characterized the transition since the beginning of the 1989 events, is slowly coming to an end.

CONCLUSION

One of the most significant processes of social change at the end of the twentieth century is the global change in the status of women. Not only have the daily living conditions of women changed, but substantial changes are emerging in their life positions, life interests, and life strategies. Within this universal trend, women in Central and Eastern Europe face specific problems with regard to the transformation of their societies. The governments of Central and Eastern Europe are trying to copy the prosperous Western model of development in order to achieve full popular support for the changes they are enacting. If the adaptation is successful, the positive elements, but also the shortcomings, of the liberal model of development will also be transferred. In this situation the experiences of women from the Western countries could be of great significance.

As a matter of principle, the transition in Bulgaria has the objective of changing the basis of the totalitarian structures. In this framework women's problems do not seem to have priority, a fact that makes women as a group quite invisible. The new model of development does not overtly discriminate against women, but it does emphasize the consolidation of the family as an economic unit rather than the interests of its individual members. This approach coincides with economic and political circumstances that have led to changes in social policy which may significantly reduce women's employment.

As change progresses, the Communist regime's predominantly economic approach to women has gradually been replaced by an underestimation of their significance as a social group. Emphasis is put on solving women's problems only as members of other groups—the unemployed, youth, or pensioners. This trend is still strong, and rapid changes cannot be expected.

The transition from a totalitarian regime is thus an ongoing challenge for the women of Bulgaria. For all of them it has brought political freedom. For some of them, it is connected with risky but prosperous entrepreneurial activity. Others, after years of guaranteed jobs, are facing unemployment. Those who find themselves in a weak position in the face of the new competitive economy feel deep frustration and a sense of injustice. The transformation of the value system is also a very important factor for women. Women are adapting to the new realities, but they are also led by illusions that may not sustain them through this period of changes. This situation leads to uncertainties and fear, especially for older women. It is predominantly younger women who are experiencing the advantages of the transitional period.

As noted above, there is no consensus today among women themselves on how the rights women had during the socialist regime should be evaluated. The economic and social crisis in Bulgaria has produced diametrically opposed views of the past and the future of Bulgarian women. In this fluid environment, the majority of the existing women's organizations are weak and have tactical rather than strategic aims. They exist to address single issues. Many are short lived, and most are quite passive.

A change in the approach of the leaders of national and local institutions in regard to the needs and the role of women in the transition period will have to occur if a legal, economic, and social framework is to be created which will guarantee the equality of men and women and give women the right to choose how they will behave and work. Such a change can be achieved if women's organizational power is translated into activity to influence national and local institutions as well as the legal system. The change from Communist to post-Communist society created hopes for a positive shift in women's position in society. However, to date, we have seen only a redefinition of the socialist goal of equal opportunities, not a new conception of women's rights.

NOTES

1. M. Pumpalova, "Diskusija za socialnite grupi," *Democratic Review* 4–5 (1996): 217–19.

2. *Statistics 1959* (Sofia: Central Statistics Institute at the Government, 1959), 60.

3. R. Gancheva, M. Vidova, and N. Abadzieva, *Sto waprosa i otgowora za bulgarskite zheni* (Sofia: Sofia Press, 1983).

4. K. Gatev, *Kolichestveni i kachestveni aspekti na konsumacija* (Sofia: National Statistics Press, 1992).

5. Nacionalen Statisticheski Institut, *National Statistics 1996* (Sofia: Nacionalen Statisticheski Institut, 1996), 72.

6. Nacionalen Statisticheski Institut, *Obrazovanie i kvalifikacija na trudeschtite se i uslovija na trud* (Sofia: National Statistics Press, 1990), 23–25.

7. P. Bozhikov, "Izsledwane na socialno osigurenita hora," *Statistics* 3 (1995): 20–33.

8. Ibid., 29.

9. *Obrazowatelna i generatsionna struktura* (Sofia: National Statistics Press, 1992).

10. *Zaeti i dohodi prez 1990* (Sofia: National Statistics Press, 1991), 80.

11. Women make up 40.7 percent of the researchers and 36.2 percent of the university science professors. Nacionalen Statisticheski Institut, *Obrazovanie i kvalifikacija na trudeschtite se i uslovija na trud*, 23–25.

12. Nacionalen Statisticheski Institut, *Naselenie* (Sofia: National Statistics Press, 1991).

13. Nacionalen Statisticheski Institut, *Ikonomika na Bulgaria* (Sofia: National Statistics Press, 1991).

14. *Kodeks na truda* (Sofia: Nauka i Izkustvo Press, 1986), 131–33.

15. Ibid., 132.

16. *Kodeks na truda* (Sofia: Confederation of the Independent Trade Unions Press, 1992), 30.

17. *Kodeks na truda* (Sofia: Nauka i Izkustvo Press, 1986), 74–79.

18. Ibid., 74.

19. Ibid., 75.

20. *Pensionen zakon—dokumenti* (Sofia: Nauka i Izkustvo Press, 1976), 8.

21. Nacionalen Statisticheski Institut, *National Statistics 1996*, 26–27.

22. Nacionalen Statisticheski Institut, *Ikonomika na Bulgaria*, 121.

23. D. Kostova, *Ikonomicheskite lideri v Bulgaria* (Sofia: Institute for Trade Union and Social Science Research Press, 1990).

24. D. Kostova, *Ikonomicheskijat elit na Bulgaria* (Sofia: Institute of Sociology, 1996).

25. Ibid., 59–60.

26. Nacionalen Statisticheski Institut, *National Statistics 1996*, 73.

27. Ibid., 73.

28. Ibid., 62.

29. B. Bogdanov, "Dohodi, razhodi i konsumatsia na domakinstvata s detsa do 18 godini," *Statistics* 3 (1996): 67, 73; R. Gancheva, "Bulgarskite pensioneri w perioda na prehod kam pazarna ikonomika," *Statistical Barometer* 99 (1996): 1–3; "Blagosastojanieto v 18 Iztochno-Evropejski strani: Statistika 1996," *Statistical Barometer* 95 (1996): 6.

30. *Socialno i ikonomichesko razvitie na Bulgaria 1990–1994* (Sofia: National Statistics Press, 1995), 7.

31. Ibid., 9.

32. Ibid.

33. Ibid., 6.

34. Ibid., 45. There was a 76 percent decrease in exports to the countries of Central and Eastern Europe between 1989 and 1994 and a decrease of 86 percent to the countries of what was previously the Soviet Union.

35. D. Gallie et al., "Employment Conditions, Labour Market Insecurity, and Work Motivation: A Comparison of the Czech Republic, Slovakia, Bulgaria, and Great Britain," manuscript, Nuffield College, Oxford, 1996.

36. Nacionalen Statisticheski Institut, *Naselenie*.

37. D. Gallie et al., "Employment Conditions, Labour Market Insecurity, and Work Motivation."

38. Nacionalen Statisticheski Institut, *Grad i selo, danni* (Sofia: National Statistics Press, 1988), vol. 3.

39. *Budzhet na vremeto* (Sofia: National Statistics Press, 1991).

40. "Efektivnost na politikata po podobbrjavane roljata na zhenata v Bulgaria," Sociological Survey, Institute of Sociology, BAS, Sofia, 1981.

41. *Zhenata v Bulgaria* (Sofia: Committee for Social Information at the Government, 1985), 66–67; Gancheva, Vidova, and Abadzieva, *Sto waprosa i otgowora za bulgarskite zheni*.

42. *Zhenata v Bulgaria*, 65–66.

43. "Efektivnost na politikata po podobbrjavane roljata na zhenata v Bulgaria."

44. N. Naidenov, P. Stoyanova, and D. Kostova, *Politicheska borba 1990* (Sofia: Institute for Trade Union and Social Science Research Press, 1991).

45. Nacionalen Statisticheski Institut, *Grad I selo, danni*, 2:280.

46. Naidenov, Stoyanova, and Kostova, *Politicheska borba 1990*; V. Tomov et al., "Presidential Elections: 1992," Presidential House, Sofia, 1992.

Chapter Ten

Contemporary Democratization

The Prospects for Women

PHILIPPE C. SCHMITTER

M uch of the recent and by now voluminous literature on democratization has ignored the role of women. Autocracies in some 50 countries and on every continent have collapsed, been overthrown, or attempted to transform themselves since 1974. Almost without exception, these transitions have involved an attempt to establish some form of democracy, and women have played a role in every one of these momentous political transformations. Descriptive accounts have occasionally singled them out as individuals (e.g., Aung San Suu Kyi in Burma or Violeta Chamorro in Nicaragua) or as movements (e.g., the Madres de la Plaza de Mayo in Argentina, the Comadres in El Salvador, or the Conavigua Widows in Guatemala), but women as a sociopolitical collectivity with distinctive interests and modes of action have not, to my knowledge, been systematically included in the theories and comparative analyses that have grown up around the topic of democratization.[1]

Having contributed to one strand of that literature, I hasten to enter a personal plea of guilty under extenuating circumstances. At least from the transitological perspective that Guillermo O'Donnell and I adopted, virtually all the usual collective suspects—classes, sectors, professions, regions, religions, ethnic groups, generations, and genders—are likely to face the very considerable uncertainty of regime change confused and divided in their preferences and, hence, unpredictable in their behaviors. One could not, we argued, presume that any of these groups would act collectively and reliably with regard to the choice between autocracy and democracy in the way that they so often did in responding to the choice between candidates of established parties or drafts of alternative policies in a stable system. Instead, it seemed necessary to us to create a new, more contingent set of categories in order to analyze the immediate outcome: for example, "hardliners" and "softliners," "maximalists" and "minimalists," regime beneficiaries and regime opponents.[2] Needless to say, in such an approach, women per se largely disappear from the analysis of transitional politics—along with workers per se, capitalists per se, landowners per se, and even the armed forces per se.[3]

We also hypothesized that, once the transition was under way, a "resurrection of civil society" involving the mobilization of a wide range of causes, including those of women and feminists, was likely to play a crucial role by compelling authorities to go beyond mere liberalization toward some form of democratization.

Admittedly, this was not a particularly appealing notion, since it implied that (1) women (along with other excluded and oppressed social groups) rarely determined the timing and mode of transition, and (2) to the extent that women got swept up in the resurrection process their impact would probably be ephemeral. Once the polity had begun to settle into the "normal" processes of liberal democracy, competition between political parties and representation according to territorial constituencies would take over and relegate movement-type activity to secondary, if not marginal, importance.[4]

In this brief chapter, I propose not to return to this question of the empirical role that women or women's organizations did or did not play in the transitions in southern Europe, South and Central America, and Central and Eastern Europe. Rather, I would like to address the perennial *political* question: *Que Faire?* What can be done, once a process of democratization is under way, to ensure that its outcome will not systematically discriminate against the interests of women—and maybe even provide them with benefits that had previously been denied them? What specific rules, arrangements, or practices are most likely to provide women with access to significant positions of authority in the emerging polity? What type of democracy is best suited for dealing with the issues about which women collectively are concerned? In other words, what can be done to make neodemocracies "female-friendly"?

To the best of my knowledge, no one writing about democratization has explicitly addressed these questions. The vast bulk of feminist political theory seems to take the basic structure of existing political institutions for granted and concentrates its effort on ensuring that more women will be empowered to occupy more and more prominent roles within these institutions. However, several scholars have indirectly offered some suggestions when referring to arrangements and outcomes in particular countries which seemed to benefit women either as individuals or as a social category with distinctive interests and passions. Although it seems self-evident that the material situations and political demands of women vary considerably across the geocultural clusters of recent regime change (and, less significantly, within South America and Central and Eastern Europe), I believe that it may still be possible to come up with some generic guidelines.

IMPROVEMENTS WITHIN LIBERAL DEMOCRACY

I begin by assuming that contemporary neodemocracies will not engage in explicit gender discrimination with regard to the criteria for citizenship. These days, all men and women over a specified age of maturity tend to have the same set of basic, "formal and equal," political rights: to vote, to join parties, to be candidates, to meet publicly, to form associations, to petition public authorities, and so on.[5] Whatever marginal differences might emerge in any specific case, these fundamental rights of the liberal democracy were regarded as universal, uncontestable, and irreversible—unless, of course, the polity were to revert to some form of autocracy.[6]

Although feminist theorists have frequently expressed dissatisfaction with liberal democracy—especially its restrictions on participation and its separation of public and private spheres[7]—their (implicit) consensus seems to be that a good deal can be accomplished within the limits imposed by it. This may be just a reluctant "tactical" concession to political realism, since one of the most striking features of the current wave of democratization is the generalized unwillingness to experiment with new rules or institutions. Whether from restricted imagination or excessive caution, very few politicians have advocated, much less implemented, measures that attempt to go "beyond" liberal democracy. There is no compelling evidence for such a demand from the female citizenry, especially in Eastern Europe.[8] Everywhere, the effort seems to be that of adopting "best practice" from existing democracies with only minor concessions to local conditions and traditions.

CONVOKING A CONSTITUENT ASSEMBLY

With this (major) restriction in mind, the first liberal measure likely to lead to an eventual improvement in the political fortunes of women is the convocation of a constituent assembly or constitutional convention. Recycling an old constitution, as the Argentines did,[9] or reforming an immediately preceding one, as the Greeks did, will offer few opportunities for the sort of basic reconsideration of rights and rules which is required. Moreover, feminists should advocate formalization of these rights and rules as early as possible during the process of transition, when expectations about equality are high, actor preferences are still uncertain, and vested interests are more likely to be on the defensive owing to their collusion with the *ancien régime*.[10] It will also be to the advantage of women if the constituent assembly is composed only of representatives specifically elected for that purpose, since this may help to overcome the prejudice that the "normal" process of governing and legislating is a masculine activity.[11] The risk of adopting this strategy is that it may open the constitutionalizing process to so many claims from specific groups that the end product will be a document of extraordinary length with many contradictory provisions and unrealistic promises.

Consider the case of Brazil, which ended up, after waiting 12 years, with the world's second-longest constitution. Admittedly, it does have many profemale provisions, along with a laundry list of other rights and entitlements, but the document as a whole is unworkable. Many of its provisions are ignored, and much of the energy of the present government is being expended in revising key provisions—although not the provisions dealing with women's rights.

Insisting upon Decentralization

As for the content of this (re)founding document, women seem to have a major interest in political decentralization, especially in obtaining the maximum possible degree of autonomy for municipalities. I have not seen any relevant data, but I suspect that women tend to do much better (certainly, initially) in local contests in which the outcomes are more dependent on personal exchanges, detailed information about needs, and small-scale solidarities. From these constitutionally protected strongholds of municipal or communal autonomy, they are subsequently more likely to be able to build a basis for later penetrating those realms of national politics typically dominated by men. Federal systems would seem of marginal utility because their states or regions are usually too large for women to reap the immediate benefits of small-scale politics, but it could be argued that they, too, could eventually provide a useful "intermediate" stage of aggregation.

Promoting Disciplined Parties

Women also seem to have good reasons for preferring disciplined, permanently organized political parties. On the one hand, such parties are more likely to make collective decisions to include women in their leadership—even to establish specific quotas for them—because they have a strong vested interest in producing majorities and because only such parties will have the internal cohesion necessary to implement such decisions about candidacies and programs reliably and uniformly. On the other hand, parties that are disciplined by principle or credible threat of sanctions, or both, will be more likely to carry through on their electoral promises and to deliver the legislative goods when they have the requisite governing majority.[12]

From this general preference it should be possible to deduce a number of subsidiary ones, namely, for all rules or institutions that tend to strengthen the disciplinary capacity or permanent organization of political parties. The literature is not exactly clear on what these conditions are, but my (admittedly imperfect) reading of it suggests that political feminists should be in favor of proportional representation;[13] closed list systems without preferential voting; candidate nomination by caucuses, not primaries; legislative committee assignments by party whip, not seniority; public financing of parties and electoral campaigns; multiple-member constituencies; high thresholds for entry of new parties; and I am sure there are others.[14]

It should be noted in passing that the imputed preferences for political decentralization and for disciplined, permanently organized political parties may not be compatible. In this case, it would be incumbent upon specific women's organizations involved in the transition and the constitutionalizing process to choose between them according to local or national conditions.

Preferring Parliamentarianism

Finally, within the options offered by existing liberal democratic practices, it seems possible to deduce that women should prefer parliamentarianism over presidentialism.[15] Not only does this way of organizing executive power generally serve to strengthen the internal structure and discipline of parties, but it also affords a means of attaining that power which does not involve exposure to the grueling demands of extended campaigning, heavily "mediatized" contact with the public, and surreptitious reliance on invisible connections (mostly "old boy" and "corporate" networks) for raising the much larger necessary sums of money. In the long run, there may be no reason why women cannot participate with equal effectiveness in the campaign for the presidency—Violeta Chamorro certainly did so successfully in Nicaragua (even if under exceptional circumstances). But in the short to medium run, I suspect that women stand a significantly better chance of making it to the top through the internal machinations of parliamentarianism. Moreover, once they are there, as prime minister with a (more or less) assured majority in the legislature, they will be in a better position to implement policies that can favor the interests of women. Presidents elected through an excruciatingly *machista* process have often had to face a legislature controlled by the opposite

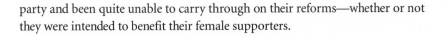

party and been quite unable to carry through on their reforms—whether or not they were intended to benefit their female supporters.

IMPROVEMENTS BEYOND LIBERAL DEMOCRACY

One of the consequences of relying exclusively on the discourse of liberal democracy is that the analyst tends to concentrate her or his attention on a single process—that of party competition—and on a single variable—the proportion of women who are elected to positions of representation or selected for positions of authority in the government. This becomes *the* indicator of how well women are doing in neodemocracies.

And in the neodemocracies, the evidence on this variable has become overwhelming. Women are simply not being elected. They seem to do somewhat better in the initial "founding elections" but usually decline in subsequent "regular" ones. This has been especially noteworthy in Eastern Europe, where their numbers already fell precipitously in the first elections from what they had been under the previous autocracy and, in most cases, have continued to diminish thereafter.[16] Everywhere, with the exception of Scandinavia, women are heavily underrepresented with far fewer seats in parliament than they deserve according to their distribution in the citizenry.[17]

Freed from the electoral fetish of liberal democracy, the theorist can shift her or his attention toward other means of citizen expression and different channels of group representation where the collective interests of women might find better and even more efficacious expression. The problem with such "postliberal" thinking is that it usually is only wishful. However compelling the abstract argument may be, it remains separated from the problem of agency. Existing actors with their established preferences and strategies may be able to see the benefits of shifting to new rules or institutions, but the costs of doing so appear prohibitive—especially for the present generation of politicians—and the benefits will be slow and uncertain in coming. One would hope that moments of regime transition in their intrinsic uncertainty might encourage more risk taking and experimentation. Alas, as mentioned above, nothing could be further from the case in South America and Central and Eastern Europe!

Nevertheless, I am convinced that it is worth discussing briefly some possible postliberal reforms that could increase gender equality, even if there does not seem much likelihood that they will be implemented in the neodemocracies in the near future.

SHIFTING TO DIRECT DEMOCRACY

A very sizeable feminist literature stresses the virtues of direct democracy based on more active and intense participation of the citizenry in political life. Distrustful of the usual hierarchical and vicarious institutions of liberal-representative-electoral democracy, it argues that women have special skills and expertise that, if applied to the microlevel of interaction, would change radically the policies adopted. Most important, such grassroots activity would have the effect of breaking down existing barriers between the public and the private, the political and the social, thereby extending the range of egalitarian principles into institutions: the family, the household, the school, the church, the neighborhood, and so on, where women possess important power resources. Were it possible to create a larger-scale polity by combining such units of intensive participation (and not just to decentralize authority within an otherwise liberal model, as advocated above), the resultant "strong democracy" would presumably go some way toward effacing discrimination by gender.[18] Whether this would be sufficient to overcome other forms of discrimination rooted in the availability of leisure time, feelings of personal efficacy, reluctance to express dissent, unwillingness to tolerate diversity—not to mention persistent differences in levels of interest in politics—is quite another matter. The core underlying assumption that direct participation will eliminate these differences and enlighten citizens about their "true" interests remains to be proven.[19] Until feminists are firmly convinced of this, it is difficult to imagine that their movements will invest much of their scarce resources during the transition in such a doubtful venture.

SELECTING BY LOT

Surprisingly, there is one institution that has deep roots in classical democratic theory and practice which could very rapidly and definitively eliminate gender as a discriminating factor in politics, an institution that has never been proposed (to my knowledge) by feminists, namely, selection by lot.[20] If all representatives were to be chosen randomly from a pool of citizens and if differences between men and women were ignored in establishing that pool, the problem would be solved—along with several other factors of systematic discrimination which have plagued modern democracies. One could even imagine carrying the principle further and selecting political executives and upper-level administrators in this fashion, perhaps from more restricted pools in order to overcome problems related to the necessity for expertise and the avoidance of potential conflicts of interest.[21]

Presumably, the absence of discussion of this alternative is related primarily to the above-noted enthusiasm of feminists for direct and participatory democracy. Nothing would be more vicarious and passive than the selection of representatives or officials randomly by computer! A bit more cynically, one could observe that such a process would effectively eliminate the relative advantage that upper-middle-class professional women have when nomination takes place through either conventional party channels or small group deliberations. Since this is the sociological group that does most of the theorizing and proselytizing with regard to women's causes, it seems doubtful that women of this group would be attracted by such an alternative—despite its manifest efficiency in eliminating gender discrimination.[22]

ENSURING CATEGORIC REPRESENTATION

A third set of postliberal reforms might be more politically appealing to feminists. They could be grouped under the label "categoric representation." By law and, perhaps, even by constitution, women would be designated as a social group whose interests deserved explicit recognition. Given their inequality of treatment in the past and their persistent difficulties in collective action, their collective access to the political process should be specifically guaranteed. The obvious historical analogy would be with the way in which so-called consociational democracies have accorded differential representation and veto powers to designated cultural, linguistic, or religious minorities. That these groups are usually concentrated spatially makes this easy to do by manipulating the territorial boundaries of constituencies and weighing them differentially. For women, who live more evenly dispersed among the general population, other solutions would have to be invented. For example, the law could simply specify that one-half of all candidates or even of all officeholders would have to be female. Already, political parties in some countries have voluntarily set aside such a quota, but to convert such a measure into an obligation enforceable by public law would go beyond the normal boundaries of liberal democracy.[23]

An alternative measure could take a corporatist direction. Rather than seeking to ensure the proportional placement of women on party lists or in territorial assemblies, it would aim at establishing a comprehensive associational structure that would officially represent the "functional" interests of women. This would, no doubt, require public funding and monopolistic certification. Authorities would then be required to take into consideration all proposals generated by this (putatively) all-encompassing "national confederation/association/union of women" and to consult it on all relevant policy issues before placing them before parliament. One could even imagine a scenario in which this association could be given the right of veto over matters of particular importance to its members.[24]

Such an arrangement would have the singular advantage in some countries of Western Europe of literally replicating existing structures of "social partnership" and "concertation" involving class- and sector-based associations of labor and capital and, presumably, would not have to counter the sort of ideological objections that would be raised in more liberal and pluralist settings. What is missing—so far—is the same degree of political promotion and ideological legitimation "from above" by male politicians and intellectuals which was so instrumental in forging a corporatist system for the intermediation of class, sectoral, and professional interest in northern and Western Europe since the 1920s and 1930s.

In line with this objective of promoting policy concertation, but without going so far as to create an entire national structure of publicly mandated and financed "women's corporations," a number of neodemocracies seem to have experimented with what one author has called "state feminism."[25] Spain, some six years after its founding democratic elections and one year after the Socialist Party (PSOE) came to power for the first time, took the lead when it established the Instituto de la Mujer. Its subsequent history in promoting profemale legislation through interministerial coordination and successive "Equal Opportunity Plans" has not been particularly successful. For example, Spain still has one of the most restrictive abortion laws in Europe. Even more problematic, according to Celia Valente, whose account I am relying on, is the Instituto's persistent connection with the PSOE and its failure to establish close working relationships with the Spanish feminist movement. It is, however, seriously involved in encouraging the formation of regional and municipal women's programs and in subsidizing various women's organizations. Whether the Instituto could survive a major electoral defeat of the PSOE and its withdrawal from government is unclear. The earlier example of the Ministère de la Femme, set up by the French Socialist government in the early 1980s and abandoned when a conservative became prime minister, suggests that its survival prospects are slim.

Apparently, Brazil, Argentina, and Chile have all created analogous *conselhos, consejos,* and *servicios* to deal with women's issues from within the administrative apparatus. Sonia Alvarez's description of the reaction of Brazilian feminists to the subsequent activities of National Council on Women's Rights (CNDM) and the State Council for the Feminine Condition (CECF) in São Paulo is strikingly similar to Celia Valente's evaluation of the Spanish Instituto de la Mujer:

According to feminists who have served on or worked with the CECF and CNDM as of 1988, many of the new women's institutions were profoundly partisan. Most had few if any links to independent, nonpartisan women's organizations and instead were created as electoral gambits by mayors and governors, providing these with a newfound source of democratic legitimacy. To the dismay of the feminists who conceived of the councils as institutions that would channel women's demands into policy arenas and monitor policy implementation, many of the new councils instead served as mechanisms for the top-down mobilization of women.[26]

MOVING TO REPRESENTATION VIA VOUCHERS

As we have just witnessed, the corporatist/concertation solution to the persistent underrepresentation of women presents many problems, not the least of which is how to ensure the autonomy of such "sponsored" associations or councils from the state or governing party and how to prevent their developing into oligarchic and overbureaucratized organizations with a particular, circumscribed view of the interests of their members-cum-clients. Elsewhere, I have proposed the creation of a set of postliberal reforms that would not only avoid these problems of dependence and closure but could even make a significant dent in inequalities of interest representation based on gender.[27]

The crux of the proposal is to sever the relationship between the need for representation and the willingness or ability to pay for it. "No Representation without Taxation" is the ironic slogan I have adopted. All (tax-paying) citizens, male or female, would be required to contribute a modest amount to the support of associations that represent their interests—in a manner analogous to public financing of parties but with a twist. Instead of allocating funds according to previous electoral performance or membership levels, I suggested the creation of a system of "secondary citizenship" in which individuals would be issued vouchers at regular intervals for the support of associations and allowed to distribute them according to her or his own self-assessed interests. These vouchers would be exchangeable for public funds from the general budget. Only organizations accepting certain restrictions—for instance, internal democratic selection of leaders, transparency of finances, no profit-making activity—would be eligible to receive vouchers and by so doing would be accorded the status of "civic" or "semipublic" institutions. This relatively simple measure would have the effect of channeling substantially greater resources into associations of all types and would also greatly reduce (but not completely eliminate) the existing inequalities in the capacity for collective actions across social groups. The sum total of this distribution would automatically and indirectly "redesign" the system of interest representation—without the need for detailed state intervention.

Especially interesting from a feminist perspective is the fact that this system of vouchers would be open without discrimination to all existing and potential interests (provided they accept the limitations of semipublic status). It would not ex ante or ex officio ensure the predominance of any specific line of cleavage, as do all existing corporatist systems. It would just equalize the conditions for self-organization across interest categories that differed initially in their resources, numbers, intensities, locations, and so on. No one could accuse it of specifically favoring or "endowing" the interests of women. Citizens would be free to choose which interests concerned them the most and which specific associations best represented them. If they were to support such a reform, feminists would have to be confident that their organizations could compete freely and effectively with alternative identities and preferences of women. Depending on the periodicity with which the vouchers were distributed, the whole system would be reasonably flexible, rewarding those that succeeded in identifying new concerns and punishing those that held on too long to outdated ones. Competition between voucher seekers would be lively, which should improve the flow of communications about the pros and cons of rival associations and could even encourage a fair amount of increased deliberation and debate among citizens. Most important, this would tend to limit the processes of internal oligarchization, social closure, and "goal displacement" which have tended to plague officially founded, recognized, and funded corporatist institutions.

A SOLUTION TO THE AGENCY PROBLEM?

Contemporary democratization is beset with a deep irony: the countries of the South and East have recently liberated themselves from various forms of autocracy and are desperately seeking to acquire the institutions of already established democracies; the advanced capitalist societies that have been practicing this form of political domination for some time are experiencing widespread disaffection with these very same institutions. The East and South want nothing more than to imitate existing practices; the North and West are bored and disillusioned with them.

In both cases, normative democratic theory has been largely shut out of the process of collective deliberation and choice. Feminism—with its distinctive critique of "real-existing" liberal democracies—could help to bring together theorists from the East-South and the North-West and might even be able to generate adequate support for significant and much needed improvements in long-established as well as neodemocracies. After all, if they were successful in convincing a large proportion of women citizens of the need for such reforms—either within or beyond the confines of liberal democracy—they will have gone a long way toward solving the "agency problem" that has plagued all other contemporary efforts at improving its sclerotic practices.

NOTES

Without the encouragement of Terry Karl, I would not have attempted to write this chapter, and without her help I would never have finished it. She is not, however, in any way responsible for the opinions expressed in it. To Jane Jaquette and Elisabeth Friedman I owe many critical comments, to which I have attempted to respond—as several notes testify.

1. I hasten to qualify this statement. There have been several comprehensive descriptions of the role that women and women's issues have played in specific transitions. Sonia Alvarez has written a model account, *Engendering Democracy in Brazil: Women's Movements in Transition Politics* (Princeton: Princeton University Press, 1992). Jane Jaquette has edited a major comparative study of the role of women's movements in Latin American transitions, *The Women's Movement in Latin America: Feminism and the Transition to Democracy* (Boulder, Colo.: Westview Press, 1990), and, with the essays in this volume, is now extending her effort to cover Eastern Europe as well. Also, Nanette Funk and Magda Mueller, eds., *Gender Politics and Post-Communism* (London: Routledge, 1993).

A more systematic analysis of secondary sources which covers the role of women in democratization in both Latin America and Eastern Europe has appeared since I wrote the first draft of this chapter: Georgina Waylen, "Women and Democratization: Conceptualizing Gender Relations in Transition Politics," *World Politics* 46 (April 1994): 327–53. It argues (unconvincingly in my view) that "women's movements played an important role in the early stages of democratization in all the countries [of Latin America]" (343) and (more convincingly, in my view) that "women were not in a good position to influence the state and the newly active political parties during the very rapid collapse of the old order that has taken place in Eastern Europe" (347).

What is missing (as far as I can tell) is an analysis of the much more limited role that women and women's movements have played in the consolidation of democracy. This parallels another lacuna in the feminist literature in general, namely, the lack of a systemic discussion concerning how different institutional configurations of democracy affect the likelihood that women's interests will get on the policy agenda and be seriously addressed by policy makers.

2. Guillermo O'Donnell and Philippe C. Schmitter, *Transitions from Authoritarian Rule: Tentative Conclusions about Uncertain Democracies* (Baltimore: Johns Hopkins University Press, 1986).

3. Since the descriptive accounts tend to focus exclusively on those women's groups promoting a democratic outcome, they often ignore the fact that a substantial proportion of women continued to support autocratic rulers and that these autocrats were occasionally successful in creating and sponsoring women's movements that had more members than the opposition. Chile is probably the major case in point.

4. This hypothesis has not, however, gone unchallenged. There are students of social

movements in Latin America, in particular, who claim that their role in provoking and guiding the transition was more significant. Scott Mainwaring and Eduardo Viola, "New Social Movements, Political Culture, and Democracy: Brazil and Argentina in the 1980s," *Telos* 61 (Fall 1984): 17–52; Scott Mainwaring, "Urban Popular Movements, Identity, and Democratization in Brazil," *Comparative Political Studies* 20, no. 2 (1987): 131–59; Renato Boschi, *A Arte de Associacão: Politica de Base e Democracia no Brasil* (São Paulo: Vertice, 1987), and Gerardo Munck, "Social Movements and Democracy in Latin America: Theoretical Debates and Comparative Perspectives," paper presented at the 16th Congress of the Latin American Studies Association, Washington, D.C., April 4–6, 1991.

Tracy Fitzsimmons and Elisabeth Friedman have recently produced doctoral dissertations at Stanford University outlining the role of women's movements in contemporary Chile and Venezuela, respectively, and both have respectfully raised doubts about my skepticism with regard to social movements in general and women's movements in particular—during and after the transition.

The evidence from Eastern Europe definitely suggests a more prominent role for social movements, although collective action by women is never mentioned. See Sidney Tarrow, "Eastern European Social Movements: Globalization, Difference, and Political Opportunity?" paper presented at the First European Conference on Social Movements, Berlin, October 29–31, 1992.

5. I believe that only Kuwait is an exception among neodemocracies—and one could question where it crosses even the most minimal threshold for inclusion in the club!

6. It should be noted at this point that one effect of this uniformity with regard to formal rights (or, more specifically, with regard to granting the right to vote equally to men and women) is to impart a conservative bias to the founding and, probably, most subsequent elections. Virtually all electoral studies have confirmed that, as a group, women are more likely to vote for rightist (but not extreme rightist or neofascist) parties than men. It is only in the (unfortunately) rare cases in which the educational levels, professional accomplishments, and everyday life experiences of women become (almost) equal to those of men that this difference in voting behavior disappears, for example, Norway and Sweden. In all of the neodemocracies, even the most economically developed and socially advantaged, women are very far from having attained this degree of informal equality. In the Eastern European cases, where women under the *ancien régime* had an equivalent labor force participation rate and level of education, the degree of de facto gender discrimination remained very high. Hence, the "women's vote" has everywhere tended to impart a decidedly conservative bias to their electoral results. This, along with the generic decline in the role of social movements in the course of the transition, helps to explain (ironically) why women as a category and feminists as a movement have done so poorly in the aftermath of recent democratizations.

7. Carol Pateman, *The Disorder of Women* (Stanford: Stanford University Press, 1989), and Susan Moller Okin, *Gender, Justice, and the Family* (New York: Basic Books, 1989), have been my basic guides on this issue.

From their analyses, I presume that they would agree with the categoric conclusion of Anne Phillips that "whatever its claims in other fields of endeavor, liberal democracy has not served women well." I am much indebted to her "Must Feminists Give Up on Liberal Democracy?" *Political Studies* 40 (1992): 68–82, for inspiration in writing this chapter, since she has been one of the few feminist theorists who have stressed the differential role of concrete democratic arrangements. Also her *Engendering Democracy* (Cambridge, England: Polity Press, 1991) and her "Democracy and Representation: Or, Why Should It Matter Who Our Representatives Are?" *Frauen und Politik, SVPW-Jahrbuch*, no. 34 (1994): 63–76. Susan Mendus, "Losing the Faith: Feminism and Democracy," in *Democracy: The Unfinished Journey, 508 B.C. to A.D. 1993*, ed. John Dunn (Oxford: Oxford University Press, 1992), 207–19, has also influenced my thinking on these issues.

8. Specifically, on the hostility to "Western Progressive Feminist" goals, see Peggy Watson, "The Rise of Masculinism in Eastern Europe," *New Left Review*, no. 198 (1993): 71–82.

9. Actually, the Argentine experience proved to be especially illustrative of this point. Initially, the Argentines recycled their venerable 1853 constitution. No feminist issues were raised, and very few women were elected. Subsequently, the Argentine Congress extensively revised the National Electoral Code and, at that time (1991), introduced a comprehensive system of quotas for women candidates (Law No. 24.012). Nelida Archenti, "Political Representation and Gender Interests: The Argentine Example," paper presented at the 16th World Congress of the International Political Science Association, Berlin, August 21–25, 1994.

10. Elisabeth Friedman, in her comments on an earlier draft, questioned this assumption on the following grounds: "A problem with emphasizing the early formalization of rules and rights is that this is the very time when women are demobilized. . . . Brazil is a rather special case here. There has been a much more highly mobilized feminist movement there and, of course, the length of the transition has given social movements time to recoup and organize for the constituent assembly."

My assumption was (and remains) that women's movements are typically more, not less, mobilized at early moments of the transition. It is only after the "founding elections" that they (and other types of social movements) tend to be displaced by political parties—admittedly, with the possibility that women's movements may be revived at some less predictable moment in the future. Holding constituent assemblies early should give these movements a better chance to exploit the momentum they built up in opposition to autocracy and an interesting window of opportunity to "hide behind the Veil of Ignorance" created by the high level of general uncertainty about future roles and resources.

11. For example, Marvin Peguese in an unpublished research paper has demonstrated compellingly that Afro-Brazilians, despite their "normally" low level of political consciousness and organization, have been able to use the periodic opportunities presented by constituent assemblies (1932, 1985) to mobilize latent support and extract significant legal concessions from authorities and adversaries who would have otherwise preferred to ignore the society's discriminatory practices by hiding behind the myth that Brazil is a "racial democracy."

12. Nothing I have suggested in this chapter has provoked as many negative comments as this one. As Jane Jaquette put it, "Your point about . . . a strong and effective party system is logically persuasive, but . . . after my (recent) trip to Peru, Chile, Argentina and Brazil . . . women complain bitterly about how closed and elitist the old parties are." Elisabeth Friedman expressed the same thought somewhat differently: "Disciplined parties often end up excluding women by virtue of their very organization, or rather, through organized means. Analyst after analyst has described how parties have marginalized women and their concerns by setting up a 'women's auxiliary' that either serves to get out

the female vote or make coffee and copies for the 'real' participants. Feminists are often more effective in small (Left) parties than in big centrist ones."

My advocacy was based on two assumptions: (1) large, disciplined and relatively centralized parties would be more likely to respond programmatically to the existence of women's issues for purely electoralist, "catch-more" reasons; (2) when they did recognize the vote-gaining potential, they would be more capable of imposing such a strategy on the party as a whole. While I admit that small leftist or environmentalist parties may seem to offer a safer and more immediately accessible haven, participation in them is likely to produce more symbolic than real benefits. Older, "traditional" parties may be more closed and elitist, but they are not necessarily more disciplined and permanently organized—especially in Peru, Argentina, and Brazil. Chile is a more damaging example, since its parties are old, elitist, closed, and disciplined—and relatively impervious to women's interests and female participation.

If one takes the German experience as emblematic, it suggests a linear correlation between party discipline and female participation in party lists. The highly disciplined (if faction-ridden) Greens have established a 50 percent quota for women. The SPD opted first for 33 percent and later increased it to 40 percent. The CDU only later got around to discussing the issue of a formal quota—and then turned it down at its 1996 party congress.

13. I have not had a chance to read Douglas J. Amy's *plaidoyer Real Choices/New Voices: The Case for Proportional Representation Elections in the United States* (New York: Columbia University Press, 1995) to discover whether he advocates proportional representation specifically to ensure a fairer representation of women's interests.

14. One intriguing area for speculation concerns the internal structures of political parties, especially the roles assigned respectively to territorial as opposed to functional constituencies. Since most trade unions, professional associations, and sectoral organizations are usually hopelessly dominated by men, it would seem that women should prefer parties with a strong, even an exclusively territorial base. Moreover, in accordance with their general interest in decentralization, they should advocate relatively small territorial units—municipalities and communes—provided each of these has multiple representatives. What is not clear (to me) is how sensitive these internal party choices are to constitutional or legislative design.

15. This is quite independent of the reasons that have been adduced for the superiority of parliamentarianism in the process of consolidation of democracy. See Juan Linz, "The Perils of Presidentialism," *Journal of Democracy* 1, no. 1 (1990): 51–69; also the subsequent critical rejoinders by Donald Horowitz, Seymour Martin Lipset, and Juan Linz in "Presidents vs. Parliaments," *Journal of Democracy* 1, no. 4 (1990): 73–91.

16. It should, of course, be noted that the relatively high proportion of women in Eastern European "parliaments" under Communist rule was a form of participation more ritual than effective in nature. There were virtually no women in the real center of power in these countries, that is, in the Central Committees of the Communist Party. Perhaps, having lived the embarrassing experience of such vacuous "quota-ism" helps to explain why feminist movements in these countries seem not to have advanced any demands for quotas subsequently when the greater presence of women might have made a more substantial difference in policy outcomes.

17. Anne Phillips in "Must Feminists Give Up on Liberal Democracy?" reports that "the women elected to the world's national assemblies make up 2–12 per cent of the

whole" (71). If that is so, one would have to admit that the neodemocracies are not doing comparatively that badly.

18. The expression "strong democracy" is taken from Benjamin Barber, *Strong Democracy: Participatory Politics for a New Age* (Berkeley: University of California Press, 1984), where it is not associated with a feminist position. Carole Pateman in her *Disorder of Women* does make the connection more explicit.

19. Certainly the example of Switzerland with its extensive and frequent reliance on direct democratic techniques is not encouraging for what it tells us about the participation of women in politics or the penetration of women's interests within the policy process.

20. Actually, one contemporary democratic theorist, John Burnheim, has revived this tradition and advocated its extension to modern democracies, although not specifically as a device to resolve gender-based inequalities. *Is Democracy Possible?* (Cambridge, England: Polity Press, 1985). As far as I can tell, no one has taken this suggestion seriously— least of all, anyone militating actively in the political life of "real-existing" democracies!

21. I recall (but cannot find or cite) a "political science fiction" short story by Isaac Asimov in which early in the next century the president of the United States would be chosen randomly from a pool of candidates, themselves chosen randomly some time previously and subjected to an intensive training experience. I cannot remember if any of the candidates in the final pool were women or, for that matter, what the punch line of the story was.

22. M. E. Hawkesworth, for example, proposes a blanket constitutional provision mandating that "women hold 50 percent of all elective, appointive and bureaucratic offices" but never entertains the notion that this might be accomplished by random selection. *Beyond Oppression: Feminist Theory and Political Strategy* (New York: Continuum, 1990), 171–97.

23. To my knowledge, only Argentina has gone this far in a postliberal direction. Not only does its 1991 Law of Quotas provide that at least 30 percent of the candidates for both the Senado and the Congreso be women (there are no quotas for other social groups), but it also specifies that they must be given equal treatment in the composition of party lists.

Incidentally, as a partial result of this law, 25 women were elected deputies in the subsequent 1993 national elections. Nelida Archenti, in "Political Representation and Gender Interests," reports that according to interviews with 17 of these female deputies by the newspaper *Pagina 12*, only 2 defined themselves as "feminists" and only 4 supported a proposed law in favor of abortion.

24. I gather from a reference in Phillips, "Must Feminists Give Up on Liberal Democracy?" that Iris Young has proposed just such an arrangement in her "Polity and Group Difference: A Critique of the Ideal of Universal Citizenship," *Ethics* 99 (1989). Unfortunately, I have not been able to obtain a copy of this article.

25. Celia Valente, "State Feminism in Spain (the Institute of the Woman), 1983–1994," paper presented at the 16th World Congress of IPSA, Berlin, August 21–25, 1994.

26. *Engendering Democracy in Brazil*, 243.

27. "Interests, Associations, and Intermediation in a Reformed Post-Liberal Democracy," *Politische Vierteljahresschrift* 35.Jg., Sonderheft 25, "Staat und Verbände" (1994): 160–74; and "Post-Liberal Democracy: Does It Have a Future?" in *Die Reform-fähigkeit von Industriegesellschaften*, ed. Karlheinz Bentele, Bernd Reissert, and Ronald Schettkat (Frankfurt: Campus, 1995), 47–63.

Contributors

Maruja Barrig is a journalist and the author of *Cinturón de Castidad: la mujer de clase media in el Perú* (1971), one of the first feminist books published in Peru. She has written widely on women's political and economic issues. She is a visiting professor in Gender Studies at the Catholic University in Lima and a consultant on development projects in Latin America.

Teresa P. R. Caldeira is a professor at the Department of Anthropology at the University of California at Irvine and is a research associate at CEBRAP (The Brazilian Center for Analysis and Planning) in São Paulo. Her research focuses on citizenship, violent crime, urban segregation, and social movements in contemporary Brazil.

María del Carmen Feijoó is a sociologist who has written extensively about the impact of structural adjustment policies on women in Argentina. She edited *Women and Society in Latin America*. She has done research for CEDES and CONICET (The National Council of Scientific and Technical Research) and served as undersecretary of the Department of Education of the Province of Buenos Aires.

Jane S. Jaquette is Bertha Harton Orr Professor of the Liberal Arts, professor of politics, and chair of the Department of Diplomacy and World Affairs at Occidental College. She has written extensively on issues of women's political participation, women and development, and the UN Decade for Women. Her most recent book is *The Women's Movement in Latin America: Participation and Democracy*.

Dobrinka Kostova is a fellow at the Institute of Sociology, Bulgarian Academy of Sciences. She has published a number of articles about the consequences for women of political, legal, economic, and social changes in post-Communist societies. She is a member of the Bulgarian Union of University Women and of the Association for Women in Development.

Philippe C. Schmitter, founder and former director of the Center for European Studies at Stanford University, is a professor of Political and Social Sciences at the European University Institute in Fiesole, Italy. He co-edited *Transitions from Authoritarian Rule: Prospects for Democracy* (in 4 vols.) and is completing a book on democratic consolidation.

Renata Siemieńska is professor and chair of the Sociology of Education and Schooling Department in the Institute of Sociology and head of the Interdisciplinary Research Division of Gender Studies at the Institute of Social Studies, University of Warsaw. She has published several books and essays based on her study of cross-national value systems and of women's political participation. She served as president of the UN International Research and Training Institute for the Advancement of Women (INSTRAW).

Julia Szalai is deputy director of the Institute of Sociology at the Hungarian Academy of Sciences and head of the External Faculty of Social Work, John Wesley College, Budapest. Her fields of research include the social history of poverty in Central Europe, and the effects of gender and ethnicity on contemporary social policy in Hungary. Among her recent publications is *Participation and Changes in Property Relations in Post-Communist Societies: The Hungarian Case* (1995).

María Elena Valenzuela is a sociologist and a consultant on gender issues at the International Labor Organization (ILO). She headed the research department of the Chilean Women's Ministry (SERNAM) from its founding until 1997, and she has authored several studies of women's roles in Chile during the military dictatorship and during the process of redemocratization in the 1990s.

Sharon L. Wolchik is professor of political science and international affairs at the Elliott school of International Affairs at the George Washington University. She has written or edited several books on comparative aspects of Communism in Eastern and Central Europe, on women's roles in the transition to post-Communist rule, and on the politics of the Czech and Slovak Republics. Her most recent book is *Czechoslovakia in Transition: Politics, Economics, and Society.*

Index

241

Library of Congress Cataloging-in-Publication Data
Women and democracy : Latin America and Central and Eastern Europe /
    edited by Jane S. Jaquette and Sharon L. Wolchik.
        p.   cm.
    Includes bibliographical references and index.
    ISBN 0-8018-5837-2 (alk. paper). —ISBN 0-8018-5838-0 (pbk. : alk.
paper)
        1. Women in politics—Latin America. 2. Women in politics—Europe,
Central. 3. Women in politics—Europe, Eastern. 4. Democracy—Latin
America. 5. Democracy—Europe, Central. 6. Democracy—Europe, East-
ern. I. Jaquette, Jane S., 1942–   . II. Wolchik, Sharon L.
    HQ1236.W586   1998
    305.42'098—DC21   98-5120
                                                        CIP